2004 02 11

Getting it Printed

THIRD EDITION

How to work with printers and

graphic imaging services to assure quality,

stay on schedule and control costs

Mark Beach, Ph.D. & Eric Kenly, M.S.

HOW
DESIGN
BOOKS
CINCINNATI, OHIO
www.howdesign.com

Getting It Printed. Copyright © 1986, 1993 by Mark Beach. Copyright © 1999 by Mark Beach and Eric Kenly. Manufactured in the United States. All rights reserved. No part of this book may be reproduced in any form or by any electronic or mechanical means including storage retrieval systems without permission in writing from the publisher, except by a reviewer, who may quote brief passages in a review. Published by North Light Books, an imprint of F&W Publications, Inc., 1507 Dana Avenue, Cincinnati, Ohio 45207. (800) 289-0963. Third Edition.

Other fine North Light Books are available from your local bookstore or art supply store, or direct from the publisher.

03 02 01   5 4

Library of Congress Cataloging-in-Publication Data

Beach, Mark.
    Getting it printed / Mark Beach and Eric Kenly.—3rd. ed.
        p.   cm.
    Includes index.
    ISBN 0-89134-858-1(pbk.)
    1. Printing—United States. I. Kenly, Eric. II. Title.
Z243.U5B4   1998
686.2—dc21   98-35378
                                                            CIP

Edited by Dawn Korth
Production edited by Michelle Howry
Cover designed by Angela Lennert Wilcox
Cover photography by Greg Grosse

ABOUT THE AUTHORS

Mark Beach holds a Ph.D. in education and history from the University of Wisconsin and has taught at Cornell University and the University of Rochester, where he was associate dean of the college of arts and science. Beach has held research grants from the Smithsonian Institution, Ford Foundation and National Academy of the Arts. His books about graphic design and production are used throughout North America for corporate training and as college texts. In addition to *Getting It Printed*, his published titles include *Editing Your Newsletter*, *Newsletter Sourcebook*, *Papers For Printing* and *Graphically Speaking*.

Eric Kenly holds a Master of Science in electronic publishing from Rochester Instiute of Technology (RIT), where he teaches digital publishing for the Technological and Education Center. In addition, RIT sponsors Kenly for in-house training at companies such as Kodak, Agfa, 3M and Xerox, and for seminars at printing and imaging meetings such as the Seybold Conference. Based in California's Silicon Valley, Kenly is also retained by George Lithograph to advise management and teach customers about digital imaging.

To reach either author, use the E-mail at our Web site (www.gettingitprinted.com).

CONTENTS

INTRODUCTION

Printing is one of the few industries in which customers take an active part in manufacturing. The success of printing jobs depends on the printing buyer as much as on the printer.

Graphic design requires decisions about inks, papers, file formats and many other aspects of production. Writing specifications, reviewing proofs and conducting press checks involve still more decisions. Customers and printers work together throughout the process.

In this book, you learn how to participate in the unique, cooperative workflow of the graphic arts. You discover the technical and business requirements needed to make printing's blend of art, craft and industry work for you.

This guide helps everyone who plans, designs or pays for printing:

• sales and customer service representatives for printers, paper merchants and imaging services

• designers, photographers and illustrators who create graphic communications

• production managers for agencies, studios and corporations

• public relations and marketing professionals who rely on newsletters, brochures, directories and annual reports

• writers and editors who produce books, magazines, catalogs or manuals

• teachers, trainers and consultants who explain how to get the most out of printing equipment, materials and processes

The skills you build using this book increase your control throughout the production sequence. You improve communication to produce more satisfactory results, on-time deliveries and lower costs. And you discover how to find the right printer at the right price for every job.

Chapters in this book follow the sequence of most printing jobs from idea through delivery. You also find information presented in several ways in addition to text:

• Illustrations, examples and photographs convey concepts that seem most understandable in a visual format

• Forms help you pinpoint needs and record individual information

• Checklists relate to standards of quality and service and help spot problems with items such as files and transparencies

• Anecdotes capture the creative flavor of the graphic arts

For ease of reference, the text refers to all illustrations, forms, checklists, charts, examples and photographs as "visuals." Each visual is numbered by chapter and sequence. For example, Visual 4-5 is the fifth visual in chapter four.

Thank you for buying this book. We hope it helps you with all your printing jobs.

Mark Beach
Eric Kenly

To improve your skills and keep up-to-date, visit our Web site at (www.gettingitprinted.com).

1. PLANNING FOR RESULTS

To keep up-to-date about planning printing jobs, visit our Web site (www.gettingitprinted.com).

Whether you are a customer of a printer, a graphic arts professional, or both, planning even the most simple printing job requires many decisions. Complex projects may demand hundreds. Each decision affects all the others in the sequence, from concept to finished product.

Careful planning helps you control the quality, schedule and cost of printing jobs. Planning sharpens your vision of the final product and improves communication among people involved in production. And planning helps you avoid costly changes after production begins.

Decisions about printing jobs involve both business and technical information. This chapter focuses on business considerations as a framework for technical decisions. You learn how to start answering the key questions found on the opposite page, and why the success of your printing job depends on your answers. We introduce you to the graphic arts services most commonly used to coordinate printing jobs.

This chapter also introduces four categories of printing quality. We refer to these categories throughout this book and summarize them in chapter seven. The categories of quality are meant to classify printing, not to judge it. Controlling costs and schedules includes selecting the quality category appropriate for each particular job.

PRECISION PLANNING

Getting printing done at the level of quality and service you want and within your budget and schedule calls for answers to fifteen key questions. Details emerge as plans develop, but the general outline applies to all projects.

1. What is your purpose?

You may want to entertain, inform, sell or inspire. Maybe your product is for keeping records, impressing clients, recruiting members or gaining customers. Goals help you answer questions about design, quality, quantity and cost. For example, a brochure to build membership in a trade association might include a postpaid response card.

2. Who is your audience?

You may want to reach customers, members or employees who already know you, or people who have never heard of you. Your readers may be anyone—old or young, men or women, active or sedentary.

Your audience affects design. Posters advertising concerts look very different from posters announcing lectures. Readers older than forty-five appreciate larger type.

Thinking about your audience and the impression you want to create suggests the quality you need. In some situations, watermarked stationery may seem pretentious. If you are an aspiring doctor, however, a quick-copy letterhead might encourage patients to think speed is your approach to surgery, too. Stay consistent with the best standards that your clients, customers or members expect from organizations similar to your own.

3. How will your piece look?

Even in the earliest phases of planning you probably have some ideas about the right mix of type and visuals. You may imagine a handsome annual report, efficient form or enticing catalog. You could have in mind the size and approximate page count you're aiming for. Knowing your goals, audience and budget shapes your vision.

Your concept of yourself, your business, organization or client also affects design. Should your audience perceive you as dignified or informal, conservative or speculative? Do you offer products or services? Answers to questions such as these help you write and design. The answers also influence decisions about ink colors, papers and printing quality.

As you think about design, don't ignore writing. Poor writing ruins a printed piece as easily as poor design. Equally important, generous use of the delete key cuts production costs faster than any other tool. Every sentence you cut saves on paper and printing.

4. How will readers use your piece?

People read books gradually, but only glance at signs. Readers sort quickly through newsletters

---

1-1 BASIC PLANNING QUESTIONS

Regardless of your printing job or the methods you use to produce it, answers to the following questions will help you control costs, ensure quality and stay on schedule.

1. What is your purpose?
2. Who is your audience?
3. How will your piece look?
4. How will readers use your piece?
5. How will other processes handle your piece?
6. How will you reach your audience?
7. Where else might you use your content?
8. When do you need the job delivered?
9. How many pieces do you need?
10. What quality do you need?
11. How much can you spend?
12. What are your workflows?
13. How will your piece reach your printer?
14. What help do you need?
15. What services do you want from your printer?

1-2 POST OFFICE PROBLEMS

The U.S. Postal Service has hundreds of definitions and rules that affect every aspect of your printing job. Following are just a few categories and only one example in each.

Content. To qualify for periodical rates, publications must include a specific percent of space devoted to advertising.

Design. Copy on the address panel must remain a specific distance from each edge.

Format. Pieces that qualify as letters cost less to mail than those considered flats.

Size. Postcards, letters and flats all have minimum and maximum dimensions.

Paper. Stock for business-reply cards must measure at least .007 inches thick.

Printing. Contrast between ink and paper must meet standards.

Folding. Folds must face specific directions, depending on format.

Packing. Pieces bundled and put on pallets according to guidelines qualify for lower rates.

Before deciding anything about design, show a dummy of your mailing to a postal official. Ask for a signature affirming that your design meets the standards of the class of mail you have in mind. Make sure the official who signs your mock-up works at the post office where you plan to mail.

and direct mailings, more slowly through brochures and catalogs. A menu must have strength at the fold, resist spills and greasy fingers, and appear attractive and readable in low light.

Thinking about use includes considering life expectancy. You may use one loose-leaf binder only during a weekend workshop, while another must last years as a reference tool. If your catalog must serve two years, consider a separate price sheet you can change every few months, or refer readers to your Web site.

5. How will other processes handle your piece?

Printed pieces often coordinate with other products and services. Labels must fit bottles, and instruction sheets fold to fit boxes. Show a dummy to people who will handle your piece to verify that it meets their needs.

Printing customers often run into problems when they take products to mailing services. Machines for folding, inserting, addressing and sealing may not handle the pieces. If you are preparing printing for direct mail, go out of your way to coordinate design carefully with your mailing service. Study Visual 1-2 to make sure you stay alert to postal standards.

6. How will you reach your audience?

Perhaps the message will go into an envelope with other printed pieces, such as a business reply envelope and flier. If so, you may need matching papers and coordinated sizes.

Some products, such as books with plastic comb bindings, need special packaging. Wrapping must protect paper goods from moisture. If the standards of your industry are to ship in dozens, tell your printer to pack in boxes with twelve, twenty-four or thirty-six units.

Consider box weight and size. Materials for common carriers and mailing must conform to requirements of size, shape, weight, folds, colors and seals.

7. Where else might you use your content?

When you prepare writing, illustrations and photos for printing, keep other purposes in mind. You may need some of the same information on your Web site, in a CD or for a TV ad or a sign. Many designers use the slogan "Any device in, any device out" to ensure flexibility.

Most applications can output files in a variety of formats. If your job duties call for a wide range of graphic messages, you may end up with several copies of the same file, each prepared for a different medium. Make sure your filing system clearly identifies the original file. When you prepare a new file, begin with the original and not with a previously modified file. And make sure to delete files used for rough drafts and trial designs.

TIMELY SCHEDULING

Most printing customers feel more stress about meeting deadlines than about controlling costs or maintaining quality. Turnaround gets top priority. But customers often don't allow enough time. Some imagine that commercial or specialty printing takes only a little longer than quick printing.

A routine job at a commercial print shop typically takes just a few working days. Time starts when you deliver files. Writing, editing, design and approvals can add another two to six weeks before that. For complicated jobs and when things go wrong, these times can easily double.

8. When do you need the job delivered?

A printer's ability to deliver on schedule depends on many factors. You control some of them: submitting files on time and according to specifications; reading proofs promptly; keeping alterations to a minimum; handling payments as agreed. Printers control others: scheduling jobs through various departments; ordering papers and inks early enough; maintaining good business relationships with prepress services, binderies and other subcontractors. Sometimes fate steps in: The printer's number one account demands priority press time; blizzards block all roads from paper mills; a photograph features an employee who just took another job.

Printers constantly juggle jobs to assure efficient use of machines and people. Good customers may get priority, but "first in, first out" proves a good rule of thumb for most shops.

Realistic scheduling demands honesty between you and your printer. If your files may arrive late, say so. If you can accept a partial shipment, don't insist on full delivery. If Monday morning is soon enough, don't insist on Friday afternoon.

To stay on schedule, set deadlines in consultation with your printer and stick to deadlines that apply to you. For every day you are late with files or proofs, expect your printer to delay delivery by at least one day. If you miss deadlines, your printer may rush too fast to achieve the quality you want. Or you may have to pay for overtime.

Print production managers often get locked into schedules that move in predictable steps from editorial to design to prepress to printer. Whether schedules come from in-house conventional wisdom or from the latest version of job-tracking software, they often hurt more than help. Creative people don't work on schedule, and supervisors don't give approvals on schedule. Even more important, new production methods—new software, networks and machines—constantly shift the relationship of people and activities, changing familiar workflows.

To keep your jobs on schedule, plan backward from the deadline, not forward from the starting date. Tell everyone when you need the job delivered, then let them help decide intermediate deadlines for the specific project.

OPTIMAL QUANTITIES

Poor decisions about quantity increase costs. If you order too little, you pay for reprinting sooner than necessary. Because of additional setup charges, going to press a second time makes unit costs higher than printing all you need in one run. Also, unit price goes down as quantity goes up, so one large order costs less per piece than several small orders. For example, 5,000 maps might cost $2.75 each if run all at once. Printing 3,000 now and 2,000 later might increase the unit cost of the entire 5,000 to $3.90.

If you order too many, you pay for printing on paper that you may never use. Generously estimating needs might save money, especially because next year printing will probably cost more than this year. Yet today's cost of the job is important. Large quantities are wasted if new information makes your piece obsolete or your market turns out smaller than anticipated. Cash tied up in printed inventory might be better invested elsewhere.

9. How many pieces do you need?

Forecasting the right quantity is one of the toughest judgments about any printing job.

To help decide about quantity, ask people who will use the product for their best guess about how many they need. Keep in mind circumstances that could mean increasing or decreasing your print run. Finally, get prices for printing two or three quantities greater than your immediate needs. You might discover a price break, a number over which unit costs drop significantly. See Visual 10-6 for guidelines about selecting quantities when you solicit quotations.

Stay conservative. More customers regret having too many than wish they had more. A year's supply is plenty. You might revise new forms in two months; established forms might become obsolete in six months.

Many customers order short press runs from printers with digital presses. Devices that print directly from computer files produce exact quantities on short notice and with fast turnaround times. For more information about digital printing, consult chapter eight.

Although the matter of quantity may seem largely guesswork, it does have a bright aspect.

Once you make the guess, you can express it clearly. But be careful. Most printers follow the trade custom allowing 10 percent over or under production on jobs up to ten thousand units. If you need one thousand folders and won't accept less, make this requirement clear when you place your order.

COMPELLING QUALITY

The market for printing ranges from simple, black-only fliers and forms to complicated, full-color books and art reproductions. Few printers, however, produce jobs spanning the entire range of quality levels. Most printers limit themselves to working within one or two quality categories.

10. What quality do you need?

Because the range of quality among printed pieces and printers is so great, planning requires decisions about how good each product must be. Customers who know exactly what quality they want can plan realistic schedules and budgets and select printers who can produce the work properly.

Throughout this book you encounter four categories of quality that help you identify specific quality features of printing jobs. You learn definitions of the categories here and refine the definitions in many other places. Visual 7-8 gives

---

1-3 CUTTING PRODUCTION TIME

Standardize. Stick with common ink colors, paper sizes and product formats.

Avoid alterations. Get files and specifications right the first time.

Exploit technology. Use digital printing, Portable Document Format (PDF) files and other techniques that reduce prepress.

Reduce buyouts. Keep the job under one roof and in the workflow of one business.

Lower quality. Give up inspired prose and perfect colors. Just get the job done.

Expedite approvals. Reduce the number of people who review copy and proofs.

Communicate clearly. Always use correct terms and symbols.

Cut dead time. Eliminate days a job waits on a desk for approval, on a pallet for binding or on a dock for delivery.

Speed delivery. Pick up the job today instead of waiting for tomorrow's delivery; pay for partial shipment via fast carrier.

Shop for speed. Find designers, prepress services and printers who can accommodate your rush work.

Pay for speed. Tell your printer you have a tight schedule and need rush service.

details about ten features of each quality category.

Basic printing. Basic quality involves standard materials and quality control at quick printers and copy centers. Using devices that print with toner, not ink, basic quality gets the job done reasonably well without losing content. Basic quality pieces are usually in only one or two colors. Photographs are recognizable but may lose details from the originals. Political fliers, business forms, newsletters and real estate brochures are usually printed basic quality.

Good printing. Good quality printing involves standard materials and quality control at commercial and publications printers. Images may be created from either toner or ink. Colors are strong, color photos pleasing, black-and-white photos sharp, register tight but not perfect. Average direct-mail catalogs, most hardcover books, retail packaging and magazines such as *Time* and *Newsweek* represent good printing.

Premium printing. Premium quality requires careful attention to detail, high-grade materials and presses using ink. Color photographs seem to match transparencies, and black-and-white photos appear very sharp. Products have few flaws and seem almost perfect to people who are not graphic arts professionals. Many commercial printers do premium printing when schedules and budgets permit. The category includes upscale clothing catalogs, annual reports from large corporations, and magazines such as *Communication Arts* and *National Geographic*.

Showcase printing. Showcase quality combines the best machines and materials with operators who give scrupulous attention to detail. Everything from design to paper is first class. Color photos come as close as possible to matching products or original scenes. The category of showcase printing consists of products that themselves are forms of art that only a few printing buyers can afford or printers can achieve. It includes museum grade art books, brochures for expensive automobiles and resorts, and the finest annual reports.

Each printing job has its own appropriate quality level. Don't take a simple catalog to a printer specializing in showcase quality. And don't pay an award-winning graphic designer to coordinate basic quality printing. Use this system of quality categories to help you decide what level of printing you want, select printers who can produce to that standard, and keep materials and production skills consistent throughout the job.

The four quality categories classify printing, not criticize or praise it. Criticism is for the printer who promises work to a certain standard, then doesn't produce it; praise is for the printer who honestly describes what the shop can make, then delivers exactly what you expected.

To make sure you get the most from your printing dollar, keep all components of a printing job, such as type, paper, print quality and design, within the same category of quality. Components below the average quality level for the job drag down the others; components above average don't look as good as they should, so waste time and money.

Consider a poster that includes photographs from top professionals who planned their work to appear on premium paper. Using ordinary paper is false economy because it doesn't reflect the quality of the photos. It makes sense to use a premium paper and to work with a printer who has precision equipment.

Quantity needs, costs and deadlines, as well as quality requirements, affect which printers are right for your job. The poster could be printed to the same quality by a small, medium or large commercial printer. The small printer might give the best unit price for 2,000 posters, the medium-size printer could prove most efficient for 10,000, and the large printer might be best for 50,000. The printer with the lowest price, however, might not feel able to get the job done on time.

MATCHING COST AND VALUE

Many professionals approach budget planning by estimating how much the job is worth to them when properly done. Brochures that sell $30,000 cars are worth far more than brochures that sell $30 books. Even if the job you have in mind doesn't lead directly to financial profit, you hope it produces specific results such as better public relations. You must decide how highly you value those results and what you are willing to pay to achieve them.

11. How much can you spend?

During early planning, you may find it difficult to say how much you will spend for a specific job. It should be possible, however, to develop some rough estimates. Experience with previous jobs and knowledge of local rates will help you make educated guesses about the cost of many products.

Unit costs and job costs. Printing processes that use plates, such as offset and flexography, have relatively high unit costs for the first few hundred copies. Units costs drop sharply as run lengths increase. Direct digital processes have a different economy. With photocopy and digital printing, unit costs stay almost identical regardless of run length.

If you need less than 1,000 copies, digital processes will probably have lower unit costs than plate processes.

Novice printing buyers often feel tempted to reduce unit costs by increasing run lengths. The directory that costs $2.00 each for 1,000 copies may cost $1.75 each for 2,000 copies and $1.45 each for 5,000 copies. In this example, the highest unit cost yields the lowest invoice for the total job.

To keep costs in perspective, do the arithmetic for the entire job as well as for each unit. Then ask yourself how many of those units you really need during the next few months.

Fixed costs and variable costs. Thinking about fixed and variable costs helps place value on the final product. Fixed costs stay the same whether you print one copy or one million and include design and prepress. Variable costs include the price of paper, press time and bindery operations that go up or down as quantities change.

Consider fixed costs when determining unit price. For example, $1,000 for a nameplate design on 1,000 monthly newsletters means the nameplate costs a dollar per copy for one month. Putting the same nameplate on 50,000 newsletters cuts the unit cost to two cents. The design that seemed a luxury for 1,000 copies becomes a bargain for 50,000.

Considering the value of your time and the unit cost of your piece leads to an approximate budget for a job. To produce a small book, for example, might take you 20 hours a week for a year, including writing, and cost $2.00 per unit for paper, printing and binding. Your cost for 1,000 books is $2,000 plus the value of about 1,000 hours of your time.

To ensure best cost control, use the following guideline: With relatively few copies, pay most attention to fixed costs. As quantities increase, shift your attention to variable costs.

Printing costs and procurement costs. Experienced printing buyers keep budgets in perspective by thinking about procurement costs, not just printing costs. Procurement costs include the value of your time and the time of people who work with you. For example, soliciting quotes from several vendors may involve a purchasing agent, accountant and manager as well as your own attention. The money you save may not be worth the effort.

It's easy to underestimate the cost of design and other work done on a project long before it gets to the printer. Don't overlook the cost of writers, photographers and illustrators when computing the total cost of the job. And keep in mind overhead in your own organization that might add 20–40 percent to direct costs.

Many printed products, such as books, magazines and technical manuals, have nearly identical specificiations from one publication to another. Printing buyers working with products such as these typically have long-term contracts with printers instead of working on a job-by-job basis. Contracts for a year or two allow you and the printer to develop efficient workflows and take advantage of quantity discounts for paper.

PLANNING YOUR WORKFLOWS

Your involvement with your printer begins with graphic design and writing specifications, continues through sending files and reviewing proofs, and may end with a visit to the bindery. When large printers produce complex jobs for large organizations, production may involve dozens of people over periods of months.

12. What are your workflows?

Both printing buyers and printers juggle many jobs at once, so are involved in many workflows. To keep success high and stress low, you need an efficient flow for each job and each relationship with a printer.

In this chapter we introduce you to the eddies and currents in the streams of digital information. In chapter five we go into detail about workflows in prepress where there is greatest overlap of customer and printer activity.

You and your printer must work together to ensure that you both meet your business goals. Close cooperation requires workflows that identify responsibilities on both sides of the relationship. Visual 1-4 helps you create such workflows.

13. How will your piece reach your printer?

Printers receive most jobs as files and art that customers prepare. Accurate transfer of digital information requires coordinating applications, formats and media. In addition to files, jobs may include art such as photos and illustrations that need scanning. You need to prepare the art correctly according to the requirements of your printer.

Many printing jobs involve legacy information: files, art or film from previous jobs. The legacies may be stored at your workplace, at the printer's or at a mix of the two. Using the legacies may involve a blend of old and new technologies, such as stripping film and merging files.

14. What help do you need?

If you lack the time or skill to manage a printing job, the graphic arts industry has several categories of professionals who can do the work for you. They include printing brokers, ad agencies and graphic designers.

Brokers. Printing brokers coordinate printing jobs at several different printers. Their profit comes from markups added to the cost of printing.

Brokers shop for printing just as you would if you had the time, skill and network of contacts. They may deal with trade printers who do not have sales reps and specialty printers located at great distances. They often get discounts based on high volume. As a result, brokers may get jobs done faster and for less money than you could.

If you spend over $250,000 per year on printing, you may find that working with a broker saves you time and money.

Printing brokers often have a much broader knowledge of graphic arts production than sales reps working with only one printer. A broker has probably worked for a few years for a paper merchant, ad agency or variety of printers. A sales rep, on the other hand, probably has worked with just one or two printers. For that reason, you can use a broker to handle a variety of printing needs. To accomplish the same objective through sales reps, you might work with six or eight printers.

Agencies. An advertising or public relations agency builds an overall plan that may range from corporate logos to television commercials, then carries out the plan by contracting with media and producing messages. Clients hiring an agency may assume the campaign will involve some printed products, but may have no specific ideas in mind.

Not all ad agencies deal knowledgeably with printing. Some specialize in broadcast media. If you have printed pieces in mind as part of your ad campaign, make sure the agency you are considering has experienced printing buyers on staff.

The staff at ad agencies that handle a lot of printing includes copywriters, graphic designers, production artists and at least one person, the production manager, who works with printers. In addition, ad agencies subcontract a great deal of work to freelance specialists.

Graphic designers. Graphic designers build on ideas from customers to create printed messages. The "graphic" part of graphic design

1-4 WORKFLOW CHECKPOINTS

Every printing job has a unique workflow with many opportunities to control quality, cost and schedule. Use the following list to identify what steps you want on your production flowchart.

Agreements
- Service expectations: communication, prepress, training, cost control, additional services, archiving
- Schedules: approvals (supervisors, other departments), files to in-house production, files to prepress, job delivered
- Quality requirements: industry guidelines, corporate standards
- Digital standards: fonts, applications, color spaces, file formats, transmission methods
- Cost control: prepress, paper, overs and unders, terms and conditions

Documents
- Descriptions: specifications, purchase orders, alterations
- Agreements: quotations, contracts
- Proofs: preliminary, contract, press sheets
- Delivery: shipping, inventory, confirm meeting specifications
- Financial: invoices, statements

Technical tests
- Calibrate: monitors, scanners, printers, imagesetters
- Preflight: software and applications

Archives
- Materials: art, photos, files, film
- Documents: descriptions, agreements, proofs, delivery, financial

---

refers to art that communicates; the "design" part to planning for production.

Designers subcontract for services and pass the charges on to clients along with a markup. Often, however, designers stop short of contracting for the printing itself. Few design studios have sufficient cash flow to broker major printing jobs; most prefer to have the customer contract directly with the printer.

If you coordinate printing for yourself, insist that your graphic designer and printer consult with each other. Unless you have agreed differently, your designer's responsibility stops when you accept mock-ups and files. To assure appropriate quality at reasonable costs, and to keep alterations to a minimum, the designer must know specifics about the prepress, press and bindery requirements of the printer.

SERVICE EXPECTATIONS
At most printers you deal with a sales representative (also called an account rep) and a customer service rep. Good sales and service reps ensure that printers produce jobs properly and on time. They suggest ways to raise quality and cut costs, pick up and deliver copy and samples, and answer technical questions.

Sales and service reps also work within the printing company on behalf of customers. They monitor estimates to keep costs down, work with prepress staff and press operators to keep quality up, and check with production supervisors to keep jobs on schedule. Your reps may compete with other reps in the same company for press time and priority in bindery.

15. What services do you want from your printer?
Many printers follow the rule of thumb that customers talk price but buy service. This guideline recognizes the fact that printed pieces influence every aspect of how organizations function, so printing customers often place a higher value on dependable schedules than on flawless production or low price.

Visual 1-6 helps you identify what services

you want. After making your own list, show it to your printer so you can both feel clear about what to expect.

INVOLVING YOUR PRINTER

For any job with workflow or specifications new for you, talk with a printer or production manager as early in the planning as possible. Describe your needs and ask whether the shop can produce your piece efficiently. Consider suggestions about alternate papers and formats as well as other ideas about how to save time and money.

When talking with a printer, show a mock-up to help visualize the final printed piece. The dummy might be anything from a simple thumbnail to a comprehensive layout that looks much like the final product.

You can make a dummy showing bindery needs by folding one or two sheets of paper to simulate your format. On larger jobs, such as books and annual reports, a paper distributor will assemble and bind a dummy to your specifications. When a printer makes a dummy for you, or gets one from a paper merchant, it costs you nothing and may save you thousands.

Comprehensive layouts, known simply as "comps," tell the printer precisely how you expect the job to look. They help printers think about practicalities such as ink coverage and accuracy of folding. You can produce simple comps with colored markers or more accurate comps on your desktop printer.

Tell the printer what aspects of the job you consider important. If you require just-in-time delivery but don't care about holding shadow details in photographs, say so. Also ask for examples of the printer's work that look similar to your job. Study them carefully, knowing that they represent the shop's best work, not its average.

The human side of production

If you're like most printing buyers, you have several projects happening all at the same time and all in different stages of production. Each project involves three or four people at each stage, so you coordinate the work of dozens of professionals every week. To make matters even more complicated, projects range from simple business forms or newsletters to complex catalogs or packaging.

Many people working on projects that you coordinate know more about specifics of the printed piece than you do. Treat them as colleagues, not subordinates. Try to help others focus on the writing, design or production that forms their piece of the puzzle. When you concentrate on setting schedules, defining quality and controlling costs, you act like a coach, not a supervisor.

WORKING WITH PRODUCTION MANAGERS

People in your own industry can recommend local brokers, agencies and designers. So can graphics consultants for paper distributors. Because these people routinely call on agencies and designers, they can recommend services suited to your needs.

Classified directories list advertising agencies under a variety of categories, such as "Advertising—Direct Mail," as well as under the main listing "Advertising Agencies." Most graphic designers and printing brokers are listed only under their own classifications.

Hiring expertise in design and production does not exempt you from planning. To get the best work from designers and agencies, explain your goals and audiences and provide rough guesses about format and budget. Don't waste a professional's time and your money because you have no idea what you want. Describe what you consider appropriate quality by showing samples of work that you find satisfactory.

There is a fine line between being specific enough to get what you want and general enough to stimulate creativity. Take time to describe yourself and your organization. The conversation may reveal needs you didn't know you had. For example, if you want presentation folders for a convention, a designer may suggest you also get name tags and notepads with coordinated logos and colors.

Accountability for the accuracy of final copy lies with you. Conscientious professionals ask

....

clients to approve all proofs. An agency, broker or graphic designer should ask you to sign proofs just as a printer would.

Agencies and designers charge for their services either by the hour or by the job. Agencies also commonly charge a retainer, which may or may not include hourly rates. Finally, an agency, designer or broker may mark up printing costs 15 to 30 percent.

Working with a creative or production service increases the complexity of electronic interface. Before entering production, verify that all the computers and software that you believe can interface actually do. Run several tests before signing a contract.

COPYRIGHT CONCERNS
Clients and vendors in the graphic arts must consider how copyright law affects business agreements. The following paragraphs present the key issues. Use this information to decide whether you need further research or to consult an attorney.

For links to Web sites that keep you up-to-date about copyright, visit the site for this book (www.gettingitprinted.com).

Intellectual property
Copyright law protects creators of intellectual property when they have placed their creations in a tangible medium of expression. Media of expression include printed products, photos and drawings, CDs, Web sites and computer software.

Both the content and the design of graphic messages are intellectual property. "Content"

generally refers to writing. "Design" means images such as logos, illustrations and photographs and the unique way those images are assembled in a publication.

The person or organization that owns the content or design may license it or sell it to someone else. If someone reproduces the property without permission, they have used it illegally.

Intellectual property is usually licensed, not sold, and the license is usually for a special purpose. For example, a photographer may license an image for reproduction in an annual report. The company that published the annual report should not use the photo in a brochure or on a Web site without paying an additional license fee to the photographer.

Intellectual property includes software, which is protected by copyright. When you "buy" software, you actually buy only a license to use it under specific circumstances, such as on one computer (single user license) or at one location (site license).

Files and fonts
Type fonts are copyrighted computer programs.

Copyright law is clear that customers should pay to use fonts. The law is also clear that "using a font" does not include sending it to prepress along with other files for a job. Prepress should pay for its own fonts, not use fonts supplied by customers.

Although the law is clear, most printers expect customers to send fonts with jobs. In fact, printers report that their most frequent problem with customer files comes from wrong or incomplete fonts.

A few printers insist that they pay for their own libraries of fonts. If a job requires a font not already in the printer's collection, the printer buys it.

Customers who want to stick to the letter of the law pay additional costs for font licenses that allow them to send fonts to vendors. Printers who want to stick to the letter of the law verify that customer fonts have such broad licenses or, as an alternative, buy their own licenses for fonts their customers use.

Work for hire

Copyright belongs to the person or organization that creates the work. If a logo, technical drawing or photograph was made by a freelance artist, the creator owns the copyright. If the work is created by an employee as part of job responsibilities, the organization owns the copyright. Even if an image was created on commission for a client, the artist owns copyright unless the contract between client and artist includes a specific provision—called work for hire—that transfers ownership to the client.

Copyright protection extends to work by prepress services. When prepress workers enhance files by correcting color and trapping images, or when they make sketches, dummies, proofs and/or film, they create new products. These products form the basis of the trade custom saying that "creative work developed or furnished by the provider is the provider's exclusive property." We discuss this and other trade customs in chapter ten.

Freelancers, agencies and printers should protect their own interests and help clients avoid disappointment by dealing with copyright issues early in negotiations for new jobs. Vendors and clients are free to negotiate any transfer of rights they find mutually agreeable, but should express their agreement clearly in writing before work begins.

Creative work is copyrighted when it becomes published, whether in print or on an electronic medium. Most publishers put their names, the copyright symbol and the year of creation on the work itself. For example, art appearing on a banner might include in small lettering "©1999 Outdoor Design Group." A

form designed by the owner of a small business could include the notice "Copyright © 2001 Quick Muffler Shop."

To establish an exact date of copyright, you can fill out a form, pay a small fee and send examples of your creation for official registration. The formal procedure is necessary before defending a copyright in court or to have it honored in other countries. U.S. copyright laws are administered by the Copyright Office of the Library of Congress, Washington, DC 20559. ■

1-5 CHOOSING A PRODUCTION MANAGER

When evaluating the print-buying skills of a graphic designer, advertising or public relations agency, or printing broker, keep in mind the following guidelines:

• Ask what procedures they use to control costs.

• Insist on references from previous customers *and* from two or three printers. If they cannot supply names of both customers and printers, keep looking.

• Ask to see actual printed products (not just designs) similar to those you have in mind. If you plan to publish books, don't plan to work with someone specializing in clothing or catalogs.

• Determine how much they mark up the printer's invoice. You need to know how much you pay for the professional's service.

• Judge whether you feel comfortable with the person. If the relationship succeeds, you're going to spend a lot of time working together.

1-6 SERVICE EXPECTATIONS

Most printing customers consider service more important than quality or price. Good service starts with a clear understanding of expectations.

- What do you expect from your printer?
- What does your printer need from you?

Use the following checklist to help you identify what service you expect. After making your expectations clear to yourself, review them with your printer. Verify that your printer will provide the service you want and that you can pay for it.

CUSTOMER EXPECTATIONS

You should assume that your printer meets the following minimum level of service:

- provides quotes and contracts based on specifications
- produces jobs with the quality and quantity specified
- delivers jobs by the contracted deadline
- charges according to the contract with any increases clearly explained

PRINTER EXPECTATIONS

Good service requires doing your part of the job. Your printer should assume that you meet the following minimum levels of expectations:

- complete specifications and purchase orders
- mock-ups showing bleeds, backups, folds, etc.
- printouts showing contents of files
- files and art that conform to specifications, mockups and printouts
- minimum alterations
- reasonable schedule
- schedule changes when you make alterations
- quotes and proofs returned within 24 hours
- prompt arrival for press checks
- prompt payment of bills

If you don't meet the expectations above, you probably are not a profitable customer.

Expectations in the following checklist go beyond these fundamental levels of service. The checklist is divided into five categories: communication, prepress and press, additional services, cost control and training.

COMMUNICATION

■ **Customer to printer methods** ———————

specifications	__in person	__fax
	__Web site	__E-mail
files	__in person	__Web site
	__E-mail	__delivery service
art	__in person	__mail
	__delivery service	
changes	__in person	__fax
	__Web site	__E-mail
proofs	__in person	__E-mail
	__Web site	

■ **Customer phone to printer** ———————

sales

office _____	fax_____
mobile_____	home_____
☐ call any time	call only __AM to __PM
E-mail _____	

customer service

office _____	fax_____
E-mail _____	
Web site _____	
comments_____	

■ **Printer to customer methods** ———————

sales	__in person	__phone	__fax
	__Web	__E-mail	
customer service		__in person	__phone
	__fax	__Web	__E-mail
proofs	__in person	__Internet	
	__intranet		
production department		__in person	__phone
	__fax	__Web	__E-mail
shipping department		__in person	__phone
	__fax	__Web	__E-mail
accounting department		__in person	__phone
	__fax	__mail	__E-mail

■ **Printer phone to customer** ———————

office_____	fax_____
mobile_____	home_____
☐ call any time	call only __AM to __PM
E-mail _____	
Web site _____	
comments _____	

■ **Speed of response** ─────────────

quotes	__1 hr	__12 hrs	__24 hrs	__48 hrs
preflight	__1 hr	__12 hrs	__24 hrs	__48 hrs
proofs	__1 hr	__12 hrs	__24 hrs	__48 hrs
job status	__1 hr	__12 hrs	__24 hrs	__48 hrs
invoices	__1 hr	__12 hrs	__24 hrs	__48 hrs

■ **Packing/shipping labels** ─────────────

__job number __bar code __count __weight

■ **Company policies** ─────────────

__quality manual   __terms and conditions

PREPRESS AND PRESS

■ **Files** ─────────────

__convert to CMYK	__adjust color
__adjust traps	__adjust dot gain
__fix in prepress	__return for fix

■ **Proofs** ─────────────

__desktops __bluelines __overlays
__integrals __remote

comment_____

■ **Press checks** ─────────────

__at any time   only ____ AM to ____ PM
__at end of press   __in proofing room

ADDITIONAL SERVICES

■ **Premanufacturing** ─────────────

__copywriting	__proofreading
__photography	__design
__layout	__illustration
__manage databases	__procure bar codes

■ **Repurposing** ─────────────

__Web pages	__compact discs
__presentations	__signage

■ **Other printing methods** ─────────────

__digital __flexo __screen
__gravure __thermography
__foil stamp   __die cut
__emboss/deboss   __engraving
__other_____

■ **Other printed products** ─────────────

__magazines/catalogs __books/manuals
__forms __annual reports __labels
__packaging __other_____

■ **Post production** ─────────────

__return edited files __return original files

■ **Archiving and storage** ─────────────

__files __film __art __proofs
__products __time to keep materials_____

■ **Packing and fulfillment** ─────────────

__assemble and package
__address, bundle and mail
__maintain/mail customer lists
__documentation for import/export

COST CONTROL

■ **Change orders** ─────────────

__proceed immediately __notify about cost
__always   __only if over $_____

■ **Overs/unders** ─────────────

within ± _____ percent

■ **Break out costs** ─────────────

__prepress __paper __bindery

■ **Work with accounting** ─────────────

__discounts __payment schedules

TRAINING

■ **Technical support** ─────────────

__answer questions	__offer suggestions
__at printing plant	__at customer site

■ **Advice about documentation** ─────────────

__specifications	__job tickets
__change orders	__purchase orders

■ **Advice about preparing files** ─────────────

__dot gain	__image trapping
__correcting color	__preflighting
__repurposing	

■ **Advice about workflow** ─────────────

__file formats __transmission options
__research new technologies

■ **Test images** ─────────────

__ RIT __GATF __FOGRA

■ **Printing standards** ─────────────

__SWOP __SNAP __GRACOL

■ **Advertisement standards** ─────────────

__managing color __file formats

■ **International standards** ─────────────

__paper weights and sizes __ink

■ **Environmental awareness** ─────────────

__use less paper	__tree-free papers
__eco-friendly inks	__use less film

2. USING TYPE AND GRAPHICS

To keep up-to-date about using type and graphics, visit our Web site (www.gettingitprinted.com).

Printers think of the visual elements of printing jobs as either line copy or continuous-tone copy. Line copy is high contrast, usually black on white. It includes all type, rules and many illustrations. Continuous-tone copy has dark and light areas, but also has many intermediate shades of gray. It includes all photographs and some illustrations.

Effective typography requires decisions about design and production. Design involves size and style, line length and spacing and alignment. Design makes type readable. Production involves ink color and coverage, and the color of paper and printed backgrounds. Production makes type legible.

As you work with type, keep in mind the graphic part of graphic design. You may have access to hundreds of fonts and faces, but don't let the wizardry of your computer carry you so far away that you mystify your readers.

FONTS, FACES AND FAMILIES

A type font is a complete assortment of upper- and lowercase characters, numerals, punctuation and other symbols of one typeface. A font is a concept, not a physical object. Most fonts are digital, but a font could also exist on a piece of film or in a box of metal type.

Typefaces are grouped into families with similar letterforms and a unique name, such as Prestige or Garamond. The "parent" of the family is the letterform in book or light; the "relatives" are derivations such as bold, italic or condensed.

Useful type families include typefaces with a variety of weights, such as light and bold, and come in both italic and roman (upright). In addition, you may find bold weights available in condensed, extended and other versions for headlines.

Whether type looks bold or italic or appears any way other than normal is called having a style or attribute. In most type families, roman is normal (no style) and every other face has a style.

Assigned styles. Word processing applications allow you to change the way type looks by selecting words, then clicking to create appearances such as bold and italic. Prepress services call this process stylizing a font, also known as assigning an attribute. Assigned styles, however, are not the same as the real fonts used by software that controls imagesetters. For that reason, type with assigned styles looks different coming from the imagesetter than it did on the computer screen or from the desktop printer.

When you prepare your jobs for prepress, make sure to convert assigned attributes to their corresponding fonts. Page layout applications such as Adobe PageMaker and QuarkXPress include dialog boxes to make conversion simple. Conversion utilities, however, only work with type in native applications. If you have imported type from one application into another, such as from Adobe Photoshop into WordPerfect, your page layout software will not identify the stylized type.

You may find specifying typefaces confusing when different manufacturers give different names to typefaces that seem identical. Helvetica, for example, may also be called Helios, Newton, Megaron or Swiss. Fonts of the same typeface from different manufacturers may vary slightly with regard to fractions and special symbols and even design of the letterforms themselves. If you must switch from one manufacturer's font to another while staying with the same typeface, ask to see complete font printouts so you can compare characters.

BASIC TYPE FONTS

Art applied to letterforms is as ancient as writing itself. Today there are thousands of published typefaces. The huge variety of fonts and almost infinite range of sizes, however, often leads to typography that confuses the reader rather than communicates.

You can design almost any publication by selecting from a handful of type families that you know well. Working with just a few type families controls costs and speeds production. You limit the risk of errors in files, make it easier to work with imaging services, enable faster turnaround time and reduce the danger of miscommunication among creative and production services.

Following is a basic list of families. You can design almost any publication by using one family from each of these categories:

• Sans serif family, such as Helvetica, Futura or Avant Garde, for headlines, in posters and display ads, for callouts and data in infographics, and for short reference listings such as in an index. Make sure the family includes the full range of bold, light, extended and condensed characters.

• Serif family, such as Bookman, Palatino or Times Roman, for text and captions and for long reference listings such as in a glossary. Make sure the family includes italic and semibold as well as roman type.

• Script family, such as Zapf Chancery, for pull quotes and on certificates.

• Modified serif family, such as Optima, for business forms and catalog sheets and as an occasional alternative to your sans serif family. Make sure the family includes the full range of bold, light, extended and condensed.

• A collection of symbols and dingbats.

To ensure the best quality from your hardware, make sure fonts are installed in your printer as well as in your computer.

....

❝ Whenever I inspect a comp or preflight a file, I try to imagine it reproduced 10,000 times. That motivates me to double check for every possible flaw I can avoid. ❞

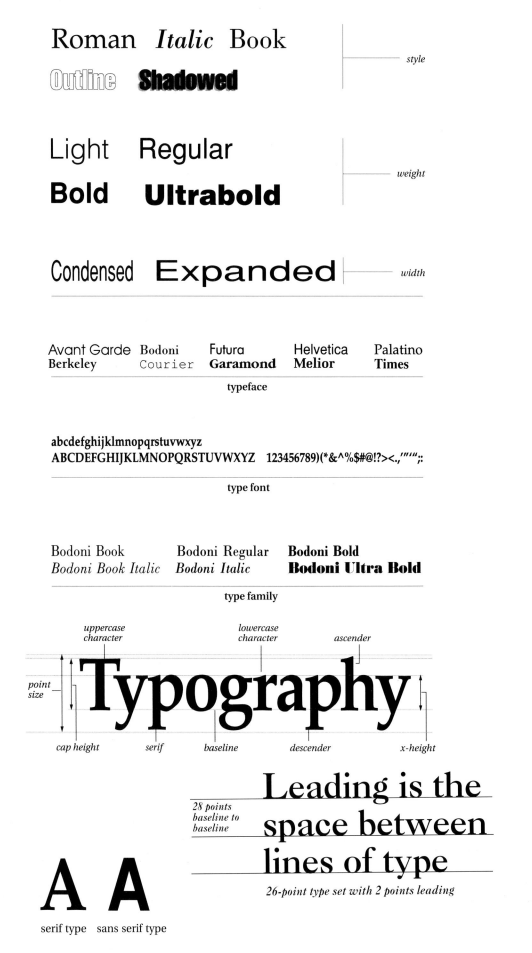

Roman *Italic* Book

Outline **Shadowed**

style

Light Regular

Bold Ultrabold

weight

Condensed Expanded

width

Avant Garde	Bodoni	Futura	Helvetica	Palatino
Berkeley	Courier	**Garamond**	**Melior**	**Times**

typeface

abcdefghijklmnopqrstuvwxyz
ABCDEFGHIJKLMNOPQRSTUVWXYZ 123456789)(*&^%$#@!?><.,'""";:

type font

Bodoni Book   Bodoni Regular   **Bodoni Bold**
Bodoni Book Italic   *Bodoni Italic*   **Bodoni Ultra Bold**

type family

uppercase character   lowercase character   ascender

point size

Typography

cap height   serif   baseline   descender   x-height

Leading is the space between lines of type

28 points baseline to baseline

26-point type set with 2 points leading

A A

serif type   sans serif type

2-2 SELECTING AND SPECIFYING TYPE

During more than five centuries of typesetting in hundreds of languages, five basic rules for readability have emerged. Modern science, using techniques to measure eye movement and comprehension, has verified these rules.

Keep typography simple. Stick with one type family. If your job calls for captions, quotes and several levels of subheads, use a type family with an appropriate variety of weights, both for roman and italic, and perhaps small capitals. Build variety by changing size, weight and slant, not by switching type families.

Stay consistent. Stick with the same typeface for each element of your publication. If you set your first major headline in 30-point Times bold, use that typeface for all major heads.

Use both upper and lower case. The shape of whole words helps people read as much as the form of individual letters does.

Words in all capital letters are more difficult to read than words using both upper- and lowercase. Words formed from lowercase letters have unique outline patterns, so readers see familiar words as whole ideas. Words in all caps have no distinctive outline and force readers to slow down to grasp their meaning.

Keep lines short. The average reader takes in three or four words per eye movement and comprehends best when making two eye movements per line. The ideal line length is seven or eight words. Figuring an average of six characters per word, lines containing between forty-five and fifty-five characters work best.

Use serifs. Materials such as books and magazines that take more than a few minutes to read call for a typeface with serifs that lead the eye from one letter to the next. Serifs make type more readable and reduce eye fatigue.

DESCRIBING TYPE

Graphic arts professionals use many units of measure to describe typography. The three most important units are points, picas and inches. Points describe the height of characters (type size) and space between lines (leading). Picas describe width of columns, alleys and gutters. Inches describe height of columns.

Printers developed the concepts of points and picas centuries ago, but their usage continues today. In practice, inches are often used instead of picas—but never instead of points. To make matters even more confusing, in France and a few other countries, there is a

2-1 Characteristics of type (opposite page) Typography has many features that affect both readability (easy to read and understand) and legibility (sufficient contrast with background). Using standard terms to describe these features helps you communicate clearly with graphic designers and printers.

system of points and picas in which the units are slightly different from points used in England and North America. The rest of the world, quite sensibly, uses metric units (millimeters) to describe typography.

You can see these units of measure on your screen along the rulers of page assembly and word processing software. Many programs allow you to switch from one unit to another. Menus in all programs ask you to specify type size in points.

One pica equals .166 inch (4.218mm) and has 12 points. One point equals ½ pica and .013875 inch (.351mm). Note that type points are different from points used to express the thickness of paper.

You often hear the terms "text type" and "display type" used to express size. Text type refers to any type smaller than 14 points; display type is any type larger than 14 points. Type that is 14 points may be either text or display, depending on its use.

Rules

Lines in the graphic arts are called rules and are described using the same system as type. Points express the thickness of a rule, and picas or inches express its length.

Try to avoid using the term "hairline rule." In addition to the large number of subjective viewpoints about the width of a hairline, there are at least four specific definitions used by graphic arts professionals that range from .003 inch to ¼ point. Always give a specific measurement—the terms "hairline rule" and "hairline register" only invite misunderstanding.

PRODUCING TYPE

Mishandling fonts creates more problems for customers and printers than any other aspect of print production. One reason is because the rules are not clearly spelled out.

We explained the legal aspect of font licenses in chapter one. The business aspects vary greatly among vendors. Some vendors expect customers to supply printer fonts along with the job. Others want both screen and printer fonts. Still others maintain their own libraries of fonts and charge extra to license fonts not already in the collection.

Regardless of how you deal with vendors about fonts, efficient production requires that you identify each font clearly and completely. You need to supply the name and manufacturer of every font in your design.

Type fonts fall into two general categories: Type One (Adobe) and TrueType (Microsoft). These two brands are vector based, which means you can enlarge or reduce the type without losing quality. Some older and custom fonts, such as Adobe Type Three, are bit-mapped, which means that enlarging characters makes their edges look jagged because of low resolution.

Adobe Type One

Most publishing applications use Adobe Type One fonts, which have two versions: screen fonts and printer fonts.

Screen fonts are loaded into the system via a font utility. Loading the font into the system allows the monitor to display the font, but only at the monitor's resolution.

Most screen fonts do not give high enough resolution for a font to look good in print, so publishing systems include printer fonts linked to screen fonts. Printer fonts are PostScript applications that a monitor cannot display. When you issue a print command, the screen font links with the printer font so the output device can produce high-resolution characters.

TrueType

Some applications use Microsoft TrueType, which combines screen fonts and printer fonts into one file. Fonts are loaded via a separate utility. More important from the standpoint of

---

2-3 COMMON MISTAKES WITH TYPE DESIGN

Printing dollars work hardest when design supports communication. Research shows that you can make type convey your message best when you avoid the following common mistakes:

- lines more than fifty characters long
- sans serif type used for body copy
- text type overprinting a screened image
- insufficient leading and tracking
- long sections of body copy in all caps
- reverses out of tints less than 50 percent
- too many typefaces and weights on one page
- highlight colors used without clear purpose
- drop caps poorly related to their corresponding word
- type of one color printed on a background of another color with the same value, such as medium red on medium blue

publishing, TrueType fonts are rasterized by the host computer, not by the printer.

Output devices must have a TrueType interpreter to use TrueType fonts. Devices without interpreters do not print the fonts correctly. Even some high-resolution output devices at some prepress services do not have a TrueType converter. If you use TrueType, make sure to confirm that your prepress service can work with your files.

SCREEN TINTS

You can use screen tints to highlight copy, accent charts and graphs, and simulate changes in the density of ink. Areas of some illustrations in this book that look shaded are screen tints. You may also hear a screen tint called a fill pattern, tint, tone, screen or shade.

Screen tints create the illusion of shading because they are printed in tiny dots instead of solid blocks. Each dot has the same density as all other ink on the sheet, but dots vary in size according to the ruling and percentage of the tint required.

Every screen tint has three features you need to specify.

Ink color. This is usually the same as used for type, most often black.

Ruling. Ruling refers to the distance between the rows of dots, expressed in lines per inch. Screens with relatively few lines per inch are coarse; fine screens have many lines per inch. You may also hear screen ruling called line count or screen value.

Countries using the metric system specify screen ruling in lines per centimeter (lpc) instead of lines per inch (lpi). For example, a screen with 175 lpi has 70 lpc.

Dot area. Dot area refers to the relative size of dots that a screen allows to print and is expressed as a percentage. Dot size determines how dark or light screen tints seem. Lots of paper showing around the dots makes the tint seem light; not much paper showing makes it seem dark. For example, a 10 percent screen allows ink to cover 10 percent of the image area.

A 90 percent screen is close to solid; a 10 percent screen seems very light.

Screen ruling affects how screen tints and halftones look when printed. When printed on coated paper, fine screens yield sharper images than coarse screens but are more difficult to print. A 100-line screen has 10,000 dots per square inch, whereas a 133-line screen has 17,689 dots per square inch—almost twice as many.

Lines per inch and dots per inch (dpi) have different meanings. With digital output, each dot consists of several pixels. A dot built from two or three pixels at 300 dpi is much less precise than one built from four or five pixels at 1,200 dpi. Visual 4-5 illustrates this concept.

Choosing screen ruling

The best screen ruling for a printing job is determined by the image to be reproduced, technique used to make the screen and the press and paper used for the job. No job has a "correct" screen ruling.

You or your printer can create screen tints while preparing files for print. Most applications let you choose ruling and density. Many programs also allow you to choose ink color and create graduated screens (vignettes).

When your design calls for screen tints, keep in mind a few rules of thumb. Some papers, especially those without coatings, absorb more ink than others, so require coarser screens. Coarse screens yield fewer dots per inch, so the dots are less likely to run together when they spread on absorbent paper.

Tints of less than 10 percent tend to disappear, especially when printed using a light ink color; tints of more than 70 percent tend to look solid, especially when using a dark ink color. Some ink colors look better screened than others. Dark blue becomes light blue, while red becomes pink.

To judge how colors look when screened, consult a tint chart available at most graphic arts stores, commercial printers and design studios. Don't judge by what you see on your monitor. Several paper mills also make tint charts showing

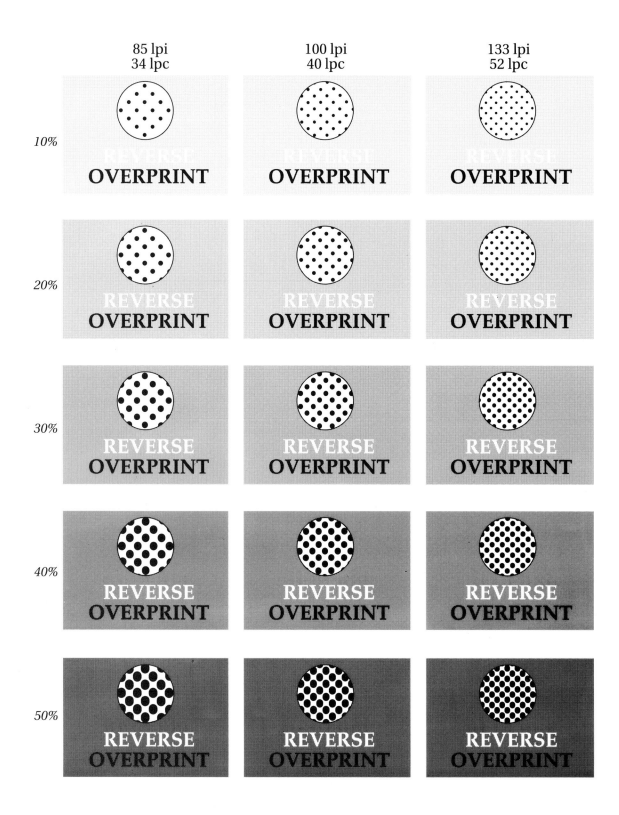

2-4 Tints, reverses and overprints *Density, ruling, ink color and dot gain determine how screen tints look when printed. Hues become lighter when screened. Paper, printing method and quality requirements determine ruling and percentage for a specific job. Plan carefully for overprints and reverses to ensure that words stay legible and fine lines stay visible.*

popular ink colors on their brands of paper.

You can screen and overlap two inks to create the illusion of a third color, as illustrated in Visual 3-7. Ink colors, paper absorbency, screen rulings and percents, and the way screens align all affect the results. Improper alignment of screens by the printer can cause distracting moiré patterns. If you are at all uncertain about the outcome, get advice from your printer.

REVERSES AND OVERPRINTS

A reverse is type, graphic or an illustration reproduced by printing ink around its outline, thus allowing the underlying color or paper to show through and form the image. The image "reverses out" of the ink color, as in Visual 2-4.

While type printed as a reverse can catch the eye, it can also lead to problems. Lines less than half a point thick may fill in with ink when reversed. Text type becomes less legible when reversed, whether or not the typeface includes fine lines and regardless of type size. Use reverses only to accent messages and as part of designs such as nameplates, never for blocks of text type.

A large reverse out of solid ink means printing a large solid that may lead to mottling or ghosting. Consult with your printer before making final decisions about design.

ILLUSTRATIONS

Line copy illustrations can come from a variety of sources. Clip art is most common.

Clip art means copyright-free drawings ready to insert into designs. Images are arranged by topic such as holiday themes, health care or family life. Extensive collections come on compact discs.

Any dark drawing on light paper works as an illustration ready to scan. Images on off-white or colored paper may lack sufficient contrast to scan well, but might be enhanced by first making

a photocopy. Images should look dense and uniformly black without fuzzy or broken lines.

When buying clip art, verify that file formats work with your software. Popular subjects come as EPS (Encapsulated PostScript) files. More specialized images, however, may remain in applications such as Adobe Illustrator or Corel-DRAW. Read the fine print before you buy.

Original drawings for line art should have sharp, black lines to reproduce without halftoning. Illustrations in continuous tones made with pencil, felt marker, airbrush, ink wash, charcoal, paint or computer must be screened into halftones or color separations. The processes are identical to those for photographs explained in chapter four.

An illustration done originally in full color may be printed in a single color but requires special attention. If you are uncertain about how an illustration will print, show it to a printer before including it in a design.

Many graphic designers also create illustrations. The best illustrators, however, tend to specialize in this single aspect of the graphic arts. Illustrators need to know what information drawings must convey and what style you want. Show the artist some drawings you like, and ask if your work can have the same style.

Clear job definition leads to satisfactory illustrations and means you can estimate costs. A good illustrator asks questions, then develops sketches for approval before drawing final art.

Fine artists produce work for enjoyment in its original form; commercial illustrators create work for reproduction by printers. A commercial illustrator's work should reproduce well on press. The art should not have delicate lines, which might disappear when images are reduced or reversed. Plan art to reduce or enlarge at similar percentages to assure consistent appearance.

When soliciting business, illustrators show examples of their work. To verify that illustrators plan for printing processes, ask to see examples in printed form as well as original art. ■

3. MASTERING COLOR

To keep up-to-date about controlling color, visit our Web site (www.gettingitprinted.com).

Adding color to your printing jobs makes them more complicated and expensive. You can control costs and support success by knowing how design, ink and paper interact to produce colors.

Color can be described objectively but is experienced subjectively. Age, gender, culture and many other factors affect the physiology of vision and the psychology of response.

The wide range of color sensation means that graphic arts professionals need proper training and tools to communicate about color. Professionals need ways to standardize viewing conditions; calibrate machinery; and control colorants, the manufacturing process and the quality of supplied material. They also need ways to speak clearly about color to people in other related fields, such as photography and packaging.

In this chapter you learn about terms and tools printers use to help make reproducing colors more precise, predictable and consistent. When you use the language and aids used by printers, you reduce uncertainty and help avoid costly mistakes.

While reading this chapter, keep in mind two of the most fundamental concepts of the graphic arts:

• No device or technique for reproducing color comes even close to the ability of the human eye to perceive color.

• Computer screens, photographs, proofs and every other device or system used to design a printing job can produce more colors than a printing press.

3-1 BASIC INK COLORS

You can design almost any publication by selecting from a handful of colors whose effectiveness you know well and that readers find attractive. While it's tempting to follow trends, the colors listed below prove most popular year after year.

Violet. Pantone Violet or Trumatch 39-b4.

Warm red. Pantone 032 or 185, or Trumatch 6-a.

Cool red. Pantone 199 or Trumatch 2-a.

Burgundy. Pantone 201 or Trumatch 2-b6.

Blue. Pantone 286 or 300, or Trumatch 36-b1 or 34-a.

Green. Pantone 347 or Trumatch 19-a.

Brown. Pantone 469 or Trumatch 49-a6.

In addition to facilitating design, working with just a few colors controls costs and speeds production. You limit the risk of errors in files, make it easier to work with imaging services, and reduce the danger of miscommunication among creative and production services. Furthermore, these hues are so popular that many ink companies keep a premixed supply as spot colors, so they cost less.

Deciding whether color is good enough requires knowing exactly how well you need it to look for a specific printing job. For example, a brochure about jewelry calls for better color than a poster about roofing materials. Furthermore, precise control means knowing what portions of a job matter most. In the jewelry poster, for example, the gems require faithful reproduction, but colors in the headlines may need little attention.

THE MAGIC OF COLOR

Color is a psychological and physiological phenomenon created by an object, an observer, context and light. Understanding these properties makes you more able to predict and control color perception and reproduction.

Object

The same color ink looks different when applied by different presses or printing systems to different substrates.

Color changes as light gets absorbed or reflected from ink and paper. Learning to predict and control printed color requires understanding how ink and paper interact. This chapter and the next two focus on ink.

Ink absorbs light. As a layer of ink grows thicker it absorbs more light, making the ink appear darker. For example, cyan ink in a can appears almost black. When a press puts a thin film of that ink on a piece of paper, it looks cyan.

Paper affects color by absorbing ink and because of its own color. Chapter six deals with how paper color and absorbency affect ink colors.

Observer

The same color ink looks different to different people. The human eye has three types of cones that each see a different color. Scientists call this arrangement trichromatic vision—"tri" for three, "chromatic" for color. Trichromatic vision means that humans can match all of the colors in the visible spectrum by mixing red, green and blue.

Because combinations of red, green and blue create so many colors, these three are called the additive primaries. The additive primary colors are abbreviated RGB.

Normal color vision means that all three types of cones operate properly. Color blindness begins when one or more of the cones loses proper function. For example, some people can not see the red in a traffic light because the cone that should respond to the red component of light doesn't work.

Approximately 2 percent of women and almost 10 percent of men have some form of color blindness. Furthermore, the ability to perceive colors accurately deteriorates with age.

In addition to physiological factors, color perception is influenced by culture, climate and many other factors. And even if everyone sees the same color, each may respond to it differently. For example, people of different ages identify with different colors just as they do with different music.

Color is relative. No matter how carefully you specify color, a significant portion of the population will see and respond to it differently. Keep this in mind before you insist on precise color reproduction that drives up costs and throws off deadlines.

Light

The same ink color looks different under different light sources.

Light affects how you see color. For example, incandescent light—ordinary round bulbs—makes orange and red seem warm. Most fluorescent tubes make colors seem green or yellow, which explains the green cast in many photos taken indoors.

Scientists use temperature as one measure of light. White light has a high temperature, and temperature becomes lower as light becomes more red or orange.

Color professionals use the Kelvin system to describe light temperature. Zero Kelvin means no heat. Fluorescent bulbs range from 1,800 to 2,500. Sunlight ranges from 4,500 to 7,000, depending on weather conditions, time of day and latitude.

The wide range of light temperatures means that a color may look different under different lighting conditions. For example, the reds on two packages may look identical in the light of your office and different in the light of a store. You can see this phenomenon by taking a shirt that looks black under artificial light into bright sunlight, where it may seem dark blue.

Whether your product ends up on an office desk, store shelf or T-shirt on the shore determines what light influences its colors. When color is critical, evaluate it under lighting in the field as well as under standard conditions.

PROPER VIEWING CONDITIONS

Because color values change from one light source to another (called metamerism), graphic arts professionals use standard viewing conditions to evaluate color. These conditions simulate daylight and other light sources and are illustrated in Visual 3-3.

Standard viewing conditions vary around the world. In North America, daylight is described as 5,000K or D50. Values elsewhere may vary anywhere between D50 and D65 (6,500K).

You can find standard conditions at printers, design studios, agencies and prepress services. They range from small booths to small rooms near printing presses.

If your work space has fluorescent fixtures, you can come close to standard conditions by replacing stock tubes with daylight tubes, available from any electric supply company. Stock tubes are coded CW (cool white) or WW (warm white). Daylight tubes are coded D. Light from D tubes seems white compared to the slightly blue or yellow light from stock tubes.

If you feel uncertain about lighting in a particular setting, you can test it quickly using a metameric ink swatch. When you view the swatch under D50 to D65 lighting, its color looks uniform. When you inspect the swatch under other lighting conditions, it shows broad stripes of dark and light.

Metameric swatches are available as press-on labels so you can easily attach one to a proof or press sheet. You can buy metameric swatches from an art supply store or from product catalogs produced by the Graphic Arts Technical Foundation.

Standard viewing conditions also entail a 60 percent neutral gray background. This background ensures adequate neutral light reflectance while not causing color shifts or casts. You may not want to measure 60 percent reflectance,

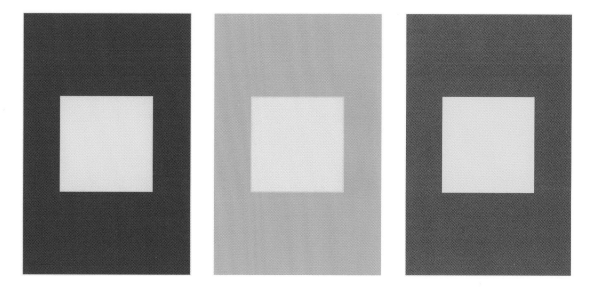

3-2 Color in context *The same ink color looks different when viewed against different backgrounds or next to different colors. The yellow square in each of the examples above uses identical ink and density but appears different because of its context.*

When you design a printed piece, consider context when selecting colors. Keep in mind that light backgrounds make foreground colors look lighter and dark backgrounds reduce contrast with foreground colors. Also remember that color may change, as when the warm hues fade from posters and displays exposed to prolonged sunlight.

but you can come close enough by placing color swatches or photos on a light gray surface.

THE LANGUAGE OF COLOR

No topic in the graphic arts has less precise language than color. Experts use different terms to describe identical features and sometimes identical terms to describe different features. This confusion often reduces quality, increases costs and delays schedules.

To make your communication about color as clear as possible, you need to know the possible sources of confusion and how to avoid them. This skill requires understanding color models and gamuts.

Color models

Scientists and artists have systems that organize colors into logical relationships. These systems, called color models, help describe, measure and control various ways of producing color.

Color models describe colors without referring to the media or device used to create the

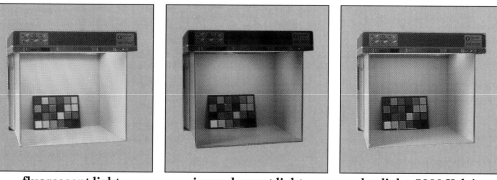

fluorescent light   **incandescent light**   **day light, 5000 Kelvin**

3-3 Standard viewing conditions *Many agencies and studios use a small booth in which to inspect color. As shown above, you can adjust lighting in the booth to simulate a variety of light sources. (Color matching booth courtesy of Macbeth Corp.)*

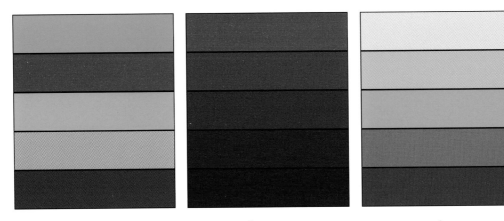

| **hue** | **chroma** | **value** |
| *color* | *saturation, depth, intensity, purity, value* | *tone, lightness, shade* |

3-4 Features of color Professionals agree that color has the three traits represented above, but they don't agree on what to call those traits. For that reason, you need to recognize each of the terms that might apply to any color and, whenever you suspect confusion, insist that communication become clear.

color or the observer who sees the color. Graphic arts professionals call this feature device independence. It means that color models help different machines, such as computers and printing presses, produce similar colors. Models also help standardize colors among brands of inks, dyes and other colorants.

The color model used most widely in the graphic arts was developed by the Commission Internationale de l'Éclairage (International Commission on Illumniation) and is abbreviated CIE L*A*B. Software such as PostScript, computer printers, press controls, spectrophotometers, and other equipment and supplies for the graphic arts rely on the CIE L*A*B system.

The CIE model is so popular in graphic arts that a group of international companies use it as the basis of their International Color Consortium (ICC). The organization sets standards so that color images created using proprietary software can travel among applications, then print accurately on a variety of output devices.

Gamuts and palettes

Color models include most of the colors humans can see, but media and devices used to reproduce color cannot create every color in the model. They have limited range.

Professionals use the word "gamut" to refer to a range of colors. When you hear that one device has a larger gamut than another, it means that the first device can reproduce more colors than the second. A desktop printer able to reproduce one thousand colors has a larger gamut than a printer able to reproduce only one hundred colors.

The concept of color gamuts applies to any device or substance able to reproduce color. Computer and TV screens, photographic film and printing presses all have different color gamuts.

Color gamut depends partially on core technology (monitors have larger gamuts than film) and partially on manufacturing standards (high-end scanners have larger gamuts than desktop scanners).

In Visual 3-1, we suggest seven ink colors that you might keep in mind when you begin designing a printed piece. These seven, or any other collection of colors, represent a color palette. The term comes from the wooden tray that artists use to hold and mix paint.

You can see color palettes in guides published by Pantone and other companies, in books from Rockport Press and North Light Books (publisher of this book) and on several Web sites. Palettes are useful to help you choose colors. Equally important, a palette from which you take colors for all your designs lets you establish color standards with your printer.

Hue, chroma and value

If you had a bag of marbles that all looked blue, you could separate them into three groups. One group would contain blue marbles with slightly different colors. This is called the hue. The second group would have the same hue that looks more or less rich. This is called chroma, or brightness. The last group would have marbles that had the same hue but that had more or less gray, making the marbles look lighter or darker. This is called value.

Visual 3-4 represents this division among hue, chroma and value. This visual represents the confusion and inconsistency in the language of color.

Try to describe the difference between the reds in the middle column of Visual 3-4. Photographers say some look more saturated than others. Fine artists say some look more pure or intense than others. Graphic designers and printers say some have more depth or value than others. Scientists say some have more chroma than others.

Notice that each professional refers to the identical group of reds. To make matters even more confusing, maybe you chose a word that no one else used.

Now try to describe the difference between the blues in the far right column. Professionals from various fields use terms such as value, tone, lightness, brightness and shade. More confusion here, especially because value was also a term referring to differences among the reds.

Confusion and inconsistency about the language of color has practical consequences. For example, many computer programs refer to HLS or HVS. In this case, *L* (lightness) and *V* (value) have identical meanings. But if you told prepress that you wanted red with more value meaning saturation, and operators gave you red with more value meaning lightness, who is responsible for producing the incorrect color?

Warm, cool and clean

In addition to terms referring to the three basic traits of color, you often hear a color called warm or cold. Temperature analogies are used to describe colors of both inks and paper. For example, a press operator might say that cool paper destroys the effect of warm reds.

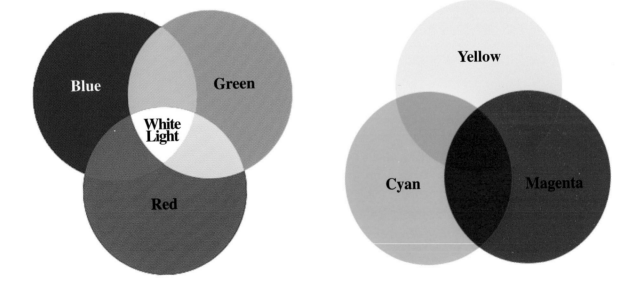

3-5 Additive and subtractive colors When the additive colors overlap, they create white (total color). When the subtractives overlap, they create black (total absence of color).

The black created by the subtrative colors isn't dense enough to produce strong contrasts, so printers add black ink. The letter "K" represents the black used in four-color process printing.

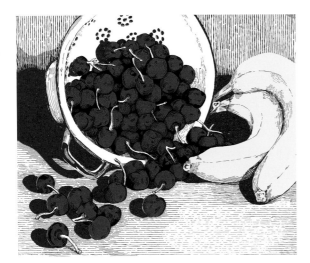

multicolor printing

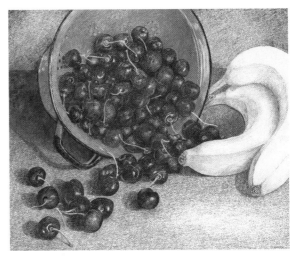

4-color process printing

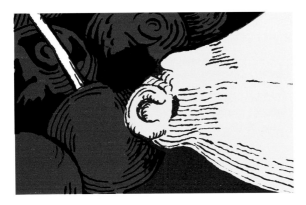

multicolor enlarged to 600%

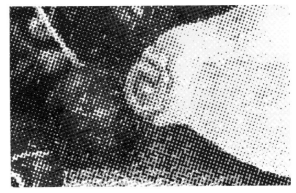

4-color dots enlarged to 600%

3-6 Spot color and four-color process *Printers can use either spot inks (also called flat inks) or process inks to create color. The multicolor image is reproduced in black, magenta and yellow printed as spot inks. The red is produced by printing 100 percent yellow over 100 percent magenta.*

Four-color process printing is for reproducing photographs and other continuous-tone copy. Printers must use all four standard ink colors and only these four. Other ink colors won't work. With multicolor printing, any ink colors work.

Cool colors are blues, greens and some grays that suggest cool places or scenes. Paper with a slight blue cast is called cool.

Warm colors are yellows, oranges and reds that suggest warm places or scenes. Paper with a slight yellow or light brown cast is called warm.

You often hear neutral hues, such as gray and beige, described by how warm and cool they seem. For example, a designer might call for a cool gray background for one ad and prefer warm gray for another. Cool gray has a slightly blue tinge, and warm gray looks slightly brown.

Notice that warm and cool are terms with cultural, not scientific, meanings. What appears warm in North America may not seem warm in Thailand.

In addition to temperature analogies, designers and printers often refer to clean color. This term has even less precise meanings than warm and cool. By clean, some designers mean free from smudges and mottles. Others mean consistent or uniform. Still others mean bright or vivid. When you hear someone refer to clean color, ask what they mean.

RGB AND CMYK

Color on a computer monitor and on a printed page consists of millions of dots, but the dots on each medium have different hues. Images on the monitor consist of patterns of phosphors that are red, green and blue: RGB for monitors. Images on paper consist of patterns of cyan, magenta, yellow and black dots: CMYK for printing.

Inks and toners create colors by subtracting light from red, green and blue. Removing light results in the colors cyan, magenta and yellow, called the subtractive primaries and abbreviated CMY.

Visual 3-5 illustrates the differences between additive and subtractive colors.

Images printed only with subtractive colors do not have sufficient contrast. For that reason, printers add black ink to parts of the image. The black ink is abbreviated with the letter *K*, resulting in the CMYK combination. Printing with the four colors of ink abbreviated CMYK is called four-color process printing.

Preparing designs for printing requires changing RGB color to CMYK color. Chapter four describes this process.

The color gamut of RGB is larger than the color gamut of CMYK. The CMYK process can't produce all the colors that are achievable by using RGB values. In other words, a printing press won't reproduce all the colors you see on your computer screen.

Plain English

Throughout this book, you learn many technical terms that describe printed color. Knowing what those terms mean helps you control quality and costs. You do not, however, have to use all those terms in everyday conversation about the graphic arts. Plain English usually works better than technical jargon.

When you speak with a printer, use everyday language to describe what you want. Say, "Colors don't seem bright enough," and let the technicians worry how to make them brighter. Unless you feel very confident, avoid requests such as, "Bring up the magenta." Describe the problem, but don't tell the printer how to fix it.

SPOT AND PROCESS COLOR

Printers have two ways to reproduce color. Spot color requires blending different inks into one ink resulting in the required hue. This method resembles blending paints for household use.

The second way to create a color is the four-color process printing we just described. Dot patterns of the four process colors simulate the desired hue as shown in Visual 3-6. You can also see the process colors printed as spot inks (without dots) in Visual 3-6.

Process colors have identical names everywhere in the world but do not have identical hues. Yellow and cyan inks used in North America are slightly less opaque than the yellow and cyan used elsewhere. There are numerous magenta hues throughout the world. If you print outside your own country and color match is critical to your job, verify that samples and proofs coordinate with the process hues on press.

Printers use four-color process to reproduce color photos and illustrations. If design requires

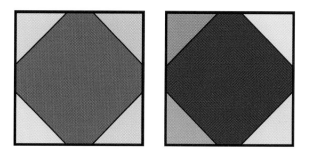
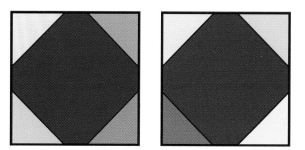

3-7 Color builds *You can overlap screens of the process colors to create thousands of additional colors.*

Dot gain and register affects colors that you build from screen tints. For best results, especially with light colors, use combinations of only two colors, not blends of three or four colors. If your design calls for an exact color match, use a spot ink instead of a color build.

3-8 Moiré pattern *Duotones, separations and overlapping screen tints may show a moiré if screens are not placed at correct angles relative to each other. A moiré may also develop when an image already reproduced as a halftone, such as a photo in a magazine, is scanned or rescreened for another publication.*

four-color printing for photos, then it's convenient to simulate spot colors using the same four ink colors. It is important to understand that if you are using a four-color process to simulate spot colors, the spot color may not look the way it was designed to look. If design doesn't require four-color printing, use spot colors. They cost less and they are easier to control.

The four-color process requires one inking station per color. Most printers use a six-color press, although some produce process color work using a two-color press (two passes through the press) or a one-color press (four passes through the press). Printing on a six-color press costs more than printing on a one-color or two-color press but produces process color jobs more quickly.

COLOR BUILDS

Graphic designers use screen tints of spot colors and process colors to create the illusion of many new colors. Visual 3-7 illustrates the concept.

Builds from spot colors. You can create the illusion of many different colors using only two colors of ink printed at various screen values and overlapping each other. The most common combination uses black plus one other color.

Printers and art supply stores have books that specify colors and screen percentages to create thousands of colors.

Builds from process colors. In addition to using the process colors for photos and illustrations, you can use them to simulate spot colors. The Pantone company and other publishers produce guides that compare spot colors and process color builds.

Some colors work better than others when created from process colors. Oranges, violets and greens are especially difficult to control. Fluorescents and metallics are impossible.

COLOR REFERENCE SYSTEMS

Whenever precise color affects the success of your printed product, you need a printed reference of all the colors available on press. Printed references help you:

- decide what colors you want
- compare colors on paper to colors created by media such as computer screens or marking pens
- determine how well four-color printing can simulate a spot color
- specify colors to graphic designers, prepress services and printers

Take each word in the phrase "printed reference" literally. Your reference requires ink on paper just as your printed product does. No matter how well calibrated your computer monitor, how sophisticated your software or how faithful your photocopier or desktop printer, they can't substitute for ink on paper.

A printed color reference is a guide, not a pretty example. It must convey exacting standards, integrate with other production tools and carry authority with everyone involved in the production sequence.

There are three kinds of printed references used throughout the graphic arts industry: swatch books that are part of color matching systems, images that are part of software packages, and references created for specific products or organizations.

Swatch books

Swatch books published by companies such as Focaltone, Pantone and Trumatch resemble books of color samples you may have seen at paint stores. Graphic arts swatch books, however, identify colors by number, not by name as in books of paint colors. Everyone in the production sequence, from design to printing, refers to colors by their numbers. For example, instead of saying, "I want bright red," you would tell a printer you want Pantone 299.

Color matching systems are communication tools, not limits on creativity. You can specify or try to match any color you find attractive. Matching systems simply help everything go smoothly and quickly by assuring that everyone is talking about the same color.

The system developed by Pantone Inc. is the oldest and most commonly used color matching system. It includes thousands of spot colors and their approximations in four-color process. Pantone guides are also available for metallic, fluorescent and pastel colors. Many Pantone colors integrate with colors in marking pens and other materials used by designers. Pantone also publishes guides showing how colors appear as builds of process colors and when printed in tint percentages with black.

Companies that produce color matching systems do not manufacture ink. Companies that make ink can license Pantone colors and mix inks to color specifications from printers.

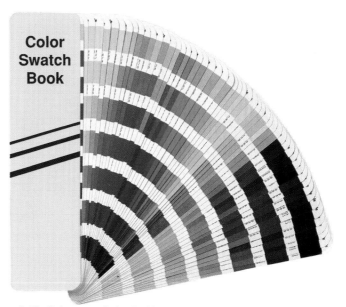

3-10 Color swatch book *Many reference guides for color matching systems appear as books that you can fan out to compare colors. Publishers identify each swatch with a number.*

Swatch books come in many versions, such as metallic inks and four-color simulations of spot colors. Prepress services, printers, ad agencies and design studios have copies of the swatch books. You can buy your own copy at an art supply store. Companies that make ink often give copies of swatch books to printers and their customers.

3-9 SPECIFYING COLOR

When you specify a color, whether created by mixing an ink or by four-color process printing, specify whether you want the printer to "use" or "match" the color.

Using a color. This means ordering ink mixed according to the formula in a swatch book. Using a color build means printing screen percentages of inks according to guidelines in a swatch book. In both cases, the printer follows your instructions regardless of how other factors, such as paper, might affect the final outcome.

Matching a color. This means that you want color on your printed piece to look as close as possible to the color you see in a swatch book or in a sample such as a piece of fabric. Your printer selects the formula for spot ink or blend of screen percentages to achieve that effect.

To help you select and specify colors, publishers of computer programs for design and illustration incorporate color matching systems into their software. You can select colors on the screen that coordinate with colors in swatch books.

When you work with colors on a computer screen and in a swatch book, keep in mind the impact of paper on ink color. Features such as ink holdout, whiteness, opacity and brightness all influence hue, saturation and value. Color matching systems make some attempt to compensate for the effects of paper by publishing swatch books on different stocks, such as coated, uncoated and newsprint. Looking at colors on paper similar to the stock for your job helps you imagine the final outcome but cannot replace evaluating color on the exact sheet you plan to use.

If a spot color is critical to your job, ask for a drawdown. Your printer applies the exact ink specified to the exact paper chosen for the job.

Color Control Bar

© Graphic Arts Technical Foundation, 1992

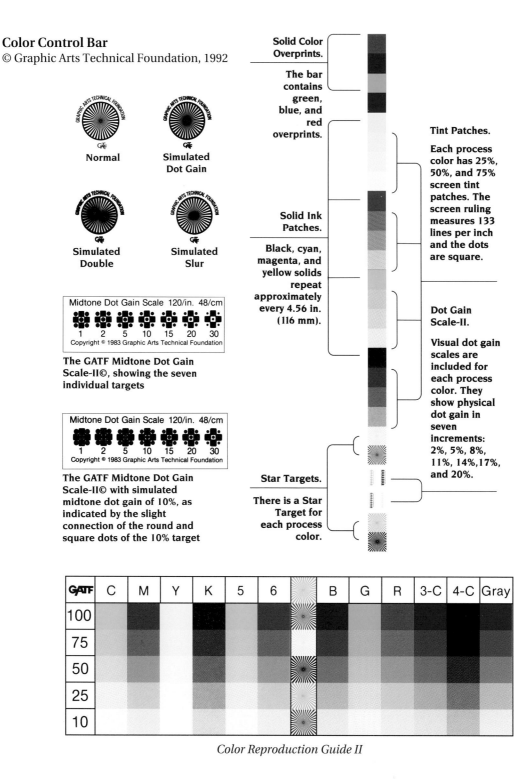

Normal

Simulated Dot Gain

Simulated Double

Simulated Slur

Midtone Dot Gain Scale 120/in. 48/cm

1 2 5 10 15 20 30

Copyright © 1983 Graphic Arts Technical Foundation

The GATF Midtone Dot Gain Scale-II©, showing the seven individual targets

Midtone Dot Gain Scale 120/in. 48/cm

1 2 5 10 15 20 30

Copyright © 1983 Graphic Arts Technical Foundation

The GATF Midtone Dot Gain Scale-II© with simulated midtone dot gain of 10%, as indicated by the slight connection of the round and square dots of the 10% target

Solid Color Overprints.

The bar contains green, blue, and red overprints.

Solid Ink Patches.

Black, cyan, magenta, and yellow solids repeat approximately every 4.56 in. (116 mm).

Star Targets.

There is a Star Target for each process color.

Tint Patches.

Each process color has 25%, 50%, and 75% screen tint patches. The screen ruling measures 133 lines per inch and the dots are square.

Dot Gain Scale-II.

Visual dot gain scales are included for each process color. They show physical dot gain in seven increments: 2%, 5%, 8%, 11%, 14%,17%, and 20%.

GATF	C	M	Y	K	5	6		B	G	R	3-C	4-C	Gray
100													
75													
50													
25													
10													

Color Reproduction Guide II

3-11 Color control images Printers add color control bars, such as the vertical strip above, to proofs and press sheets to help evaluate features such as density and dot gain. Control bars have screen rulings appropriate to the paper and press used for the job. Typically they contain 25 percent, 50 percent and 75 percent screen tints of each process color in addition to solids, gray balance targets and overprints to test ink trapping.

Printers use guides such as the one above to calibrate equipment and establish standards for their shops. Notice that the Color Reproduction Guide II allows space for fifth and sixth spot colors and shows the RGB outcome of overprinting pairs of process colors.

3-12 CONTROLLING COLOR QUALITY

Many factors influence color on a printed product. When you produce a printing job, you control some of them, such as:
- quality of originals and separations
- paper surface, coating and color
- ink color and density
- register and dot gain
- effect of varnish or coating

Your printer controls additional factors, such as:
- ink tack
- pressroom humidity
- paper conditioning

Neither you nor your printer influences other factors, such as:
- color blindness
- light source for viewing printed pieces
- coating that yellows with age
- inks that fade in sunlight

Regardless of how hard you try, you cannot ensure that people who see your products will perceive the same color that you controlled so carefully throughout the production process.

Drawdowns are the only way to see how ink and paper interact before going to press. Printers and ink manufacturers make free drawdowns at your request.

You can specify any color to match a sample, but remember that printers may have a hard time or may not be able to match colors made from pigments not found in printing inks. Matching an ink color to a sample of paint, dye, colored paper or fabric may require extensive consultation between printer and ink manufacturer to reach a satisfactory result. You pay for that extra attention.

Reference images

Many designers use color images printed on reference sheets to calibrate digital devices and promote efficient workflow. The sheets are part of the documentation of color management utilities from companies such as Apple, EFI and Kodak.

Color management utilities use spectrophotometers to read the color values. After selecting the reference image that best suits your needs, you can calibrate your scanner, monitor, digital camera and output devices to the image you selected.

Reference images do not have standard names or numbers as do patches used with color matching systems. You must tell everyone in production what utility and image you used.

Custom references

Referencing for specific products or organizations means that you calibrate everything in your production process—equipment, software, paper and printing—to your own standards. The task may seem daunting, but it is much easier than it appears when it's carried out for appropriate products.

A product is appropriate for custom referencing if you produce it over and over again, as you would a newsletter or magazine. Even if you don't produce a periodical, you could custom reference a series of books, brochures or manuals—any printed piece whose design specifications remain constant.

The more people and products you have in print production, the more important it becomes to establish color standards. People see color so differently and color varies so much with substrate and lighting that consistency requires using every possible technique.

Custom referencing requires running tests and keeping detailed records about design and printing. For example, you might design a logo calling for overlapping tints of process colors, as shown in Visual 3-7. You could develop a test pattern using various combinations of screen percentages, produce film or plates for the pattern at two different imagesetter outputs, then have a printer reproduce the pattern on eight or ten candidate stocks. The printer would keep ink density uniform throughout the run. In this case, you might learn that the exact right hue is 20/60 black/cyan printed on 80# Vintage dull running the black density at 1.60 and the cyan density at 1.35.

Producing your own references demands painstaking effort—only worth the work when color is critical or you feel fascinated by statistical process control. Making the effort, however, can give you command over quality not available from other procedures.

ENSURING COLOR QUALITY

When you can describe the color quality you want, you control cost and schedule as well as satisfactory appearance. But not all colors that you can see will reproduce well on press. Even the best printers need you to tell them what colors in the piece are critical. Exact color match involves much more money and time than many projects require.

Graphic arts professionals think of three quality levels of color. Printers and prepress services use the levels to estimate how much attention a job requires. As you learn in chapters four and five, each level points to starting with different originals, using different methods to prepare them for printing, and evaluating different kinds of proofs.

Pleasing color

Red looks red, not orange or brown. Whites are white and skin isn't purple. Pleasing color is also known as newsprint quality color and production color.

You accept pleasing color in products with modest budgets, such as your employee newsletter or staff directory. You can see pleasing color in rack brochures and newspaper inserts. Basic quality and many good quality printing jobs produce pleasing color. Most desktop systems can produce proofs, film or plates for pleasing color.

Match color

Match color requires matching a specified spot ink color, such as found in a Pantone swatch book, or matching color photos. You can see match color in clothing catalogs, coffee-table books, travel magazines, and brochures for automobiles and appliances. Premium and some good quality printing jobs produce match color, sometimes known as magazine quality color.

Match color requires production techniques beyond the capabilities of most desktop systems. You need to work with an imaging service or printer with (1) imaging devices that can capture the full range of color and tone and (2) skilled operators.

Match original

Match original, the most demanding level of color, requires matching an original scene, product or unique swatch. You can see color printing at this level in upscale annual reports, calendars from large art museums and catalogs for expensive clothing and jewelry. Designers often bring samples of fabrics to press checks to get ink colors as close as possible to product colors. Showcase printing jobs produce match original.

Match original requires production techniques found only at the best imaging services and printers. You can expect to pay top dollar, take lots of time and have close involvement in evaluating color. ■

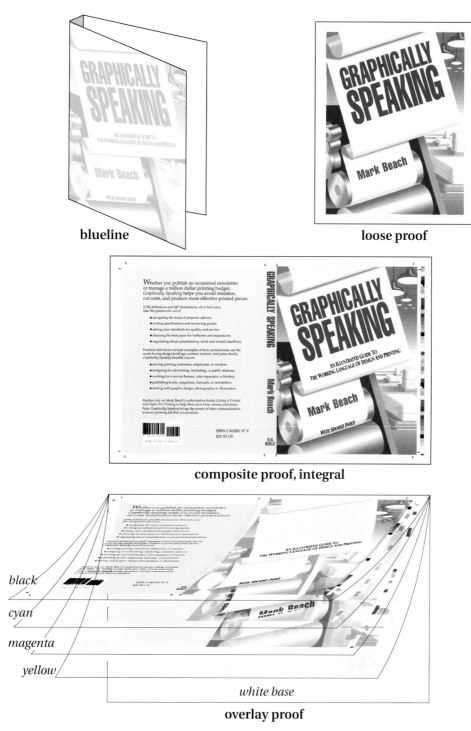

blueline

loose proof

composite proof, integral

black

cyan

magenta

yellow

white base

overlay proof

3-13 Common proofs *Proofs help you control color quality by predicting how images on files or film will appear on paper.* Pages 71–73 explain how to use each kind of proof most efficiently.

4. CONTROLLING PHOTOGRAPHS

To keep up-to-date about reproducing photographs, visit our Web site (www.gettingitprinted.com).

Controlling photos for reproduction requires further understanding of the relationship between design, prepress and printing. This understanding helps you predict how images will appear when reproduced and leads to lower costs and dependable schedules.

Original photographs on film are continuous-tone copy, with many hues from dark to light. Continuous-tone copy must be converted into halftones before printers can reproduce it. Original photos from digital cameras, photo compact discs and the Web are already digitized, which is the first step in the halftoning process.

In this chapter you learn what to look for when examining photographs for printing, and see differences between images that will reproduce well and those that will not. You also learn how to make the transition from RGB to CMYK to ensure the quality you want in parts of the image you consider important.

Photographic terms are so similar to printing terms that you need precise language to avoid confusion. We refer to black-and-white prints, color prints and transparencies simply as photographs to make it clear that these are originals. To identify reproductions made on a printing press, we use the standard graphic arts terms halftone, duotone and separation.

Although this chapter is about photographic images, much of its information also applies to continuous-tone illustrations. They, too, must be converted into halftones or separations before printing.

4-1 EVALUATING ORIGINAL PHOTOS

To ensure halftones and separations that meet your goals, start with good originals. Don't try to salvage images unsuited to your publication. When examining photos, get your images off to a good start by using the following guidelines.

For basic quality printing:

Focus. Important features instantly recognizable.

Grain. Enlargement to publication size doesn't make the image look too grainy.

Flaws. No scratches, dirt or stains.

Tonal range. Contrast and some middle grays.

Color. Colors identifiable.

Photos for basic quality jobs are often made using snapshots from inexpensive cameras and produced at automated photofinishing services, so the prints may meet these standards only marginally. Other photos begin as images in consumer-priced digital cameras that capture only a small percent of the information in the original scene.

For good quality printing:

Focus. Important features look sharp.

Grain. Enlargement to publication size doesn't make the image look too grainy.

Flaws. No scratches, dirt, blemishes or stains. No distracting features in the image.

Tonal range. Good contrast and a full range of grays showing detail in both highlights and shadows.

Color. For pleasing and production standards. Colors look saturated. No distracting cast.

You can use a single-lens reflex 35mm camera or midpriced digital camera to make photos for good quality jobs that meet these standards with only occasional exceptions.

For premium quality printing:

Focus. All features look sharp throughout controlled depth of field.

Grain. Enlargement to publication size doesn't make the image look grainy.

Flaws. No scratches, dirt, blemishes or stains. No distracting features in the image. No patterns that might cause moirés.

Tonal range. Dmax 1.7 for black-and-white prints, 2.0 for color prints and 2.4 for transparencies. Tonal range visibly consistent for all photos throughout the publication.

Color. For match photo standards. Colors close to original scenes or products.

Photos for premium quality jobs are made by professional photographers and should meet these standards with rare exceptions.

For showcase quality printing:

Focus. All features look sharp throughout controlled depth of field.

Grain. Enlargement to size for publication reveals no grain.

Flaws. None.

Tonal range. Dmax 1.8 for black-and-white prints, 2.1 for color prints and 2.5 for transparencies. Tonal range measurably consistent for all photos throughout the publication.

Color. For match original standards. Colors true to original scenes or products.

Photos for showcase quality jobs are made by top professional photographers and should meet these standards with no exceptions.

IMAGES FROM FILM

Preparing photos for reproduction should start with the best quality originals you can provide. Contrast tends to decrease during printing, so originals need good contrast and a full range of tones. The original should not look flat (low contrast) or have either highlights or shadow areas without detail (high contrast).

The emulsion coating of photographic film consists of grains of silver salts that are sensitive to light. Films with rather large grains capture images using less exposure to light than films with smaller grains. Because of this versatility, photographers refer to large-grained film as fast and smaller-grained film as slow.

Images made on fast film don't look as sharp as those made on slower film. Moreover, enlarging photographs makes grains bigger. The lack of sharpness carries over into printing plates, detracting from the clarity of the image.

Prints

When considering photos for black-and-white printing, you evaluate enlarged prints or contact prints of unenlarged negatives. The groups of unenlarged images on one sheet of paper are proof sheets. Choosing photos from proof sheets (also called contact sheets) lets you see every image, not just those the photographer wants to show you.

Use a loupe to inspect images on proof sheets from 35mm film. Place the magnifier directly on the surface of the print to examine focus and detail.

Even using a magnifier, it is difficult to detect on proof sheets the distractions, such as white coffee cups and reflected flashes, that can ruin a picture. If you plan to enlarge an image more than 150 percent or feel uncertain about focus, flaws or distractions, order a photograph made to size. The new photo reveals whether the image is worth reproducing.

When using proof sheets, specify choices and instructions in red. Use a permanent felt marker or grease pencil to show cropping and areas to lighten or darken during darkroom printing. Remember that all the images on the proof sheet were made at once with one exposure. Some may not look as good as they would if made individually.

When ordering prints, keep in mind that semigloss photographic paper looks more like the printed piece than gloss, so it gives a better idea of the final outcome.

If you have original images on disc, you examine them on a computer screen rather than on paper. The screen gives the image much higher contrast than it can have on paper. To simulate the image in your printed product, output it using a laser printer with at least 600-dpi resolution.

Transparencies

The best separations originate from transparencies, because they have greater tonal range than prints. Photos originating on film have greater tonal ranges than photos taken with digital cameras.

When you examine color photos, use a correct light source, as described in chapter three. Standard viewing conditions are the first key to color quality control.

When projecting transparencies or viewing them on a lightbox, be cautious. Backlighting helps to examine sharpness and study key elements, but the intense brilliance may deceive you about how bright images will appear when reproduced. Backlighting also shows more shadow detail than a press can reproduce.

Transparencies are viewed properly with emulsion side away from you to assure that you see the scene the same way the photographer did. Put the emulsion side down on a light table or toward the screen during projection.

There is a direct relationship between size of the original film image and sharpness of the image when enlarged for printing. A 35mm slide enlarged to 8″ × 10″ grows by 700 percent. If the image is cropped even slightly, enlargement can be over 1,000 percent. Enlarging decreases sharpness because it magnifies the grain structure of the film. Keeping enlargement to a minimum guarantees the sharpest possible printed image.

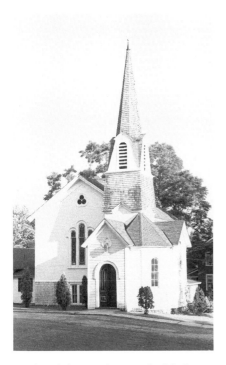
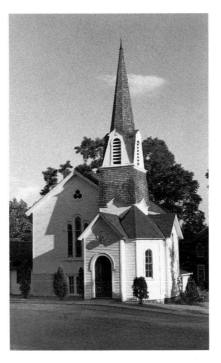
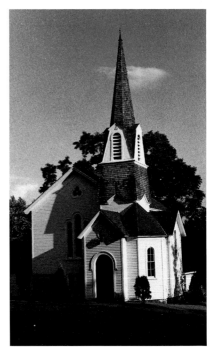

detail dropped out in highlights   *good contrast and detail*   *detail lost in shadows*

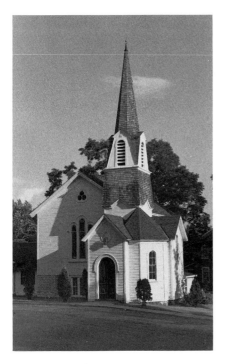
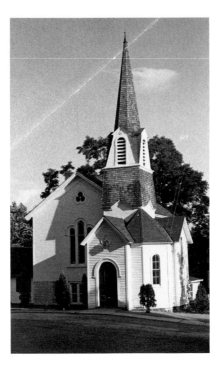
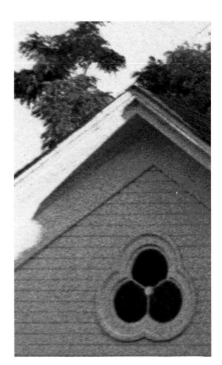

flat contrast   *flaws*   *grain enlargement*

4-2 Black-and-white photos To get good halftones, start with good originals. Four of the photos above were poorly exposed, developed or printed, so they would not look good if reproduced. Look for full tonal range and good contrast. Good originals show details in their highlights (lightest areas) and shadows (darkest areas). Photos with too much contrast may lack detail. Low-contrast images reproduce as flat and lifeless. Images made on fast films or inexpensive digital cameras may not look sharp when enlarged.

All printing should begin with the sharpest possible photographs. Ideally, showcase and premium printing should begin with large-format transparencies. In the parlance of photography, 35mm is small format, $2\frac{1}{4}'' \times 2\frac{1}{4}''$ is medium format, and $4'' \times 5''$ and $8'' \times 10''$ are large format. It is not likely, however, that you will get $8'' \times 10''$ photos under conditions of aerial or wildlife photography, but you should expect to receive large-format images from studio work.

Color films are made for exposure under specific lighting conditions. If the light wasn't right, photographs may have a color cast that was obviously not part of the original scene. Photographs made with outdoor film, for example, may have a gold cast if exposed under tungsten light and a green cast under fluorescent light.

Color photographic prints made for reproduction are known as C-prints when made from negatives and R-prints when made from trans-

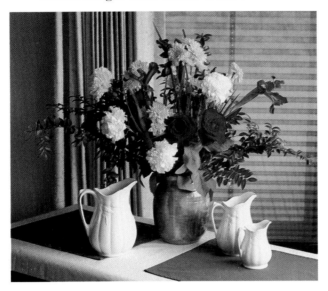

normal exposure, good detail

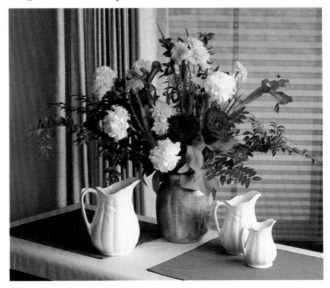

blue color cast

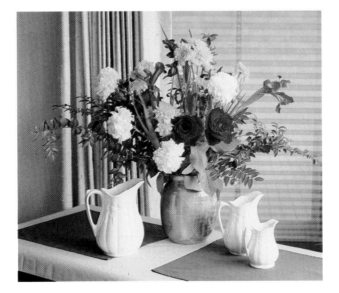

overexposure, poor highlight detail

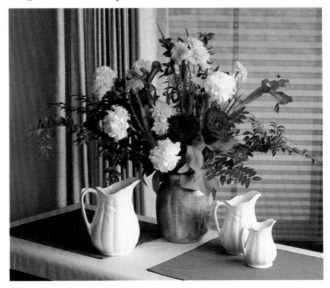

underexposure, poor shadow detail

4-3 Color photos *Color images exposed under improper lighting may have a color cast. Underexposure or overexposure can also lead to loss of detail in shadows or highlights. Pre-*

press services may eliminate casts when making separations, but can't put details into separations when none exist in originals. (Photo by Kathleen Ryan.)

parencies. C-prints and R-prints are already second-generation images when given to a printer or imaging service.

DIGITAL ORIGINALS

Digital originals are photographs made with digital cameras or downloaded from photo compact discs or the Web. The quality of the image-capturing device used to digitize the image gives you a hint how well the image will print. The section of this chapter about scanners gives guidelines.

When evaluating digital images, don't rely on your monitor to judge color. In addition to examining the image itself, use image-editing software to examine the image's histogram. Each section on the histogram's scale represents one gray level or color. If the histogram appears smooth, you can expect good tonal reproduction. If the histogram looks like a comb with missing teeth, you won't get a full range of tones.

Using an image-editing application also allows you to look for neutral grays. Use the application's on-screen densitometer to view CMY values. Images with neutral grays need less color correcting than those whose grays are out of balance.

HALFTONES

Images for reproduction must be changed from continuous tones to halftones before a printer can reproduce them on press. Halftones consist of thousands of tiny dots that create an illusion of the original image. The pattern of dots tricks the eye into thinking it sees continuous tones. In areas of the image with small dots, more paper shows through, creating highlights; the portions of the image with large dots show less paper, thus reproducing shadow areas.

Black-and-white photographs converted into dot patterns are called halftones; color photographs prepared for printing in color are called separations. Use these terms for all images converted to dot patterns, whether they appear as negatives, proofs or in the final printed product.

Color photographs may be scanned as a halftone for printing black-and-white, but they don't

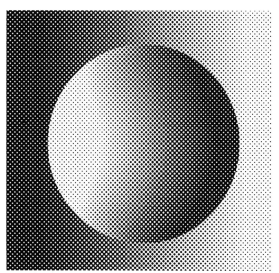

4-4 Continuous tones to halftones *The ball and background screened at 30 lpi makes halftone dots easy to see. You can also see that dots in the bright (highlight) area are smaller than dots in the dark (shadow) area. As you move the image farther from your eyes, individual dots seem to connect to form one image. Halftone dots stay the same distance from each other but change in size to create the illusion of continuous tones.*

look as good as starting with a black-and-white photo of the same image.

Halftones and separations are produced by imagesetters that output files originating from any of the following devices:

- a scanner, which converts images on film or paper into digital information
- a video camera, which has the original photo on tape (you select one frame at a time that a computer digitizes for print output)
- a digital camera, which captures the original photo as digital information

If you don't have a scanner and want to work with film photos on your computer screen, take your film to a processing service that can output results to a photo compact disc or place them for pickup from the World Wide Web. Use disks or a Web archive to store a library of photos ready to insert into newsletters and brochures. Stock photo services also offer images on disks and Web sites.

You can specify halftone negatives at a variety of standards depending on whether your job prints good, premium or showcase quality. Some of the quality distinctions come from extra care by scanner operators. Make sure to tell your imaging service if you plan premium or showcase printing.

SCANNING

Halftones and separations begin with scanners. Some scanners have light that passes the copy four times to make CMYK files. Other scanners scan images in one pass to make an RGB file. To allow four-color process printing, operators must separate the RGB file to CMYK files. Separations are made by the scanner's software or by using an application such as Adobe Photoshop.

The quality of the scanner that captures and digitizes the image affects the output. Scanners use one of two types of input technologies: charge-coupled device (CCD) and photomultiplier tube (PMT).

CCD scanners, also known as flatbed scanners, have an array of photosensitive diodes. When light hits the array, the diodes give off charges equal to the levels of light. The light is digitized and the diodes' output value becomes part of the image data.

PMT scanners, also known as drum scanners, are like television tubes in reverse. A television tube emits light when charged, while a PMT emits an electric charge when light hits it. The

photomultiplier tube sends the charge to a converter that changes the energy into digital data.

To ensure quality separations, a scanner should use at least twenty-four bits per scan. In addition, the device should be capable of high resolution, density range and dynamic range.

Resolution

Both input devices (digital cameras and scanners) and output devices (desktop printers and imagesetters) use tiny points to build images. Resolution refers to the number of points per inch used for input or output.

Graphic arts professionals use many terms to describe resolution. You hear the resolution of scanners described in elements per inch (epi), spots per inch (spi), dots per inch (dpi) and pixels per inch (ppi). You also hear the resolution of printers and imagesetters described in epi and dpi. To make matters more confusing, you also hear halftone resolution described in lines per inch (lpi).

To help you understand the rest of this chapter, the following is how we use the terms:

Spots per inch (spi) refers to points used for input by scanners and digital cameras. You cannot see a spot. When the resolution of a scanner is expressed as 3,000×3,000, the numerals refer to spots per inch.

High-end scanners have resolutions of 8,000×8,000 spi or greater. Low-end devices might have resolutions of 600×1,200 or even 300×600.

Pixels per inch (ppi) refers to the resolution of a computer monitor. Pixels consist of spots. You can see a pixel. When you hear about a 2,400-ppi scanner, try to think spots per inch, not pixels per inch.

Dots per inch (dpi) refers to the spots made by desktop printers and imagesetters. When you read about a 300-dpi laser printer or 1,200-dpi imagesetter, try to imagine a tiny digital point, not a halftone dot.

Lines per inch (lpi) refers to the relative size of halftone dots. High screen rulings, such as 175 and 200 lpi, have relatively small dots.

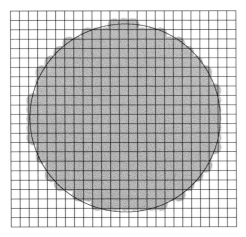

4-5 Spots and dots *Imagesetters and desktop printers make round halftone dots from square digital dots (spots) arrayed on grids such as the one above. High-resolution devices use more spots to make each halftone dot and thus offer more precise control over the size of the halftone dot and the smoothness of its edge. A 2,400-spi printer has 2,400 spots in the grid that it can use to create each halftone dot.*

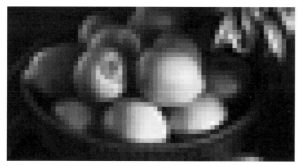

—*scanned at 20 spi, output at 150 lpi*

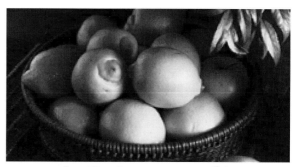

—*scanned at 72 spi, output at 150 lpi*

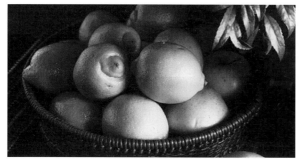

—*scanned at 150 spi, output at 150 lpi*

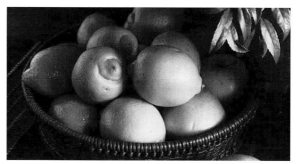

—*scanned at 225 spi, output at 150 lpi*

4-6 Spots per inch (spi) *Scanning the original image at 20 spi and 72 spi did not capture enough information to result in a pleasing reproduction. Even the 150-spi scan lacks detail.*

Only the 225-spi scan—1.5 times the lpi—results in sufficient detail and tonal range.

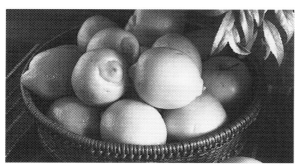

—*scanned at 225 spi, output at 85 lpi*

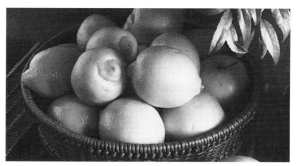

—*scanned at 225 spi, output at 133 lpi*

4-7 Lines per inch (lpi) *The examples above were both scanned at the same spi but output at different lpi. The scan*

captured more information than the 85-line screen can reproduce and merely slowed down output and wasted file space.

Low rulings, such as 85 and 100 lpi, have relatively large dots. Visuals 4-4 through 4-7 illustrate the concept.

Keep in mind the difference between digital dots (dpi) for output and halftone dots (lpi) for printing. Halftones dots consist of digital dots. You can see a halftone dot but not a digital dot.

The best and least costly separations begin as scans that require a minimum of adjustment. To ensure correct resolution, you need to tell scanner operators the design size of the image

(how big it will appear in print) and the screen ruling (lpi) of the printing job. With these two facts, operators can give you the best scans available from their equipment.

Input resolution affects output resolution. The goal when scanning is to capture just the right amount of information. Resolution that is too high (too much detail) wastes memory and processing time. Resolution that is too low won't produce satisfactory halftone dots or detail.

You can get satisfactory scans almost every

time by using the following guidelines:

- Scan the image at the size it will appear in print.
- Scan at 1.5 times lpi for images with average detail. For soft images, use 1.3 times lpi. For images with lots of detail, use 2 times lpi. You can see an example of 1.5 times lpi scanning in the lower right image of Visual 4-6.

Interpolation. If output resolution requirements are higher than a scanner can deliver, the computer in the scanner interpolates the digital data upward to deliver the required resolution. Interpolation has little effect on parts of an image containing little detail, such as the sky. Images with lots of detail, however, such as textiles or jewelry, may lose sharpness when interpolated.

Screen ruling

Like screens for tints, screens for halftones and separations are measured in lines per inch (lpi). Coarse screens, such as those used by newspapers and quick printers, are 85 to 100 lpi; medium screens in newsmagazines and company publications are 133 or 150 lpi; fine screens in premium or showcase quality brochures or annual reports range from 150 to 300 lpi.

The paper you specify for the printing job affects screen ruling. Uncoated paper absorbs ink quickly: Dots soak in, spread out, become fuzzy at their edges and touch. A coarse screen helps shadow areas retain detail on uncoated paper. Coated paper holds ink on its surface, so you can use a finer screen.

With most jobs at commercial printers, 133- or 150-line screens give effective results. As screen rulings get finer, every step in the process takes more care and therefore costs more. Shadow detail is especially hard to reproduce when using fine screens. Showcase quality pieces printed offset might use 300-line screens with 90,000 spots per square inch—nine times the number of a 100-line screen. While yielding extraordinary results, 300-line screens are very difficult to print by offset.

Your choice of screen ruling affects quality, cost and schedule. Consult with your printer.

For specialized help, ask your printer or paper distributor for demonstration materials made by paper manufacturers. Paper mills such as S.D. Warren and Hammermill publish free booklets and charts showing photographs in many screen rulings and colors on a variety of papers.

Density

Scanners and digital cameras have ratings for density and dynamic range that help you know the quality of the device. High-end scanners have higher values than less costly devices.

Density describes darkness and is measured using a densitometer found at most printers and prepress services. The lightest possible density is zero—totally clear. The darkest density is 5.0—utterly opaque.

Few images have highlights of zero and shadows of 5.0. In practice, a photo with highlights approximately .1 and shadows approximately 3.5 shows lots of contrast. A photo with relatively dark highlights or relatively light shadows has a small density range and thus looks flat.

Most scanners and digital cameras can capture the brightest parts of images—densities close to zero. The difference between high-end and low-end devices lies in how well they capture the darkest parts of images—densities approaching 5.0.

Manufacturers use maximum densities, abbreviated Dmax, as one measure of the quality of devices. Dmax ratings range from 2.5 for low-end scanners to 3.8 for the most costly machines. Scanners with Dmax ratings close to 5.0 can capture almost the full range of tones from white to black.

Dynamic range. Scanners have practical limits within their theoretical ranges. These limits, called dynamic ranges, express the devices' ability to capture data from any given image.

Dynamic range is less than density range. For example, a scanner might have a Dmax of 3.5 and the dynamic range of 3.0. This means that operators must choose where to lose the .5 density, in the shadow or in the highlight.

Dynamic range relates more closely to practical issues of printing than Dmax does. No press

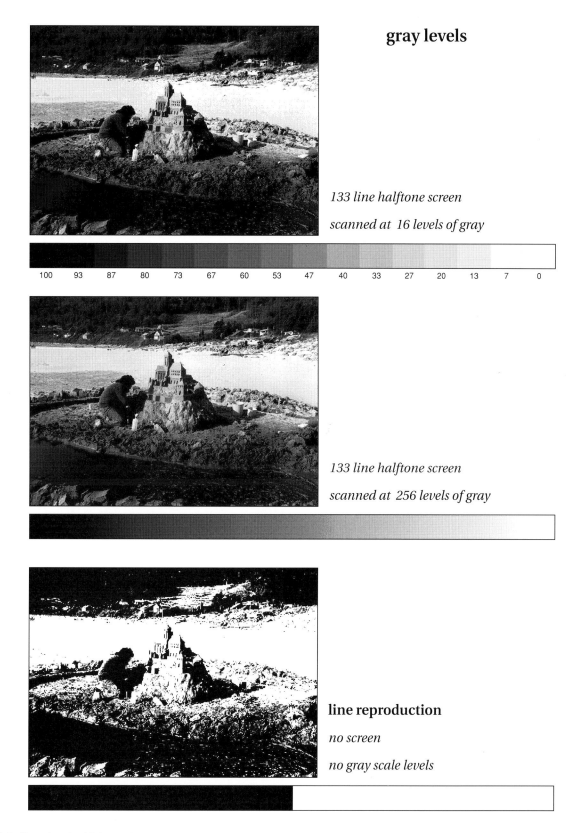

133 line halftone screen

scanned at 16 levels of gray

| 100 | 93 | 87 | 80 | 73 | 67 | 60 | 53 | 47 | 40 | 33 | 27 | 20 | 13 | 7 | 0 |

133 line halftone screen

scanned at 256 levels of gray

line reproduction

no screen

no gray scale levels

4-8 Gray levels High-resolution devices produce a wider range of halftone dot sizes than low-res devices, and yield a wider range of tones. The top image was scanned at only 16 levels of gray. You can see breaks between levels of gray in the tone scale. Breaks such as these are called banding. The middle image was scanned at 256 levels of gray, resulting in more detail in the halftone and eliminating banding from the tone scale. The bottom version of the image shows what happens when a photo is reproduced without being halftoned. Sometimes photos are reproduced as line reproductions for a special effect known as posterization. Here the tone scale shows no gray levels, only black and white. (Photo by Kathleen Ryan.)

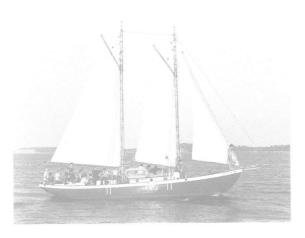

cyan impression

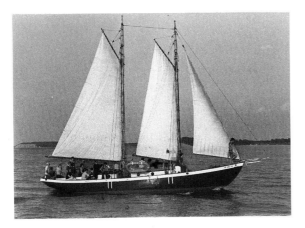

black impression

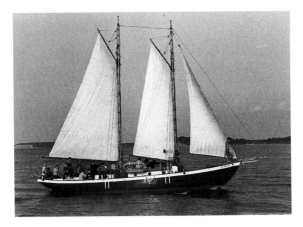

cyan and black duotone

4-9 Duotones *Printers create duotones from halftones produced to expand the tonal range or yield a special effect. In the example above, highlight dots are dropped out from one plate to print cyan in the water without printing cyan in the sails.*

or paper can reproduce a density of even 3.0. And no paper is white enough to yield a density reading of zero. As a rule of thumb, newsprint can reproduce black ink densities up to 1.2, offset papers up to 1.8 and coated papers to 2.2.

Tone compression

Printers use the term tone compression to describe the loss of contrast as images move from real world to printed page.

The ratio between the lightest whites and the darkest blacks in sunlight may be as much as 1000:1. The human eye can perceive this difference. Photographs are limited to a difference of approximately 100:1, and halftones on premium coated paper to a difference of approximately 20:1. The darkest blacks on press sheets are much lighter than on photographs or than in nature; the lightest whites on press sheets are much darker than in photos or nature.

Measured photography. You cannot avoid tone compression, but you can predict its effects by applying techniques of measured photography.

Viewers notice loss of details in highlights more easily than in shadows. Measured photography deliberately compresses tones by reducing densities in shadows and holding densities in highlights.

In measured photography, the photographer visualizes the image on a press sheet. The photographer then controls lighting to produce a photo whose critical details fall within the tonal range of the paper and printing process planned for the specific printed product. In addition to ensuring more predictable results on press, the technique produces consistent images for scanning in groups (ganging).

Guidelines for measured photography are expressed using the f-stop system familiar to photographers. If you use the Zone System to plan exposures, you will find measured photography easy to understand. For more information, consult GATF (Graphic Arts Technical Foundation) or a professional studio photographer.

DUOTONES

Printers produce a duotone using two plates made from two separate halftone negatives printed in register. One plate prints the black, and the second plate prints the other color. Duotones cost more than simple two-color printing because they require more precise register. Black-and-white photos result in better duotones than color photos.

There are two reasons to use duotones. First, a plate made from a single halftone cannot print shadows dark enough without sacrificing quality in highlights. Using two scans, printers can make one to favor highlights and the other to favor shadows.

The second reason to use duotones is to achieve a color effect different from black and white, as shown in Visual 4-9. Sample books from paper companies show a variety of color combinations. Samples also help you specify whether you want normal duotones using both ink colors about equally or whether letting one color dominate might yield a more pleasing effect.

Because you can use duotones to create such a variety of effects, you need to tell your printer or imaging service what effect you want. Show printed examples to convey the outcome you seek. When you specify a duotone, write the percentages of each ink color. You might write "50 black/50 cyan" or "40 black/60 brown."

SEPARATIONS

Printers use halftone dots of four ink colors to simulate the full range of colors in photos and illustrations. To begin this process, prepress must change original images into four files. After creating the four files, they are output either as film or as printing plates.

The act of dividing a color image into four files is called color separating. The film, and also the final printed images, are called separations. The printing procedure using separations is called four-color process printing.

Specifications often abbreviate four-color process printing as 4/4, meaning four colors on each side of the paper.

Technically speaking, color separations are halftones. Plates made from each separation could be printed with black ink or ink of any other color. It is only because the four halftones are printed in register with each other using specific colors of ink that they simulate the original full-color image.

Once the four separation files are made and composed with type and graphics, printers use them to make plates. When on press, one plate is inked with yellow, one with magenta, one with cyan and one with black. Printing the dots onto the press sheet puts the separation back together and gives the illusion of a continuous-tone photograph or illustration. Visual 4-10 illustrates this concept.

Printing color separations is much more difficult than printing single halftones. The dots of each color must align correctly with the dots of the other three colors. Visual 4-11 illustrates the effects of printing a separation out of register.

The process of separating and printing compresses the color gamut, losing detail and contrast. A good transparency appears twenty times brighter than ink on gloss paper. There is no way that even the best printing company can come close to reproducing its vivid tones. Even color prints are about twice as bright as four-color process printing on glossy paper.

To get an idea of how the image will appear after separating and printing, first make a photographic print or printout from a high-end desktop printer. That image looks much more like the printed piece than the transparency or the image on a monitor.

The process of creating separation files includes many steps that allow operators to improve the images. Adjustments are usually made using software applications after images have been scanned. Visual 4-12 illustrates this concept and describes the steps in proper sequence.

Printers can make some colors more vibrant by adding a fifth color of ink. For example, red areas already printed magenta become much brighter when printed again with another type of red. This technique requires a separate halftone negative, plate and inking station for the fifth color.

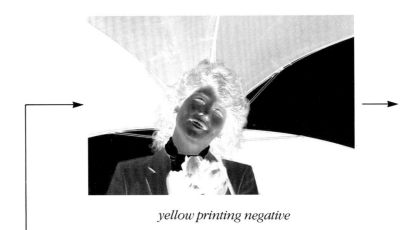

yellow printing negative

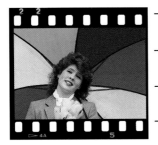

original transparency

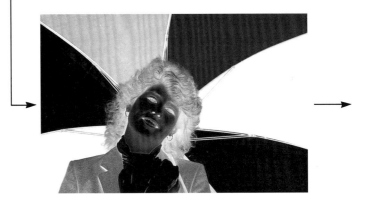

magenta printing negative

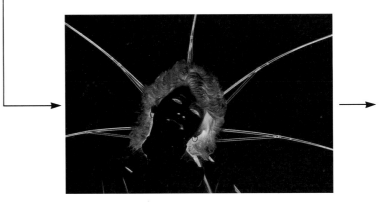

cyan printing negative

4-10 Color Separations *When prepress separates a transparency or print, it is scanned to create four halftone negatives or plates. Light from the image passes through a blue filter that creates the negative whose plate prints with yellow ink; a red filter makes the cyan plate; a green filter yields the magenta plate. Because an image reproduced using only yellow, cyan and magenta would lack sufficient contrast, prepress makes a fourth negative to add black ink.*

The four ink colors yellow, magenta, cyan and black are the process colors and are abbreviated CMYK. Their halftones are called color separations. (Photo by Kathleen Ryan.)

black printing negative

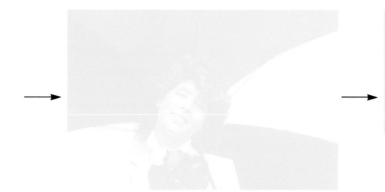

impression from the yellow plate

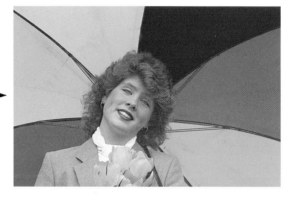

yellow impression

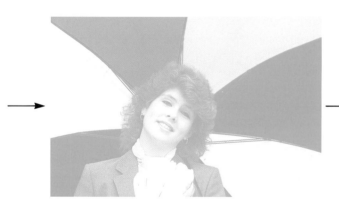

impression from the magenta plate

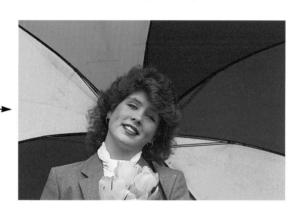

yellow and magenta impressions

impression from the cyan plate

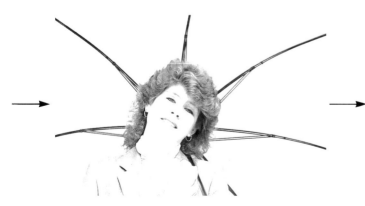

yellow, magenta, and cyan impressions

impression from the black plate

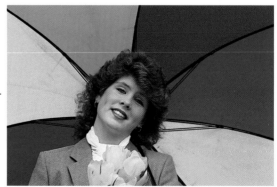

yellow, magenta, cyan, and black impressions

A few prepress services and printers can separate color photos into five, six and even eight halftones. Combinations known as high-fidelity color might include a second hue of yellow and a second and even a third shade of red in addition to the standard process colors. High-fidelity color costs much more than four-color process prepress and printing.

Color looks most vivid when printed on coated, white paper. Coatings prevent ink from absorbing and thus give sharp images. White paper provides a background that interferes very little with ink colors to affect the outcome. Like color, whiteness is subjective. If in doubt about the whiteness of a particular paper, ask your printer for comparative samples.

Prepress services can separate paintings and drawings as well as transparencies. Printing inks, however, cannot match the color of many artist pigments and dyes. If in doubt, consult your printer and consider making test separations of artists' samples.

Works of original art are often too large or awkward for scanning. In such cases, the image is photographed and the resulting photo is separated. Colors in flat products such as wood paneling and fabric can be separated when the products are placed on a flatbed scanner.

Size, quality, turnaround time and the kind of originals you submit determine the cost of separations. Transparencies cost the least to separate, followed by color prints and other reflective art. Rigid art that must go on a large flatbed scanner costs the most.

RGB TO CMYK

Many printing buyers prefer image-editing software to convert RGB to CMYK instead of letting scanner operators make the change. Making separations on the desktop gives you maximum control over the final image because you can adjust black substitution, total ink coverage and dot gain.

Black substitution

When an original has a shadow area that appears dark gray or black, the normal combination of CMYK inks may not simulate the gray values well enough. Substituting some black for CMY adjusts tones. Black substitution also means more stable colors on press and faster drying times for press sheets.

Black substitution happens during the conversion from RGB to CMYK and involves either under color removal (UCR) or gray component replacement (GCR).

UCR subtracts neutral amounts of CMY values, mostly out of the shadow areas, to improve contrast. GCR improves colors by substituting some black for small amounts of CMY. For example, if an image has a deep red color that has a cyan value, GCR might take the cyan value out and substitute black. With the black dot taking the place of the cyan dot, the hue change from ink fluctuations is not apparent.

UCR works best for images with lots of color because it functions in the shadow areas, not in the whole tonal range. This leaves more CMY inks to give color to the rest of the image. GCR works best for more neutral images, such as those with sand or wood, because GCR affects the whole tonal range by reducing the inks used to make images colorful.

Total ink coverage

Specifications for printing often include requirements for total ink coverage, also called maximum ink density. For example, specs for a card deck insert might call for total coverage of 260 percent.

Total ink coverage refers to the dot percentages of the process colors. Each color has the potential of printing at 100 percent. If each color prints at 100 percent, the total ink coverage is 400 percent. But 400 percent overwhelms a press sheet. Too much ink fills the shadows and makes colors hard to manage.

Color separators and printers compute total ink coverage by adding CMYK dot percentages in shadow areas. For example, if cyan, magenta, yellow and black each equal 75 percent, total area coverage equals 300 percent. Operators set total ink coverage before converting images from RGB to CMYK.

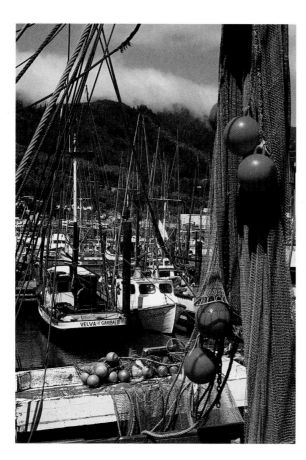 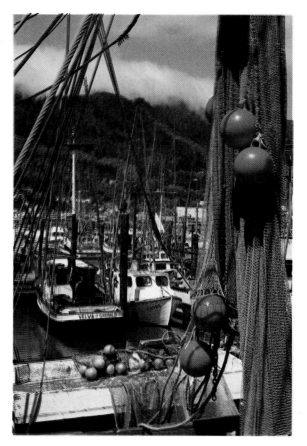

four-color process printing in register   *four-color process printing out of register*

4-11 Register of process color *Register affects color as well as sharpness. Whenever you inspect proofs or press sheets, verify correct register before evaluating color. If color changes* *during printing, check register before looking for other possible causes. (Photo by Kathleen Ryan.)*

Publications printed on relatively porous paper, such as newsprint or uncoated reply card stock, specify a total area coverage less than publications using stock with high holdout. Maximums help ensure that shadow areas hold detail.

Following are guidelines for total ink settings:
- newsprint, 180–220
- uncoated stock, 240–280
- film-coated stock, 270–290
- matte-coated stock, 280–310
- gloss-coated stock, 300–340

Your printer or paper merchant can advise you about total ink coverage for specific paper stocks. You can also find total ink recommendations in industry guidelines such as SWOP and GRACOL (see chapter ten).

Specifications for total ink coverage prevent problems with too much ink, but they should also prevent problems with too little ink. If color on press sheets seems correctly balanced but looks overall too weak, increasing total ink coverage by 5 or 10 percent may solve the problem.

Dot gain

Applications for editing images require adjustments for dot gain. Those adjustments, however, are poorly explained in technical manuals and help menus. In addition, adjusting images before exporting them for page layout means that other design elements, such as type and illustrations, do not receive dot gain compensation. This inconsistency leads to unsatisfactory results with showcase and many premium quality jobs.

When dot gain affects critical aspects of a job, we recommend that you rely on prepress operators to make adjustments. For that reason, we deal with dot gain in chapter five. ∎

Applications for editing images, such as Photoshop, let you control tones and improve colors. Producing satisfactory results requires knowing the limitations of the press and paper for the job, following a specific strategy and making disciplined judgments.

Limitations. Every combination of printing technology and substrate imposes limits on features such as minimum dot size and total ink density. Understanding these limits for specific jobs helps you plan the best possible reproduction of images.

Strategy. Use the following sequence of steps to improve images. The six steps go from most important to least important. Following the steps in this specific order gives you maximum control.

1. Set highlight point.
2. Set shadow point.
3. Adjust for color cast.
4. Correct tones.
5. Correct color.
6. Apply unsharp masking.

When working with halftones, follow steps one, two, four and six. Color separations require all six steps.

Discipline. Following the strategy requires relying on technical information, not the image on your monitor. Use the image to place the eyedropper and other menu tools, but look at curves and other guides to confirm decisions until you get to unsharp masking. Don't trust your monitor during the first five steps.

Images on these two pages begin with raw scans and progress through the steps. Note the improvements from originals to finished images.

B/W HALFTONE

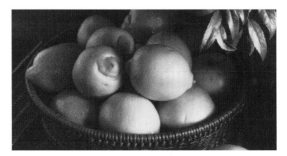

Original image. Black-and-white darkroom print produced to 150 percent size needed for this illustration, then scanned at 225 spi and output at 2,400 spi for a 150-lpi halftone.

When editing halftones, follow steps 1, 2, 4 and 6 described on the opposite page.

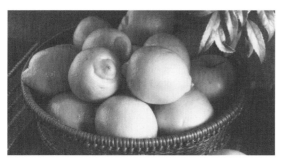

1. Set highlight point. Select the lightest area that still has detail. Avoid specular areas, such as reflection in water, that don't need dots. Putting dots in specular highlights reduces overall contrast.

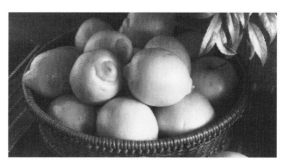

2. Set shadow point. Find the darkest part of the image, in this case under the leaves. If your image has no strong shadow, use the dark edge of the print or some other dark solid.

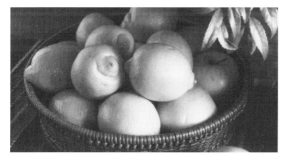

4. Correct tones. Adjust general brightness or darkness. Removing density from quarter tones adds brightness to highlights. Adding density to three-quarter tones makes the shadows a little darker.

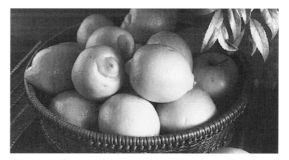

6. Apply unsharp masking. Unsharp mask heightens contrast at the edges of objects and blurs solid areas, resulting in enhanced detail. You can adjust unsharp masking in either the scanner or the separation software.

FOUR-COLOR SEPARATIONS

When editing separations, use the following sequence of steps to improve images. The six steps go from most important to least important. Following the steps in this specific order gives you maximum control.

1. Set highlight point.
2. Set shadow point.
3. Adjust for color cast.
4. Correct tones.
5. Correct color.
6. Apply unsharp masking.

For best results, color separations require all six steps.

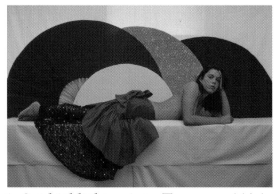

1. Set highlight point. To get good highlights in separations, set cyan at seven, magenta and yellow each at five. Too much magenta makes highlights look pink; too much yellow turns highlights greenish.

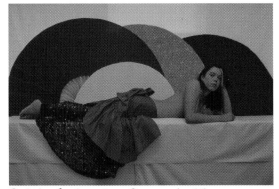

Original image. Scanned 35mm transparency at 225 spi and output it at 2,400 spi for 150-lpi separations.

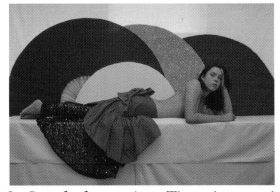

2. Set shadow point. The values used above to print a shadow point without a color cast are ninety-five for cyan and the high eighties to very low nineties for both magenta and yellow.

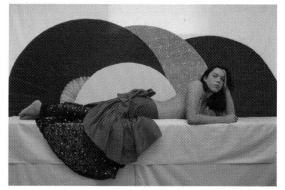

3. Adjust for color cast. Use the gradation tool to compensate for casts, then shift numbers in the offending channel until they represent a neutral gray. In this image we removed the slightly green cast.

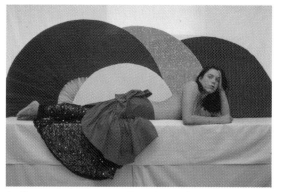

4. Correct tones. Good density throughout the image makes adjusting individual colors easier. For this example, we removed 6 percent of the dots in the quarter and three-quarter tones to unplug those areas.

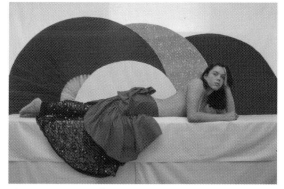

5. Correct color. Use gradation, colorize, paint and edit tools to adjust hue and saturation. Correcting color as step five ensures that you don't change neutral grays, highlights or shadows. For this example, we adjusted the fleshtones.

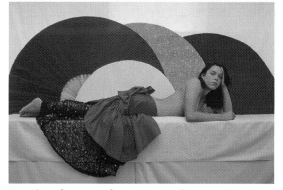

6. Apply unsharp masking. Unsharp mask heightens contrast at the edges of objects and blurs solid areas of color, resulting in enhanced detail. We used unsharp masking to improve contrast at the edges of the red fan pattern.

5. PREPRESS WORKFLOWS

To keep up-to-date about prepress and proofs, visit our Web site (www.gettingitprinted.com).

Graphic design combines art, skill and technology for purposes of communication. The designer decides how a piece will look and work, then plans the route from vision to reality. This chapter deals with the technical plan. It explains the stages known collectively as prepress and describes ways to take each step.

To understand each step of document manufacturing, you need to know about the available tools. When you understand the relationship between digital files, film, plates, digital presses and offset presses, you have more control over the quality, schedule and cost of printing.

Most printing jobs enter prepress as digital files. Printers use files as the starting point for the manufacturing process. You are probably using a computer to assemble type, graphics and images, and then transmitting the files to a prepress facility. Digital workflows help speed production, cut costs and ensure quality.

As a printing buyer, your digital workflow involves many people before jobs go to prepress. You deal with files created or edited by writers and photographers, people in marketing and manufacturing, your supervisor and your employees. The keystrokes and applications used by all these people influence how well your jobs move through the production process.

Savvy printing buyers know how to use film as well as digital files. In fact, efficient production often requires merging the two technologies. Film remains an integral part of print production, and we discuss it in this chapter.

APPLICATION FILES

A digital document usually represents creative work done using several applications then merged into yet another application before final output. Documents may begin as word processing files, illustration files, image-editing files and/or database files. Files from any or all of these sources may be combined in a page layout application, such as PageMaker or QuarkXPress.

Word processing files

For products such as directories, proposals and in-house newsletters that have rather simple design requirements, you can produce a file using a word processing application, such as Microsoft Word or WordPerfect.

Printing buyers create more jobs in word processors than in any other application. In addition to being familiar to millions of users, word processing applications:

- include an ample selection of type and graphics,
- support imported graphics created in other applications (such as for illustrations),
- merge with variable information, such as mailing lists, created by their own utilities or by database applications.

Word processing applications offer many ways to use keystrokes to assign type attributes, such as italic or bold. When you export these files for page layout, PostScript or directly to prepress, remember to substitute real fonts for the attributes. Imagesetters can't work with your stylized fonts.

Illustration files

Illustration applications, such as Adobe Illustrator, Altsys FreeHand and CorelDRAW, let you create original drawings and manipulate drawings imported from other sources. Illustration applications' key features include:

- editing lines
- excellent type control
- filling shapes with color
- graduation of colors
- converting type to a path

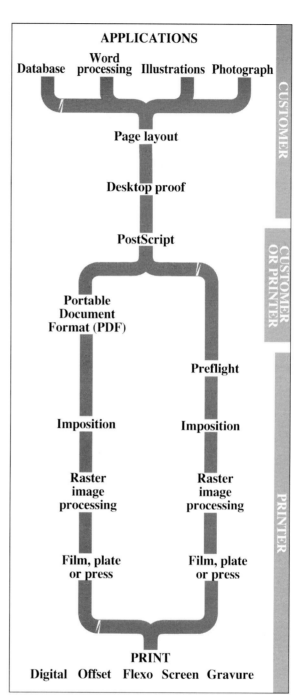

5-1 Prepress workflows *Printing jobs originate as application files that move through a digital sequence from creation to production. Printers who receive jobs as PostScript files must check them carefully before imposition. Files output in Portable Document Format (PDF) can skip preflighting and go directly to film, plate or press.*

Occasionally a printing job calls for producing a mechanical.

Production artists create a mechanical by assembling type and graphics onto a mounting board and overlays made of tissue or acetate. The name of the procedure and its end product vary from one part of the country to another. We refer to the procedure as pasteup and to its end product as mechanicals. Some professionals use the terms keylines, artboards or pasteups instead of mechanicals.

When you check a mechanical, your eye makes it appear as your brain wants it to look. Dust and smudges disappear along with typos and confusing instructions.

Use the following list to verify that mechanicals are ready for printing.

Identification. Mark each mechanical and each photograph or illustration with your name and phone number, and the name or number of the job. Place information on the front of the board outside the image area.

Correctness. Verify that words, photos and art are accurate.

Completeness. Check that each board and overlay includes all the type, art and graphics it is supposed to have. Keep the job together by giving all mechanicals, loose art, dummys and files to the printer at one time.

Accuracy. Verify marks for cropping, corners, folding, trimming, scoring and perforating. Register and trim marks must align correctly on mounting boards and overlays.

Security. Tightly adhere and burnish all copy. Mechanicals should have strong backings protected by heavy tissue during handling, transit and storage.

Cleanliness. Inspect boards, overlays and tissues to ensure they have no smudges, fingerprints, bits of glue or wax or stray guidelines.

Coordination. Examine loose copy such as photos, graphs, maps and illustrations to verify they are clean, cropped, scaled and keyed according to some system understood by the printer.

Communication. Look at each board and overlay to ensure it includes specifications about ink colors, screen rulings and densities, masks and reverses.

Proofs. Make sure that you have two photocopies of each board and overlay so you and the printer each have a proof.

When you deliver mechanicals, make a final check of job specifications. Your printer should agree that mechanicals represent the work described in specifications. If not, determine differences, decide on how they affect production and costs, and write the new information on the specifications sheet.

Image-editing files

Image-editing applications, such as Photoshop, CorelPaint and HSC Software's Live Picture, give powerful control over images. They let you change colors, merge and enhance photographic images, and create professional-level effects on the desktop computer.

In addition to their design features, image-editing applications have many prepress functions, such as control over dot gain, RGB to CMYK conversion, resolution, black generation and total ink coverage. Understanding the impact of these functions helps your output look like your vision.

Database files

Database applications allow you to store, edit and compute. They include products such as accounting applications, spreadsheets, database, and mail-merge utilities.

From the standpoint of print production, database applications perform three important functions: produce infographics, control personalization and allow electronic collating.

Infographics. Accounting and spreadsheet applications can create charts, graphs and tables to include in documents produced in other programs. For example, you might bring a chart from Lotus 1-2-3 into a manual written using Microsoft Word and designed using PageMaker.

Personalizing. Often a parent document needs individual information. For example, you might write a sales letter, then print the letter with one hundred different addresses and salutations. Mail-order companies personalize catalogs not only by printing addresses but by adding notes about sales or recent purchases.

Electronic collating. Publishers often store components of documents, such as chapters in a textbook, then print on demand. Components are assembled differently for each customer. For example, a manual having five chapters might be drawn from an archive holding fifty chapters. Another customer might want a similar manual to contain a different blend of chapters.

Printing on demand is done using digital presses as described in chapter eight.

Successful publishing from database applications requires extensive testing by everyone in the workflow to ensure accurate merging. Mistakes become obvious and costly.

Page layout files

Page layout applications, such as QuarkXPress, PageMaker, Frame Technology's FrameMaker and Microsoft Publisher, are used to create and compose parts of a page into a single digital document. Layout applications allow you to import text from a word processing document, a drawing from an illustration application and a photo from an image-editing application.

Although page layout applications can handle many prepress functions, files are only as good as their native components. For example, if the image file is not properly processed, the page layout application will output the image poorly. Another example is if the chokes and spreads have not been set properly in the illustration file, the page layout application can not change the settings to make it print better.

Page layout applications include print information commands that prepare reports about documents. The reports show file names, applications used, and lists of fonts and special effects that will help you and your printer plan the printing job.

FILE FORMATS

Professionals use various file formats to exchange information among applications and across platforms. For example, you might create a drawing on a Macintosh using an illustration application, then send it as an EPS file to a page layout application running under Windows.

PICT. PICT is the original Macintosh format used to exchange images among applications. Because it was early in the development cycle of electronic publishing, PICT I supported only eight bits or only 256 colors (indexed colors). PICT II files can contain gray scale and files from four to twenty-four bits—more than enough color information to output the highest quality level.

TIFF. TIFF stands for Tagged Image File Format and has been adopted by the American National Standards Institute (ANSI) and International Standards Organization (ISO). TIFF files form high-resolution images of digital pages by converting vectored images to bits. TIFF files are large but are easily compressed.

There are six possible varieties of TIFF files. Some contain information that gets sent to a RIP (raster image processor), which in turn gets processed into spots. Some TIFF files, including TIFF/IT, have already been converted to spots. Many advertisers like TIFF files because they print the same regardless of imagesetter and are easy to archive. An ad sent to ten publications in TIFF should look the same in every publication.

PostScript. PostScript converts images and keystrokes in application files to coordinates used by laser printers and imagesetters. Because it works with pages and documents created using application software, it's called a page description language.

The value of PostScript comes from its flexibility. Any output device using PostScript can print any document converted to PostScript, meaning that files are printer and resolution independent.

The flexibility to create documents using various machines or applications and then print them using any output device is referred to as having open systems. Device independence makes PostScript one of the cornerstones of desktop publishing.

EPS. Encapsulated PostScript files are a subset of PostScript files that supports both rastered and vectored data. This means that you can crop and scale EPS images without destroying the integrity of the file created in the original application. For example, you could edit an image in Photoshop, crop it and place it on a page in WordPerfect, then output the WordPerfect file to a PostScript device.

EPS files also support embedding halftones and transfers, functions normally performed during raster image processing. Halftone embedding allows an application to set the frequency and shape of a halftone dot. Setting the halftone in the application overrides similar functions in a RIP. Embedding of a transfer function allows you to make the image look lighter or darker when printing without affecting the original values in the image itself. If the transfer function is removed, the image will print with the original values.

JPEG. Joint Photographic Expert Group files are compressed to save storage space and increase transmission speeds. JPEG files usually begin as EPS files.

Compression results in loss of image quality. JPEG offers many compression ratios. The highest ratio results in a small file but with the most lost data. A low compression ratio results in a less compressed file with less loss to image fidelity.

DCS. Desktop Color Separations files have five separate files, not one file as with EPS or TIFF. The first file is a preview or placeholder file for placement into a page layout application. The corresponding four files are the high-resolution CMYK data not needed to display on the screen but required for the RIP. The low-resolution file is small enough to serve as FPO (for position only) proofs.

When dealing with DCS files, put all five files in the same folder before output. If the five files are not in the same folder, the output device will produce the low-resolution file. Outputting to a digital color proofer may require combining the DCS files into a single EPS file. RIPs of color proofers look for a single color file, not an image with four supporting files.

PDF. Portable Document Format files are best created after application files have been exported to PostScript. Visual 5-1 illustrates this sequence.

PDF files allow users to view and print documents independently of the applications used to create them. Viewing is especially important: Alternative formats such as PostScript do not allow on-screen preview.

Adobe Distiller, the utility that creates the PDF file, interprets PostScript code and creates a display list. With these functions done, any device that creates halftone dots can display or image the dots from the PDF file. Resolutions are not determined until output on a RIP. Resolution independence means that you can repurpose PDF files for media other than print. For example, PDF images can appear on CDs and Web pages.

PDF files have the additional advantages of being searchable and relatively small. They also help avoid errors caused when a RIP cannot interpret PostScript. Correctly made PDF files minimize the need for preflighting and other prepress work. To ensure this benefit, consult with your printer to make sure you set Distiller's preferences properly.

Miscellaneous formats. Some of the other file formats are Graphic Interchange File (GIF) and Continuous Tone Line Work (CTLW). GIF formats are files that were founded by CompuServe. These file formats are limited to eight bits or 256 colors. The reason GIFs are still valuable is the Internet can use this format. The second type of file format is Scitex's CTLW. This file format has two components. The Continuous

5-3 INFORMATION TO ACCOMPANY FILES

When you transmit files to a printer or imaging service, verify that you supply all the following written information and a hard copy example of each:

- job name and number; purchase order number
- customer name, address and contact person; fax, phone and pager numbers; E-mail address
- printer name, address and contact person; fax, phone and pager numbers; E-mail address

- list of loose art (photos, illustrations)
- mock-ups or dummies
- color specifications and swatches
- list of proofs required
- hardware used (platform and models)
- software used (brand name and version)
- all fonts used (manufacturer, name and style)
- number and names of files for output
- file formats (EPS, DCS, etc.)
- laser printouts that match electronic files
- list of special effects (such as graduated screens)

Tone (CT) part of the file is rasterized; the vectored part of the image is called Line Work (LW). The two components of the CTLW are merged in the Scitex RIP and output as a single file.

WORKING WITH PREPRESS SERVICES

When you have your digital files ready for prepress, you can transmit them to your printer or to a separate prepress service. The separate service may be known by one of several names, such as service bureau, color house, imaging service or prepress service.

Equipment in prepress departments includes light tables, imagesetters, scanners, computers, servers, digital proofers and platemakers.

Skills and equipment for prepress departments at printers and imaging services can overlap. A large printer can match the capacity of a large imaging service, while a small printer may have no prepress facilities at all. A large prepress department at a commercial printing house may have specialists rarely found at independent imaging services, while a small imaging service may duplicate what half the printers in town can do.

Prepress services change faster than any other phase of production, so insiders use many terms with imprecise meanings. For example, you often hear prepress systems referred to as high end and low end. Each phrase relates to the power and cost of hardware and software

currently available. Generally speaking, low end means what you have in your organization and high end means what a printer or imaging service has. Today's high end is tomorrow's low end.

Prepress has a major influence on the success of your printed piece. Once you have decided which printer(s) you want to work with, establishing a smooth workflow and predictable output may require months of experience with a variety of jobs.

When you evaluate a prepress service or department, keep in mind the following considerations.

Compatibility. Verify that files print the way they look on your monitor. Test, then test again. Don't take a sales rep's word for it. Test at least two files created by every application you might use.

Legality. Prepress should have its own copies of all the applications and fonts you use.

Training. Will the service's staff take time to help you avoid mistakes and take advantage of new technologies?

Documentation. Look for job tickets, file information sheets and especially proofs that help you describe and evaluate your job.

Recommendations. Ask other customers if their jobs ran smoothly through prepress and printing. Listen especially closely to stories about problems (you'll hear lots) and how the staff handled them. Everyone is a pioneer on the digital frontier, so expect some mistakes and confusion.

Focus on output. Ignore brand names of equipment. Concentrate on your own specific interface, whether the kinds of proofs supplied match the press and what the prepress delivers to your printer.

Prepress can represent a large fraction of the cost for a printing job, especially jobs that involve relatively short press runs. Following are some ways to hold down prepress costs.

Simple designs. If color breaks don't involve image trapping, graduated screen tints or complex illustrations, prepress could be simple.

Modest quality. If you have complex designs and need match original colors, prepress will take longer and may cost just as much as printing.

Regardless of who does prepress, make sure you keep track of costs separately from paper, printing and binding. Exact reprints only require making new plates and should cost less than the original job. Knowing original prepress costs helps you evaluate quotes and invoices for reprints.

Imaging services making separations need to know the name and phone number of printers using their film. Close communication is imperative. For premium and showcase quality printing, prepress needs to know what paper and press your job calls for.

Separations for advertisements must conform to specifications about file formats and screen rulings supplied by the publication in which they will appear. If you don't know those requirements, tell the imaging service the name of the publication. Prepress services own guidebooks in which they can look up specifications for thousands of newspapers and magazines.

Prepress services have a variety of practices regarding ownership of materials made in the course of preparing jobs. If you anticipate any dispute about ownership, settle it in writing before authorizing work to begin. And make sure to read the terms and conditions on the back of any contract before you sign.

To locate prepress services, look in classified directories under "Color Separations" or "Printing—Prepress Service." Ask for recommendations from your printers and from other printing customers who buy jobs similar to yours.

PREFLIGHTING FILES

Prepress operators need to know whether customers have prepared files properly. To gain this information, operators analyze files and art before allowing production to begin. The analysis is called preflight, borrowing a term from aviation. Preflight takes an inventory of electronic documents to avoid problems after the job enters production.

Many printers divide preflight into two levels.

Level one preflight. Level one preflight compares predictions with reality. Printers review files and art to make sure they match specifications used to quote and plan the job. This preflight is done by a customer service rep and takes place within an hour of receiving the job.

Level two preflight. Level two preflight examines files to make sure they will print consistently with specifications and proofs. This preflight is done by prepress operators and takes place within twenty-four hours of receiving the job.

Using information from preflight, printers can tell you what's wrong with specs or files, how you can fix problems or how much prepress will charge to fix them.

You cut costs and speed production when printers know that your files get A grades in preflight. You build this reputation by preflighting your own files. Prepress will still check your work but will learn to regard you as a dependable customer.

Good files mean profitable workflows for printers. Consistently good files deserve discounts from prepress costs.

To preflight your own files, use the following four-step process.

1. Create a job folder containing all the application files you plan to send to the printer.

2. Send the folder to a computer that was not used to create any of the files. Use a machine

having no electronic link with your desktop.

3. Make desktop proofs of the job from the new machine.

4. Compare the proofs to your specifications. If everything looks right, send the proofs and the folder to your printer without making even one additional keystroke.

Printers and prepress services have lists called "most common problems with customer files" that they would like to put into a permanently open window on your monitor. In addition, several companies make preflight software with names such as FlightCheck, FlightPro and Download Mechanic. The software scans application and PostScript files to identify errors and omissions and create job tickets. For example, preflight software can alert you to stylized fonts needing replacement with real fonts.

Sometimes a file may not print even though it passed preflight. In addition, information that was correct at the time of preflight may become wrong later in the production process. Alterations often cause problems. Any change supplied as a digital file brings the risk of contaminating other files already OK'd by preflight.

PREPARING FILES FOR PRESS

Customers and printers are often unclear about who is responsible for each aspect of preparing files for press. Efficient workflow requires this understanding.

Each printing job has a set of unique features that influence how it runs on press. The features include design and technical aspects of the file as well as which press and paper will produce the job. Prepress operators need to know these factors to adjust the files so they print with predictable results.

The three major prepress tasks deal with dot gain, chokes and spreads, and imposition.

Understanding dot gain

During the many steps from design to printing, dots tend to get bigger. Printers call this growth dot gain, also known as tone value increase.

Dot gain may influence the outcome of printing jobs in the following ways:

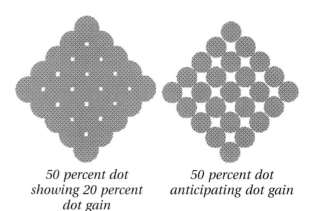

50 percent dot showing 20 percent dot gain

50 percent dot anticipating dot gain

5-4 Dot gain *Many factors make dots grow in the transition from design to paper. To ensure that colors and tints print as planned, you need to compensate for dot gain by making dots smaller in files and film than you expect them to reproduce on press.*

- Halftones and separations lose detail.
- Colors shift in separations.
- Screen tints print too dark.
- Color builds don't match swatches.
- Chokes and spreads don't function properly.
- Fine lines drop out when printed as reverses.

Many aspects of print production influence dot gain. The following are most important.

Paper. Different papers absorb different amounts of ink. Uncoated paper has more gain than coated paper, and uncalendered paper has more gain than calendered.

Printing method. Each printing method, such as offset, screen, flexography, and gravure, has different guidelines.

Type of offset press. Web presses usually have more gain than sheetfed presses.

Ink. Petroleum inks usually have more gain than soy inks.

Screen ruling. Higher screen rulings show more dot gain than lower screen rulings because smaller dots grow more than larger ones.

Screen pattern. Stochastic screens generally have different dot gain than conventional screens because stochastic screens use smaller dots.

Press chemistry. Waterless printing usually has less dot gain than conventional printing.

Professionals describe dot gain using the

same system used to describe dot size. A 50 percent dot with 10 percent dot gain becomes a 60 percent dot. A 20 percent dot with 15 percent dot gain becomes a 35 percent dot.

When printers refer to dot gain, they usually have in mind the midtone dots. But dots of different sizes expand by different amounts under the same printing conditions. For example, a 50 percent dot might have an 8 percent dot gain, but the 25 percent dot in the same image might have a 5 percent gain.

Dealing with dot gain

We wish we could give you a clear rule of thumb for dealing with dot gain, but we can't. The reason is that applications vary in the amount of control they allow. Word processing, illustration, database and page layout applications allow no control. Image-editing applications allow control but require you to use it. You can adjust it but not turn it off.

Dealing with dot gain is simple for printing jobs created using only one application. Most jobs, however, include files from several applications. When you assemble a page, you typically import some images (tints, illustrations) with no adjustments and other images (halftones, separations) with some adjustments.

To make matters more complex, some devices for raster image processing allow control for dot gain but others don't. This inconsistency means that some prepress services can adjust files for dot gain but others can't. Finally, when prepress RIPs your pages, either the whole page gets adjusted or none. RIPs can't work on just part of the page, so adjustments you made while editing images get made again.

To work your way through the maze of dot gain, ask your printer for dot gain predictions related to the quality level of your printing job.

• For basic quality, don't worry about dot gain.

• For good quality, adjust halftone dots for midtones and don't worry about other aspects of the job.

• For premium quality, adjust halftone dots, quarter tones, midtones and three-quarter tones.

Supply image-editing files separately from page layout files, with prepress to insert images and make further adjustments. Ask prepress to adjust dots in screen tints, color builds and image traps.

• For showcase quality, follow guidelines for premium, except adjust dots for each process color separately.

Imposition

Magazines, catalogs, books and many other printing jobs are printed on sheets that will be folded and collated before binding. Individual pages must be arranged on the sheets so they appear in proper sequence. The arrangement is called imposition, illustrated in Visual 5-5.

Correct imposition takes into account the number of pages, sheet size, printing technique, folding and binding methods, and many other factors. To experience some of the possible variations, try folding a piece of paper into eight-page or sixteen-page signatures. Every variation you can devise is also found in folding machines.

Impositon software is made for printers and prepress services, not for printing customers. We recommend that you arrange your files as single pages or as reader spreads and let prepress plan imposition. To help prepress understand your needs, make sure that dummies and layouts show accurately and completely how you want the job to appear when finished.

Chokes and spreads

Colors that are supposed to appear as if they touch sometimes show a thin border between them. The border appears because the press prints the colors out of register. To avoid this problem, prepress slightly overlaps the colors either by choking one or spreading another. Visual 5-6 illustrates the concept.

Image trapping is device-specific, not device-independent. For that reason, we suggest that prepress, not customers, makes chokes and

5-5 Imposition The illustrations on the opposite page represent three ways a printer could lay out a sixteeen-page booklet. These are typical ways, not all the possible ways.

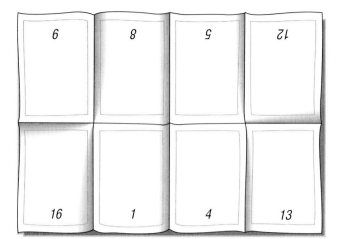

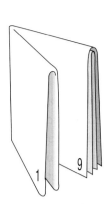
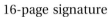

16-page press sheet on 23″×35″ stock

16-page signature

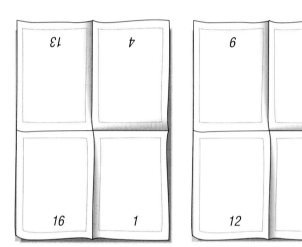

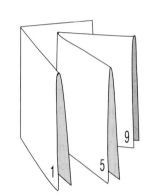

Two 8-page press sheets on 17″×22″ stock

Two 8-page nested signature

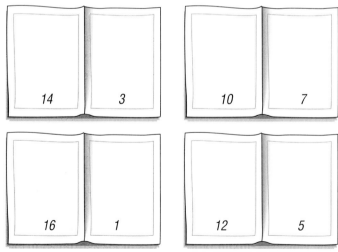

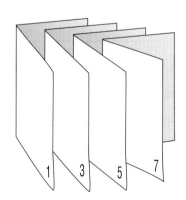

Four 4-page press sheets on 11″×17″ stock

Four 4-page nested signatures

spreads. Letting prepress handle trapping is especially important with flexography, screen printing and other methods whose register requirements are different from offset.

Keep in mind that image trapping is necessary only when designs call for close register, such as colors that appear to touch or photos that overlap keylines. You can avoid chokes and spreads completely by placing design elements far enough from each other that register variations make no difference. You can also eliminate the need for trapping by designing dark elements as overprints instead of reverses.

FILM AND FLATS

After prepress has prepared files, operators use an imagesetter to output them as either film or plates. In both cases, all the images to print in one ink color appear on one piece of film or one plate. Four-color process jobs call for four pieces of film and four plates.

Film is an intermediate step between files and plates. Many printers use film to make plates instead of making the plates directly from digital files.

Small pieces of film are often assembled into

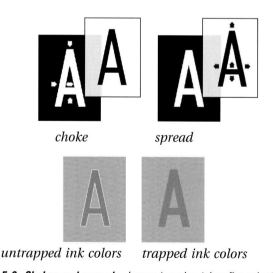

choke   *spread*

untrapped ink colors   *trapped ink colors*

5-6 Chokes and spreads *Image trapping takes five minutes to learn and a lifetime to master. In the example above, the light color beneath is choked to trap the dark color above.*

Whether to choke one color or spread another, and by how much, depends on quality standards and printing process. Correct traps depend on the type of paper and on which press will run your job.

a larger unit to match the plate needed for the job. The process of assembly is called stripping and the resulting unit called a flat. Strippers produce flats on light tables found in most prepress departments.

Imagesetters include software that places dots in patterns called rasters. For that reason, the devices are also called raster image processors and go by the nickname RIP (pronounced as a word, not letters). When printers output a file, they often speak of RIPping it.

Imagesetters vary greatly in how precisely they output files. One machine may output the same file ±.0001 inch, another ±.0002 inch. The same machine may vary ±.0001 inch today and ±.00015 inch tomorrow.

Top-quality imagesetters have almost dot-for-dot repeatability. If prepress services assure you they calibrate their imagesetters every day or every shift, you might wonder why the machines need such frequent attention.

Pros and cons of film

If film is an intermediate step between files and plates, why bother making it? Why not output every job directly to plate?

Proofs. Film provides more reliable proofs than files. When you produce showcase jobs, and many premium jobs as well, you need film proofs.

Plate size. Imagesetters vary in the sizes of images they can produce. Some can output only 9″ × 12″, big enough only for letter size. Others can output as large as 25″ × 40″, big enough for eight-up letter size as well as for almost any poster or other flat sheet. But imagesetters able to produce plates for the biggest presses are more expensive and less accurate than smaller machines. Making large plates from film costs less and gives higher quality.

Legacies. Many printing jobs involve a mix of new and old information. You may put the new information on files, but you inherit some of the old information on film. Few printers have scanners powerful enough to convert film to files, but most printers can output files to film.

This book offers a typical example of using

5-7 PROOFS FOR TYPICAL JOBS

Following are some printing jobs and the kinds of proofs each would typically require.

Newsletter two-color with halftones for quick or digital printing
- laser printouts of type and scanned halftones
- duplex photocopies of 11″×17″ imagesetter printout in printer spreads

Newsletter two-color with halftones for commercial printing (metal plates)
- laser printouts of type and scanned halftones
- blueline; also possibly loose whiteprints of the halftones

Book, directory or manual with one-color text and two-color cover
- digital blueline
- laser printouts of text type and cover art
- overlay of cover

Catalog or magazine with separations scanned by customer and provided as PDF files for pleasing color quality
- laser printouts of files
- overlays of imposed flats
- blueline of entire job
- routine press check

Brochure or poster with separations scanned by prepress for match transparency quality
- laser printouts of assembled pages
- composite digital color printouts
- loose laminates of separations
- blueline
- careful press check

Brochure or annual report with separations for match original quality, fifth flat color to match swatch and foil embossing on cover
- laser printouts of assembled pages
- two or three rounds of composite digital color printouts
- two rounds of loose laminates of separations
- two rounds of composite laminates
- production proof of dies and foil on actual cover stock
- ink drawdown on actual text stock
- blueline
- scrupulous press and bindery checks

---

legacy film. It includes many illustrations from the first and second editions that exist on film from those printing jobs. The new illustrations as well as all the type were prepared on files then output to film. The plates for this edition were made from a combination of old and new film.

It made sense to produce this book from film because many of the illustrations from prior editions did not exist as digital files. In other situations, both old and new information is digital. In those cases, it usually makes sense to output the entire job again either on film or directly to plates.

Cost and impact. Film is expensive and requires time and chemicals to prepare for platemaking. When possible, outputting files directly to plates saves time, money and environmental impact.

PROOFS

A proof is a test sheet to reveal errors or flaws and predict results on press. Notice the word "sheet." Proofs relate to printed products, not images on a monitor. Don't do a final proof of a printing job on a computer screen.

There are two verbs in the definition of proof:

reveal and predict; they define two uses for proofs: preliminary and contract.

Preliminary proofs reveal errors or omissions such as typos, wrong images or incorrect colors. When you inspect a preliminary proof, you identify corrections to make in files and art.

Contract proofs predict how a document will look when printed. They are facsimiles of the final product. When you sign a contract proof, you authorize production.

Business considerations, not proofing technology, determine whether a particular proof is preliminary or contract. A desktop laser printout could serve as a contract proof for a simple one-color job. On the other hand, the most costly color proof is still preliminary if it reveals a problem that requires fixing and making another proof.

Specifying proofs

Controlling quality and costs requires knowing how to read proofs and understanding how much work is involved to make various types of changes. For that reason, most printing jobs go through many rounds of internal proofing before going to prepress. Careful attention to desktop proofs helps reduce prepress expenses.

You can avoid feeling confused or intimidated when producing printing jobs by learning how to ask for the right proofs. Knowing what proof goes with what job helps you verify quality, stay on schedule and prevent costly mistakes. And knowing what to look for at each proof stage helps establish who's responsible for what, which becomes important if things go wrong.

Typically, a print job passes through three or four proofing stages. The first stage may be a desktop proof of an electronic file created using a word processing or page layout application. Second and third proofs may be created by a prepress department to show color, imposition, folding and trimming.

Checking proofs as the job progresses is the only way to verify that the electronic files are correct before making plates. Having proofs at press time means you can efficiently check the first printed sheets. Proofs also help determine who is responsible for mistakes and who should pay for corrections.

When examining a proof, verify that it represents the latest version of the file. Even one keystroke or mouse click can change the file to make the proof irrelevant.

Some proofs show only portions of a job, such as photos. Printers call them loose, random or scatter proofs. Others called composite proofs show fully assembled type, graphics and art.

5-8 THREE LEVELS OF PROBLEMS WITH PROOFS

When a proof reveals a flaw, assign it to one of the following categories. Defining the importance of flaws helps you decide quality questions and control costs and schedule. Whether a specific situation calls for signing an imperfect proof depends on the nature of the flaws, your confidence in the printer, your budget and schedule.

Critical flaw. A critical flaw ruins your job so you cannot use the printed product.

A critical flaw means the job is unacceptable. It requires fixing the problem then getting another proof. If it appears on the final product, the job must be reprinted.

Major error. People notice a major error, and it may detract from the value of your product.

A major error means the job is acceptable, although not satisfactory. Whether you fix a major error depends on the cost of repair, your deadline and your guess about its impact on the printed piece.

Minor problem. Probably only you and your printer notice a minor problem. If others notice, they don't care.

Almost every job contains minor problems that could have been avoided if you had more time, money or skill.

You can see how color images will appear when printed by ordering loose proofs of separations. Loose proofs reveal needs for color correcting before separations are assembled with type and graphics. In addition, loose proofs show images scaled to finished size, thus revealing whether cropping was properly done.

Loose proofs of separations, however, do not show overprinted or reversed type. For a prepress evaluation of how electronic document and photographs have been combined for the job as a whole, ask for a composite proof.

PROOFING TECHNOLOGY

You can think of proofs in three categories, depending on which step in the production process you want to analyze.

Film proofs. Film proofs reveal what's on the film that will be used to make plates.

Digital proofs. Digital proofs reveal what's on an electronic file. You might want to see digital proofs before making film. Or you might want to see a digital proof when going computer to plate.

Press proofs. Press proofs reveal what's on plates.

The three core technologies result in many types and brands of proofs. Which you use for a specific printed product depends on what you consider important about that product. If your catalog must have zero typos, output from a laser printer is a sufficient proof of type. If the products must match photos of those products, you need a color proof made from final film or a high-end digital proofer. And if flat colors must match corporate color standards, you can only trust a press sheet to reveal whether you have attained that goal.

Desktop proofs

A laser print or other desktop printout shows low-resolution contents of computer files or portions of documents, such as layers, charts or photos.

Use a desktop proof to check:
• text and headline type and placement
• keylines or halftone cropping, size and position
• placement of rules, reverses and tints

• guide marks for trims and folds
• pleasing or production color

Desktop proofs are the most common kind of proof for quick and digital printing. Make two copies, one for you and one for the printer. If possible, use a desktop printer that can duplex so you can give the printer the pages exactly how you want the job to look. Collate, fold, trim, staple or drill just as you expect the job from bindery. Leave nothing to imagination.

Bluelines (film or digital)

Printers make bluelines on photosensitive paper with the same dimensions as the press sheets for your job. Operators fold and bind the sheets so you can check crossovers, backups, page sequence and photo placement.

Use a blueline to check:
• text and headline placement
• halftone cropping, size and position
• placement of rules, reverses and tints
• page sequence
• crossovers and backups
• scores, perforations and drills
• trims, folds and binding

Most bluelines are contact prints of plate-ready negatives, but some are digital printouts. The two versions serve identical purposes. You may also hear a blueline called a silverprint or by the brand name Dylux.

Digital bluelines are used to proof imposition after files have been RIPed. But bluelines require large-format devices usually found only at prepress services.

Whiteprints (film)

A whiteprint is a contact print of plate-ready negatives. Whiteprints are typically used as loose proofs, not composites.

Use a whiteprint to:
• check halftone fidelity
• compare a variety of screen tints
• back up a hard mechanical

You may also hear a whiteprint called by the brand name Velox.

Full Bench Press
Haystack OR 94782

(423) 598-3000 • Fax (423) 598-3119

job# _____   job name _____

☐ first proof   ☐ second proof   ☐ third proof

☐ OK to print with no corrections.
☐ OK to print with corrections.
☐ **DO NOT PRINT.** Make corrections and supply new proof.

Art returned with this proof.

☐ all art
☐ correction art only
☐ no new art

Type of new proof needed.

☐ blueline of form # ___
☐ complete blueline
☐ loose whiteprints
☐ whiteprint of form # ___
☐ overlays of form # ___
☐ loose laminates
☐ laminate of form # ___

**Customer must sign
before work can proceed.**

_____   _____
signature   date & time signed

5-9 Proof approval slip *An approval slip such as the one above accompanies proofs from your printer or prepress service. The job is on hold until you sign the slip and return it with the proofs. Here's how to decide which box to check: (1) If you spot a critical flaw, ask for another proof showing corrections. (2) If you identify a major error, authorize printing after changes are made. (3) If you see minor defects, approve printing without changes. But circle the defect. Often prepress can correct a minor defect as simply as blowing dust off the flat.*

Overlays (film)

An overlay proof shows each color on a separate sheet of polyester film. Sheets are laid over each other in register and taped to backing paper.

Overlay proofs for four-color process jobs have four pieces of film taped together, one for each process color, as shown in Visual 3-13.

Overlay proofs are fast and inexpensive to make but have the disadvantage that the overlays themselves have a slight color cast, either yellow or gray. Looking through three or four layers can distort colors and sharpness.

Use an overlay proof to check:
• placement, trapping and register of flat colors
• pleasing color or production four-color
• position of varnish or other coating

Overlay proofing material is available in colors that simulate popular flat ink colors. Proofs are known by brand names, such as Color Key, Cromacheck and Color Check.

Integrals (film or digital)

Integral proofs look similar to color photographs or to finished printing done on glossy paper. Printers can match dyes and toners to inks, ensuring the best possible parallel between proof and printed product. Some integral proofs are made on the paper stock specified for the printing job. Other proofs use proprietary substrates.

You can use a desktop printer to make simple integral proofs, but the best come from film or from high-end digital proofers. Film proofs are made from either working film (for loose proofs) or flats (for composed proofs). Digital proofs come from complex machines that require careful calibration for linearization and dot gain compensation. Producing these high-quality proofs requires extensive prepress skills.

Integral proofs sometimes look better than the printed product because they do not show dot gain. If made from film adjusted for dot gain, on the other hand, color in integrals may look too weak.

Use an integral proof to check:
• image trapping and register of process colors
• match original four-color process

Integral proofs made by prepress services are known by many brand names, such as Agfaproof, Cromalin, Color Art, Matchprint, Iris and Rainbow.

Press proofs

Press proofs come from plates put on press, inked and run on paper specified for the job. Only press proofs show the true effect of dot gain or the way in which the paper color affects ink colors. For these reasons, some customers regard press proofs as essential to showcase four-color printing. Press proofs, however, are costly in both time and money and are becoming less necessary as technology makes overlay and integral proofs increasingly accurate.

Use a press proof to check:
• wet ink trapping
• trapping and register of process colors
• match product four-color process
• ink density and gray balance

A printer gives you a press proof as part of an event called a press check, described at the end of chapter seven.

5-10 HOW TO READ A PROOF

Use proofs to help control quality and cost and ensure good service. When examining a proof, keep these items in mind.

Slow pace. Take your time. Don't let a deadline make you careless.

Individual features. Make a list, then check each feature throughout the entire proof. For example, go through once just to confirm page sequence. Next check borders and rules for alignment and crossovers. Continue to examine headlines and display type for typos and placement. Finish by studying areas of critical register and color.

Photos. Check every photograph to verify that the correct image is in the correct space, is scaled and cropped properly, and faces the proper direction. Look for sharp focus, especially in portions of the image farthest from the center.

Flaws. Boldly circle every blemish, flaw, spot, broken letter and anything else that seems wrong.

Previous corrections. Double-check any corrections made on previous proofs.

Instructions. Write directly on the proof in a clear, vivid color. Be very clear and explicit in your instructions.

Finishing. Anticipate bindery problems. Measure trim size. Check that folds are in the correct direction and relate to copy as planned.

Correct colors. Confirm that you know what copy prints in what color. Double-check to make certain.

Memory colors. Verify that grass looks green, sky looks blue and other familiar colors look the way readers remember them.

Overview. Stand back to view the proof as a whole. Everything should work well together, and the message should be presented in a clear and attractive manner.

Questions. Ask about anything that seems wrong. Asking questions that seem stupid is a lot better than printing mistakes.

Costs. Discuss the cost of changes, and agree about who pays for what.

5-11 WHAT TO WRITE ON A PROOF

To make proofs most useful to you and your printer, use a dark pen to write the following information directly on a proof.

Your name. Make sure that people in your own organization can identify who examined the proof.

Date and time. One printing job might have many proofs. Make sure you know which is the latest.

Printer and press. Don't risk losing track of which vendor made the proof.

Densitometer readings. Ask for densities for each color at several points across the sheet.

Critical areas. Circle the problem area, then write what changes you want in colors or any other features.

Preliminary or contract proofs. Note whether you consider this the final proof or want another. If this is a contract proof, ask your printer to sign.

REMOTE PROOFING

To help cut production times, many clients and printers build remote proofing into workflows. Remote proofing means that printers send RIPed files for output at the client's site.

Whether you regard a remote proof as preliminary or contract depends on the critical aspects of the job, the quality of your output devices and how much you trust your printer. Remote proofs for one-color books or newsletters might save thousands of dollars and hundreds of hours.

Remote contract proofing works best when you and your printer invest time to develop proper workflows. If you publish many documents with essentially identical specifications, such as books, magazines and newsletters, remote probably works for you. For the occasional job, such as a poster, and for jobs with critical color requirements, contract proofs from prepress work better than from your desktop.

We recommend that you use remote contract proofs only if your job goes from computer directly to plate or to a digital press. If your job goes to film first, ask for proofs made from film.

COSTS AND BRANDS

Proofs gobble dollars and hours. Meeting your budget and deadline requires evaluating only proofs that relate to critical aspects of your printed product. If you know what matters most to you in a given job, you can choose the proofs that show it to you most cost-effectively. Careful choice keeps costs down and lets you fix problems at the least expensive stage possible.

Three things happen relating to proofs as a printing job moves from concept to press: Proofs take longer to make, they represent the final result more accurately and you pay more to make changes. Regarding cost, many production managers use the 5-50-500 rule: It costs $5 to correct a mistake on the desktop; $50 to correct the same mistake when found on a blueline and $500 when it's found on a composed laminate proof. Paying to correct a critical flaw discovered during a press check requires access to corporate gold reserves.

Your service bureau or printer includes the cost of proofs in the estimate for your job. Every job using plates made from film should include a blueline; for color process jobs, most printers want a laminate proof in addition and may produce one even if you don't ask for it.

Normal costs for good quality printing include one round of proofs. If you need a second or third proof, expect to pay additional as you would for any alteration. Another blueline costs more time than money; another overlay absorbs the extra dollars you stashed in case of trouble; another composite laminate trashes your entire budget.

Normal costs for premium printing include two rounds of proofs, loose and composite. Showcase printing may involve three or four rounds.

Printers often refer to color proofs by the brand name of the system they use. Until you learn the brands, simply ask whether it's an overlay or laminate so you can decide whether you need it. Differences among brands of proofing systems influence the profit of printers and imaging services but mean very little to you. As a customer, you face larger issues of quality, service and price that convince you to use one shop and avoid another. Unless your jobs involve the best possible color reproduction, pay little attention to brand names.

PLATES

After you have approved a contract proof, prepress makes the plates that form the last link between design and presswork. A printing plate carries the image that the press transfers to paper. No amount of adjustment on press can improve the quality of images coming off poor plates.

To understand how plates for offset printing work, think of a fresh printing plate as you would a fresh piece of photographic paper. Each comes from its package with no image and each has a light-sensitive coating. Exposure to light produces an image on the surface of either the paper or the plate.

Lithographic plates are relatively smooth: both image and nonimage areas lie on the same plane. Water and chemistry attract ink to image areas and repel ink from nonimage areas. Plates for letterpress, flexography and gravure printing (explained in chapter eight) feel rough and carry ink mechanically, not chemically; image and nonimage areas lie on separate planes.

Most lithography plates are based on the incompatibility between ink, which is oily, and water. A plate on press gets a thin coating of water each time the cylinder on which it is mounted revolves. Water adheres to the nonimage area, giving it a coating to prevent ink from also adhering. The image area has exactly the opposite reaction: It repels water and accepts ink. Plates used for waterless printing have a silicone surface that repels ink.

Once exposed, plates are developed by placing them in a plate processor that bathes the plates in chemicals. The chemicals remove portions of coating that were not exposed to light, leaving the image behind. Watching the image emerge as a metal plate develops is much like watching the development of an instant photo.

Printers make plates either from film or directly from files.

Plates from film. Light passing through the clear areas transfers the image from the negative to the plate. When portions of a printing plate are exposed to light, the exposed coating fuses to the metal backing and becomes receptive to ink.

The clear area of the negative through which light passes is the image area. Technically speaking, image areas may be as small as one dot in a halftone or as large as the entire plate. Printers, however, refer to the image areas as the portions of the plates that carry ink. The margins of this book page lie outside its image areas.

Printers refer to exposing a plate to light as burning it. Making one plate from one flat requires a single burn (one exposure). Using two flats to make one plate is double burning (two exposures). Strippers may make separate flats for reverses, tints or corrections and thus might burn some plates three, four or more times.

Plates from files. Some offset plates are made directly from files without the intervening steps of film. Printers call this process computer-to-plate.

Digital plates may be paper, plastic or metal, depending on the press and quality requirements for the job. They are burned by laser beams that form images similarly to a laser printer or imagesetter.

Paper and plastic plates for quick printing

....

66 If I had to choose a new prepress service (thank goodness that I don't), I'd find the one with the best guru—part nerd, part magician, part robot. My guru would know my software better than I do and could run a printing press if necessary. Finding that person would cut my headaches in half. 99 are made by an automatic platemaker. The quick part of quick printing refers in part to the fact that plates are made directly from files without the intervening steps of making negatives.

Quick print plates work well for jobs not needing fine detail. Designed for short runs, quick print plates typically show signs of wear after about five thousand impressions. They also stretch and wiggle on press, making tight register impossible.

Plates made from computer-to-plate systems can move a job from design to press in a few days. Because they don't require film, however, you pay for speed and you lose some forms of proofing.

Combining film and files. Some situations call for plates that carry images from both film and files. These jobs call for double burns, one for each medium. The plate would be imaged once from the file then again from film. For example, prepress might use this technique to place a separation on film into keylines from the file. Or a designer might create a new logo on a file to overprint a duotone on film.

SAVING PREPRESS WORK

If you're like most people, you're careless about filing materials and keeping records. You move on to the next job before the printer delivers the last one. Later—perhaps months or years later—you or your replacement wastes hours trying to figure out, locate or re-create something that you should have kept.

You can avoid waste and stress caused by poor document management by following the advice in the next few paragraphs.

....

❝ We use to think that time mattered more than money. We'd give files and art to prepress and let them figure out how to put them together. We could always run late. Now we think money matters more than time. Every file going out of here is complete down to the last dot. ❞

Delivery of your printing job should include materials that originated the printed product. If you don't have physical possession, you should know where they are stored for you. Materials could include files, photographs, loose art, working film, proofs, final film (flats) and sample press sheets.

Proofs and art. Few printers want to store your loose art or photos. If you want them stored at the printing company, make special arrangements. If not, make sure the printer returns them promptly. Check to confirm they are complete.

If you store any property at a printer's building, examine storage conditions to feel confident your materials are reasonably safe from fire, humidity and water damage. Most printers take good care of your materials while using them, but storage conditions vary widely.

Film and flats. Printers save flats but not plates. Negatives stay usable almost indefinitely, but plates can bend and get scratched during storage. In addition, you can easily update negatives but not plates. Even for exact reruns, printers prefer to make new plates.

Flats store easily in horizontal file folders. For jobs frequently reprinted at a shop you know you will continue to use, ask that operators write print quantities and dates on the folder holding flats for each job. As the record builds over the years, it helps you plan and budget by telling you how many you printed in what months and years.

Few printers store flats indefinitely. If you think you will ever go back to press, ask about company policy. Some printers throw away flats after storing them for a year or two, but the printer should notify you first.

Keep digital media, loose art, proofs and press sheets together with your specifications form and other notes about the job. You need large, flat boxes to avoid folding some of the materials.

Digital files. Prepress staff probably worked on your files, so their versions went to film or plates, not your versions. You should receive duplicates of the files from prepress clearly identified with information about your job. Store backups of computer files along with the paper records.

Many printers have sophisticated file servers and save the files for a determined amount of time and cost. First the files need postflighting to make sure the files that are stored are the ones that got printed. Then the files are digitally archived.

The format of these files is very important. If you save the application files, when you decide to reprint, the version may no longer be supported. Try to archive final files in the same format used to produce film or plates.

Computer disks and flats aren't worth much as physical objects but are priceless because of the effort required to replace them. Insurance on your property while in the shop varies among printers but ranges from none to marginal. Don't discover too late that computer files or photo-graphs waiting for processing are not insured. Check whether your business insurance covers the cost of making new flats or the value of your time to furnish new mechanicals.

Ownership. The question of who owns files and flats is different from the question of where they are stored. Generally speaking, the organization that creates the item owns it. That might mean that you own application files and loose art but a service bureau owns PostScript files and film.

Despite the claim of trade customs to the contrary, the issue of ownership remains cloudy unless it's part of a contract. Furthermore, building good business relationships with service bureaus and printers renders the issue meaningless. To avoid any question, specify with each job that you own files and film even though they are stored elsewhere. ■

6. PAPER AND INK

To keep up-to-date about printing papers and inks, visit our Web site (www.gettingitprinted.com).

The cost of paper represents 30 to 40 percent of the cost of your typical printing job. With larger jobs, such as long runs of magazines, books or manuals, paper can represent 50 percent of costs. A thorough knowledge of paper lets you cut costs faster than at any other point in the production process.

Upgrading papers is an easy and often dramatic way to improve an entire publication. The cost difference between routine and outstanding paper might be tiny compared to the cost of the job as a whole. Upgrading paper adds little to the cost of writing, design or printing.

In addition to cost, your choice of paper affects every aspect of printed products from design through printing to delivery. It pays to choose carefully.

In this chapter you learn about papermaking, the paper business as it relates to you and your printers, and major types of papers and their uses. Using this information, you can control paper costs and select papers best suited to your products and deadlines.

Printing papers fall into five major grades: bond, uncoated book (offset), text, coated book and cover. In addition to these major categories, there are many other grades, such as board and newsprint. Each grade has characteristics appropriate to specific applications. You have greater control over quality and cost when you know the features that distinguish one grade of paper from another and how to coordinate papers from different grades.

Although paper seems expensive, keep in mind that it is a relatively small expense when viewed from the standpoint of the total cost of a printing job. Total procurement costs include research, writing, design and distribution as well as printing and binding. When viewed from this standpoint, paper becomes a minor percentage of the overall budget.

HOW MILLS MAKE PAPER

About three dozen major manufacturers in North America make printing papers. One manufacturer might produce fifteen or twenty brands of printing paper plus industrial and sanitary papers.

Companies that make paper typically operate several mills. Each mill concentrates on making only one type of paper, such as bond or newsprint.

Mills make paper from cellulose fibers from trees, cotton or other plants, or from recycled paper.

Fibers from softwood trees, such as pine, are long and produce strong, relatively rough paper; those from hardwoods, such as maple, are short and yield weak, relatively smooth paper. Commercial printing papers contain a blend of softwood and hardwood to combine the best features of both. Papers made with long, supple cotton fibers are durable and smooth.

After removing bark, mills cut trees into chips. Mechanical grinders pulverize the chips for groundwood pulp; chemical digesters break up the fibers for chemical pulp.

Newsprint and other inexpensive papers, such as tissue, come from groundwood. They are called coarse papers. Printing and writing papers, called fine papers, come from chemical pulp. Fine papers are also called free sheets because they don't have the impurities found in groundwood.

Both groundwood and fine papers come from the same raw materials, processes and machinery, except that pulp for fine papers passes through the digester. Bleaching makes pulp white and chemically stable. White pulp yields white paper and is easily dyed to make colored papers.

6-1 THE MOST RELIABLE PRINTING PAPERS

Paper merchants offer thousands of combinations of grade, rating, color, surface and weight. You can, however, create most of the printed products your organization needs by using thorough knowledge of only seven sheets.

Following these guidelines increases your control over schedule, quality and cost.

1. Letterhead, envelopes, certificates and legal documents: **white 24# wove 25 percent cotton bond.**

2. Everyday photocopies and laser printing, and for notepads, fliers and statement stuffers: **white 20# wove #4 bond.**

3. Newsletters, brochures, direct mailers, booklets, staff directories and any product with mostly type and spot ink colors: **white 60# smooth #1 offset.**

4. Newsletters, brochures, catalogs, labels, calendars, maps, small posters and other products that require bright colors and faithful halftones: **white 70# matte coated #1.**

5. Covers of books, calendars and programs, and for membership cards, menus, dividers in binders, large posters and table tents: **white 8-point or 10-point C1S cover.**

6. Announcements, envelopes, presentation folders, coupons and tickets: **light blue or gray 80# felt text.**

7. Business cards and covers for premium presentations and booklets: **light blue or gray 65# felt cover** (matching the felt text above).

Consult with your printers to select one brand representing each paper, then learn all you can about its availability, how it reacts on press and what it costs in various amounts.

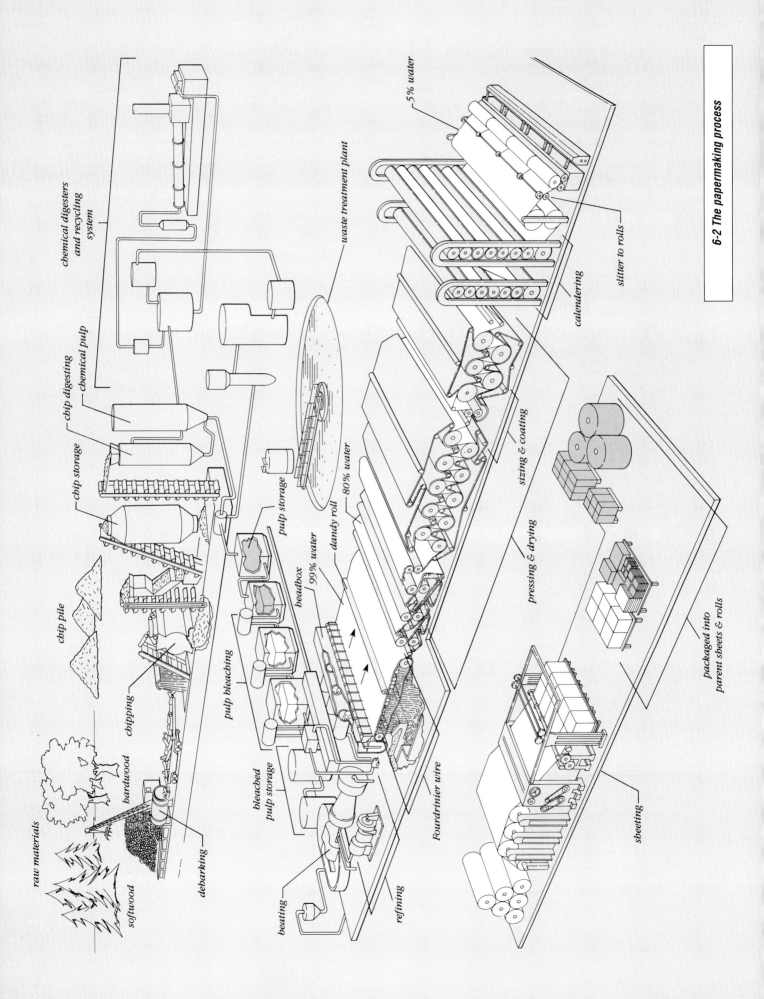

raw materials

chemical digesters
and recycling
system

chip digesting

chemical pulp

chip storage

chip pile

pulp storage

hardwood

chipping

pulp bleaching

softwood

debarking

bleached
pulp storage

beating

refining

headbox

99% water

dandy roll

80% water

Fourdrinier wire

waste treatment plant

5% water

slitter to rolls

calendering

sizing & coating

pressing & drying

packaged into
parent sheets & rolls

sheeting

6-2 The papermaking process

The papermaking process begins with beating, refining and bleaching to prepare pulp for the kind of paper desired. Refining is the most important step. Minimum refining yields thick, rough paper, such as that in shopping bags. Maximum refining yields thin, smooth paper, such as the glassine in envelope windows.

After preparation, mill workers mix pulp with water. The mixture, called furnish, flows onto the Fourdrinier wire, a wide, continuous belt of material similar to fine-mesh window screening. The wire shakes slightly from side to side as it moves forward. Fibers catch on the wire, but water falls through. The shaking ensures that fibers settle and lock together. When fibers reach the end of the wire loop 20 or 30 feet away, they contain about 90 percent water and can support their own weight. They have become paper.

The press and dryer sections remove more water, make the paper smooth and can impose texture on its surface. Later in the sequence, mills may apply sizing and coatings. Sizing makes paper better able to interact with water on press. Coatings make the surface stronger and improve ink holdout.

As steel rollers in the calender section press paper, it becomes smoother, thinner and more shiny. Many uncoated papers and all coated papers are calendered.

Mills make paper in huge rolls called reels or logs. A typical reel could measure 18 feet long and 5 feet thick and weigh several tons, much larger than even the largest web press can print. Mills cut sheets and smaller rolls from these master rolls.

Recycled papers

Paper accounts for approximately 40 percent of the solid waste that overflows landfills in North America. In addition, making paper consumes energy and pollutes air and water. The health of our environment calls for using recycled fibers instead of virgin fibers whenever reasonable.

Mills can put old paper back into the pulping process and blend it with virgin pulp from trees or other plants. Old paper that mills recycle into new paper comes from two sources.

Pre-consumer waste is paper that has never reached the user of a printed product. It includes unprinted paper such as trimmings left over from making envelopes, roll ends, damaged paper that printers couldn't use and waste from the mill itself. Pre-consumer waste also includes some printed paper, such as printer makeready and unsold books and magazines.

Post-consumer waste is printed paper that has been discarded by the end user. It includes publications, office paper, bags and hundreds of other products. Post-consumer waste is gathered from end users and returned to paper mills instead of going into a landfill.

Guidelines, laws and goals regarding recycled paper deal with the percentage of recycled fibers in paper and the source of those fibers. A paper listed as 50 percent recycled may use entirely pre-consumer waste and no post-consumer waste.

The recycling process shortens fibers and may not remove 100 percent of the ink. As a result, recycled papers have slightly different characteristics than comparable grades of virgin paper. We discuss those characteristics throughout this chapter.

Concern for the environment includes producing printed products than can be recycled as well as using recycled paper. Uncoated papers with little ink coverage are easiest to recycle. Coated papers and papers with dark dyes are hardest. Staples, foil-stamping and plastics make recycling much more expensive.

The language of recycling is not standard. For example, mills disagree about the difference between pre-consumer and post-consumer waste. Some mills call press makeready pre-consumer waste and others call it post-consumer waste.

Tree-free papers

As demand for paper increases along with concerns about vanishing forests, paper mills seek new sources of fiber. Research concentrates on two sources: (1) plants, such as hemp, kenaf and bamboo, that yield fiber faster than trees and

6-3 MANY USES OF "GRADE"

You may hear the word "grade" as a general term used to distinguish between printing papers but with specific meaning depending on context. Grade can refer to the category, class, rating, finish or brand of paper. All the following examples represent correct and common usage.

Category. One of the major groups of paper determined by how it is made. "I prefer groundwood grade for this job, not free sheet."

Class. One of the major categories of paper, such as bond, uncoated book, coated book, text, cover, bristol and board. "Bond is a better grade for letterhead than cover."

Rating. One of many ratings of paper,

such as 100 percent cotton or #4 gloss. "Our separations look better on a #1 grade than a #4 grade."

Finish. One of several finishes, such as wove or laid. "Which grade do you want, antique or vellum?"

Brand. One of thousands of brands of paper. "The mill makes twenty-seven grades of paper, but SilkSmooth is most popular."

Other. Any paper that differs from any other paper in any one respect. "Grain long is a better grade for this job than grain short."

To avoid confusion in this book, we use the word "grade" only to refer to a category of paper, such as bond or text.

---

(2) agricultural waste such as sugar cane, straw from wheat and rice, and by-products from coffee, banana and coconut plants.

Pulp from sources other than trees can yield strong, bright papers. Mills using tree-free pulp, however, consider it experimental both technically and economically. As customers and printers gain experience, the market for tree-free papers will result in rising supplies and shrinking costs.

For sources of recycled and tree-free papers, visit our Web site (www.gettingitprinted.com).

GRADES, RATINGS AND BRANDS

Professionals divide papers into large categories according to their end use, method of printing and pulp content.

End-use categories include:
• fine paper made for printing and writing
• industrial paper made for wrapping and packaging
• sanitary paper made for cleaning and personal hygiene
Method of printing categories include:
• sheet papers for sheetfed presses
• web papers for web presses

Pulp-content categories include:
• groundwood made from mechanical pulp that has impurities (used for newspapers and general newsmagazines)
• free sheet made from chemical pulp with the impurities washed and bleached away (used for most commercial printing jobs)

Fine papers are divided by grade, rating and brand name, the categories used most frequently when discussing printing jobs. These categories remain the same regardless of whether the paper comes from trees, other plants or recycled fibers. The source of the fibers has no effect on how papers are classified in price books and samples rooms.

Grades

Mills make printing papers in five major grades: bond, text, uncoated book, coated book and cover. Most of your printing projects use one or more of these grades. We describe each grade in detail later in this chapter.

Mills make bond for individual products such as letters and legal documents. Bond is also used for photocopies, laser printout and business forms. Sometimes you hear the terms "business papers" or "communications papers" used to refer to bonds.

Graphic designers specify text paper when surface pattern and paper color form integral parts of design. Text is used for annual reports, announcements, brochures, presentation folders and other products that must be elegant and durable.

Printers use uncoated book for everyday products such as books, newsletters and direct mailers. You often hear the term "offset" used interchangeably with uncoated book.

Printing jobs needing vivid ink colors and faithful reproductions of photos and drawings call for coated book paper. Those jobs include most magazines, calendars, catalogs and posters and many brochures.

Book covers, presentation folders, postcards and similar products call for cover paper, which is sturdy and durable. Cover paper is available in both uncoated and coated surfaces and in colors and patterns that match sheets in other grades.

Ratings

Manufacturers rate papers based on characteristics such as brightness, opacity and fiber content. You often see these ratings in swatch books, ads, specifications and price books. People rate papers so they may conveniently think, talk and write about them. Consider the ratings as guidelines, not rules.

Knowing how papers are rated makes communication among graphic arts professionals more precise and cost control easier. Rating systems help you focus on papers suited to your specific printing job.

Ratings use numbers from 1 (highest) through 5 (lowest) and words such as "premium" and "commodity," although not every grade uses every number or descriptive word. In your day-to-day work, you probably select from only one or two ratings within each grade.

Sometimes ratings seem arbitrary and inconsistent. Mills assign ratings to their own papers, so one mill's #2 dull may look similar to another mill's #1 matte.

Brands

Every paper has a brand name given to it either by a mill or a merchant. Names assigned by mills remain the same from one merchant to another; private brands assigned by merchants are unique to that distributor.

Mills choose names to build respect and brand loyalty. For example, names for lines of recycled papers include Retreeve, Evergreen and Renewal, which suggest responsibility to the environment. Names for sheets engineered for laser and ink-jet printers include Exacta and TechReady.

Private names are given most commonly to bonds and offsets packaged for small presses and office machines. Many paper merchants and office supply stores, and even some large corporations such as Xerox, feature their own brands. Private brands and mill brands come from the same mills and may even be identical except for name and price.

Preprinted papers available in office supply stores and from catalogs identify the brand name of the sheet. Brand names of the preprinted sheets are identical to brand names of unprinted paper available through printers and paper distributors. The preprinted sheets offer the advantage of colorful printing in sizes and quantities convenient for desktop machines.

SAMPLES AND DUMMIES

Mills sell paper to merchants who sell to printers and print buyers. Paper merchants operate

....

" Until I actually visited the sample room of a paper distributor, I never realized how much they can help. I thought they only worked with printers, not with buyers like me. Once I needed a dummy of 128 pages, 8½" × 11", 60# ivory vellum, perfect bound with a 10-point cover. I felt reluctant to ask for something so complicated, but they said 'No problem' and delivered it the next morning. "

locally and regionally. Several merchants in a region may carry the same brand of paper. Merchants sell mill brands but may also sell their own private brands.

To find paper merchants in your local area, look under "Paper Distributors" in a classified directory for businesses (not consumers).

Paper merchants often employ a specialist to advise buyers. Known as specifications consultants or graphic arts consultants, these experts meet with individuals and groups to discuss the paper industry. They report trends concerning cost, availability and design and explain how those trends affect the products that most interest buyers.

Large paper merchants and the mills they represent occasionally sponsor events where they exhibit new brands and colors. These events attract printers, graphic designers and print buyers eager for samples and information. Ask your printer to make sure you are invited to such events in your area.

Paper mills supply distributors with swatch books, printed samples, training materials and other sales aids. Distributors keep the materials in a samples room with its own manager. Sales reps for distributors work with the samples manager to give materials to printers and printing buyers.

Printed samples are useful for checking opacity and noting how a stock receives the ink colors you like. Printers and merchants have printed samples of various papers, although samples of printing on paper of uncommon weight, finish or color may be hard to find.

A swatch book shows small, unprinted samples of a brand of paper and tells what sizes, weights, colors and finishes the mill makes. Swatch books are especially useful for examining a range of colors.

A few mills make swatch books showing their entire lines of papers organized by brand, color and weight. These swatch books are especially popular with mills that make text/cover or writing/cover papers.

Paper merchants put labels on swatch books to identify who sells the paper locally. When you get a swatch book from a printer, note the name of the shop and the merchant. The typical print shop buys most of its paper from one merchant, so it's useful to know which printers deal with which merchants and which merchants sell papers you like.

Unprinted sample sheets come in cut sizes provided by mills and larger sizes that merchants take from inventory. Large sheets help you think about ganging jobs because you can visualize two or three pieces printed on one large sheet.

Dummies are blank sheets folded and bound to simulate the product you have in mind. They are important to any job involving binding because they let you see, feel and weigh the final outcome. You can also use paper dummies for preparing comprehensive roughs so clients, supervisors and vendors know exactly what you have in mind.

Whenever a printer suggests unfamiliar paper, ask for a printed sample. Ideally, images and ink colors on the sample resemble those you have in mind. If you have any doubts about how the paper suits your job, ask the printer to get additional samples from the merchant or mill.

PRINTER/MERCHANT RELATIONSHIPS

For most printing jobs, let the printer order paper for you. You can take advantage of samples and advice offered by merchants, but in most cases you have greatest control over quality, schedule and cost when buying through your printer.

66 When I took over coordinating all the printing jobs for our company, the first thing I did was plan how to use paper. I reduced the quality of paper for internal publications such as reports that don't need to impress anyone. The money saved by that step let me specify better quality stock for brochures for our potential customers. 99

Printers typically buy most of their paper from one merchant. They cut costs by consolidating quantities, and they build trust relationships with sales reps and people in customer service and accounting.

Buying paper through a printer saves you the time required to get dummies, check on availability, compute quantities and write specifications.

You can benefit from printer/merchant loyalty by learning about papers offered to your printers by their favorite merchants. Knowing what's available and what your printers like on press helps make production go smoothly.

When buying quick printing, you select paper from the sheets the printer offers and don't normally consult a swatch book. Quick printers keep a variety of standard weights and colors in stock and can get alternates easily. These printers include the cost of paper in their per-hundred printing prices, so you have only two or three cost decisions.

Commercial printers use paper in much greater variety and quantity than quick printers do. When buying paper as part of commercial printing, your printer's sales rep or a merchant's graphic arts consultant can help you decide what stock to use. Either can give you samples and dummies and give you information about costs and availability.

Most commerical printers keep an inventory of two or three types of paper they call house sheets. A #3 offset, a #1 matte and a #2 gloss would be typical. To keep costs down, printers buy house sheets in large quantities for routine jobs. Specifying the house sheet may mean printing on paper that isn't quite what you had in mind. On the other hand, often the house sheet is perfectly adequate and costs less than other similar possibilities.

When you specify paper for a commerical printing job, your printer checks with one or two distributors to determine that it's readily available. If the stock is locally warehoused, printers may not even order until a few days before press time. Never assume, however, that printers can get any paper you want in a matter of days. Stock that must come from a distant warehouse or directly from the mill may take several weeks.

Specialty printers buy paper in large quantity but small variety. You might choose from among four or five stocks, each suited to the special product the printer manufactures. For example, a book printer typically offers uncoated paper in three weights (50#, 55# and 60#) and two colors (white and natural) and may not offer any bond, text or coated stocks.

When you ask printers to quote on a job, tell them you want the cost of paper itemized on the estimate. Breaking out paper costs helps you consider the costs of alternate sheets. Equally important, itemized paper costs highlight the different amounts that different printers charge for the same paper.

To get lower prices by increasing the amount of paper you specify, compute your needs for several jobs at once. Resist the temptation to increase your print run simply to reduce unit costs. For example, if you produce four rack brochures every few months, write specifications for a full year so your printer can commit to that much paper.

Specifying on a job-by-job basis keeps your orders to a minimum and drives up unit costs. Specifying for several jobs at a time lowers the unit cost of paper and lowers your printer's costs because it ensures your continuous business.

You can also increase quantities by working cooperatively with other print buyers. Talking to the folks down the hall or around the corner often reveals paper needs similar to yours. Joint planning and specifying may save everyone thousands of dollars.

Like other businesses, paper distributors have sales. Orders get cancelled, specifications change, color and weights go out of style, discontinued items are closed out. If you have a job for which precise color or weight and availability for reruns aren't crucial factors, check for bargains on specials or closeout lists or have your printer check for you.

You can reduce printing costs by using many techniques to cut the cost of paper. Most techniques also save trees, energy, air and water quality, and landfill space by reducing consumption. It pays to think green.

Reduce trim size. Shaving ¼ inch off your book, magazine or catalog might save thousands of pounds—and dollars—per year. Lower weight reduces postage costs as well.

Reduce basis weight. Heavier basis weight sheets cost more per sheet than lighter ones.

60# costs 20% more than 50#
70# costs 15% more than 60#
80# costs 12% more than 70#
100# costs 20% more than 80#

Use house sheets. Design routine jobs for paper that your printer buys in huge quantities, not on stock that you specify on a job-by-job basis.

Learn price breaks. The more paper you buy, the less you pay per unit. When you plan a printing job to take advantage of price breaks, you ensure the lowest possible unit cost per printed piece.

Prices for paper decrease at specific quantity levels as follows:

partial carton costs	15-60%	above base
1 carton costs		base price
4 cartons cost	6-15%	below base
8 cartons cost	7-19%	below base
16 cartons cost	9-23%	below base
24 cartons cost	24-26%	below base
5,000 lbs cost	29-32%	below base
10,000 lbs cost	30-38%	below base
20,000 lbs cost	33-40%	below base
carload costs	37-43%	below base

Shop the sales. Paper merchants provide printers with closeout lists showing stock available at significant savings.

Consolidate needs. Work with others to merge printing jobs. When you gang runs or cooperate on long-term contracts, your printer can commit to quantities of paper that may reduce prices as much as 25 percent.

Reduce print runs. Look in your supply closet, back room and warehouse to identify printing jobs for which you ordered too many units. You may have to look in your dumpster, too. Make an extra effort to specify quantities you're sure you need.

Avoid overruns. Slight overruns are inevitable, but you can work with your printer to keep them to a minimum. Don't get stuck with a lot of printed paper you can't use.

Avoid coated paper. Uncoated paper costs less and is easier on the environment than coated paper. Coated paper is more difficult to make and recycle. Recycled coated paper contains a lower percent of recycled fibers than comparable uncoated paper.

Avoid dark-colored paper. Dark paper costs more to make and more to recycle than light paper. Produce dark colors with ink, not paper.

Print less often. Encourage readers to save items for reference or to use items a few weeks or months longer.

Reduce page counts. Use fewer words, photos and illustrations to get your message across. Choose the most efficient typefaces and sizes. Put specialized information in separate publications that only a few readers need. Let E-mail and Web sites replace paper.

Use standard sizes. Design your printed pieces to take maximum advantage of common sheet sizes. Don't fill dumpsters with trimmings.

Use the sheet efficiently. Plan jobs to use as much of the sheet as possible.

Reduce makeready. Specify quality in measurable terms. Simplify design to run printing jobs on the fewest possible machines. Make final decisions about color on proofs, not on press. Gang projects by running two or three projects on the same sheet.

Avoid bleeds. Bleeds require larger sheets and create more waste.

Reduce paper quality. Change from premium to #1, from 100 percent cotton to 25 percent cotton, or #4 free sheet to #5 groundwood. In addition to cutting costs, lower quality paper is more likely to contain recycled fibers than stock that must look bright and flawless.

Write and design carefully. Make sure your printed piece communicates clearly and completely to reduce the need for additional publications.

Consider nonprint media. Think about using voice mail, intranets, meetings, videos, E-mail or Web sites instead of printed products.

Use digital printing. Print manuals, catalogs, newsletters and even books as needed. Digital printing reduces makeready and produces only the quantity you need.

Think twice. Does the entire staff really need a copy of the whole report? Do you really need to send five hundred holiday cards? Will every legislator and related organization really read your newsletter?

Target distribution. Make your publication available only where readers want it. Don't put it on counters, newsstands or bulletin boards where it's ignored.

Clean your mailing list. Don't print items that the post office can't deliver. And don't send free copies to everyone whose name exists on some database of VIPs. Use the National Change of Address (NCOA) system and your own common sense to keep your list up-to-date.

Reject dirty mailing lists. Don't send duplicate items to the same person or household. Examine lists that you rent for matching names, job titles and addresses.

Ask readers if they care. Don't send materials to people who just throw them away. Provide business-reply cards that let readers notify you to delete their names. Encourage readers to call you or use your Web site if they don't want your publications.

Negotiate a lower cost. Ask your printer or paper merchant for a lower price on stock you currently use. The worst you can hear is no, and maybe you'll hear yes.

Ask for better credit terms. Many paper merchants invoice 2 percent/10 days instead of net 30 days. Maybe you can get 2 percent/30 days or net 60 days. Save by protecting your cash flow.

Mark Beach and Eric Kenly © 1998. From *Getting It Printed*, published by North Light Books, Cincinnati, Ohio.

REDUCING WASTE AND SPOILAGE

You can cut your costs for paper by reducing waste and spoilage.

The terms "waste" and "spoilage" represent very different concepts. Waste is unusable paper or paper damaged during normal printing or bindery operations. Spoilage is paper that, due to mistakes or accidents, operators must throw away instead of delivering to the customer.

Printers anticipate waste, most of which is makeready, and plan for it when buying paper. They do not anticipate spoilage that should have been prevented.

Printing estimators express waste as a percent of the paper needed to produce the quantity specified. If a job calls for 10,000 sheets and the estimator predicts 4 percent waste, the printer orders 10,400 sheets.

The amount of waste a printer forecasts for a specific job depends on many factors. Some general guidelines: Shorter press runs produce a higher percentage of waste than longer ones; web printing yields more waste than sheetfed printing; waste increases with number of colors printed, complexity of bindery operations and quality expectations. Spoilage could result from poor conditioning, defective plates or blankets, poor presswork, poor operation of bindery equipment, or many other unintentional situations.

Many of the cost-cutting tips in Visual 6-4 help reduce waste and spoilage. In addition, you can help your printer use paper efficiently by providing measurable quality guidelines.

Precise specifications for quality reduce waste. When you specify quality in subjective terms, such as "saturated colors," you invite extended discussion during setup or a press check. During the discussion, paper runs through the press into the dumpster. More precise language, such as "meet SWOP target ink densities," tells press operators exactly what you expect. Less paper goes into the dumpster before you see a sheet you can approve.

HOW PAPER LOOKS

Paper has many characteristics that determine its cost and influence its suitability for a particular printing job. When you understand these traits, you add to your control over the cost and quality of your printing jobs.

Color

Most printing papers are white, but not all whites look the same. Examine four or five samples of white paper. Try to decide which is whitest or "true white."

Mills use many names to distinguish one white from another. You can buy white called bright, radiant, colonial, polar, elegant, cloud and many more. You can also buy colors simply called pearl, oyster, foam or birch, all of which are white. Experts claim that white is warm when it tends toward yellow and cool when it tends toward blue.

A very white sheet helps ensure wide tonal range in photos. Contrast between the lightest and darkest parts of an image creates tonal range. A white sheet results in lighter lights, thus increasing details in highlights and making dark inks seem darker.

Keep in mind that paper comes from trees and other plants, so its natural color is light brown, not white. Mills use bleaches and other strong chemicals to make pulp white. Some chemicals cause less pollution than others, but all damage the environment.

Paper that is slightly off-white comes in many shades with many names. In addition to the obvious shade "natural," names include cream, ivory, eggshell, mellow and soft white. These shades have little glare, so they are popular for novels, technical manuals and other publications that readers hold for long periods at a time.

Mills add dyes and pigments to create paper of virtually any color. Color varies from mill to mill and there is no standard for naming hues. What one mill calls ivory another mill may call buff or cream. Colors from the same mill might show slight variations from one run to the next.

When you evaluate color, put samples next to each other so you can view two or three at once. Don't rely on memory. And use the proper lighting conditions described in Visual 3-3. If you don't have standard viewing conditions, use sunlight.

Bulk and finish affect color. Your favorite gray may seem a shade lighter in 24# bond for letterhead than in the 80# cover stock for business cards designed to match.

Colors go in and out of style. Mills add and drop colors every couple of years, following color trends in fashion and interior design.

If you're choosing paper whose color must appeal to readers over many years, as when selecting corporate letterhead, resist any temptation to follow trends. Safe, basic colors cost least and last longest.

Because color is subjective, color match can change from run to run. The mill supervisor may think sky blue made in August is an acceptable match to that made in March, but you may disagree. If you print half your brochure on the March run and the other half on paper made in August, you may not have a perfect color match.

Color match is especially difficult to achieve with recycled paper because of inconsistency of raw materials. In the case of recycled sheets, it's easier to match darker colors than lighter ones and most difficult to match whites.

White is the least expensive paper. Colored paper costs more because it is in less demand and because dyes are expensive. Light colors, such as cream and natural cost slightly more than white, and costs increase as colors get darker. Coated stock tends to come exclusively in whites, with a few mills making tones they call cream or natural; uncoated stock, in white plus light colors; and text papers, in white plus a full range of intense colors. Color in paper increases opacity and decreases brightness.

Tree-free and recycled papers are available in many whites and colors. Color matches for paper containing high percentages of post-consumer waste may vary more from batch to batch than on comparable virgin stock.

Brightness

Mills measure the light that white paper reflects and report results as percentages. The brightest possible paper would reflect 100 percent of the light striking it. Most papers have brightness ratings between 60 and 90 percent.

Whiteness and brightness are different features. Brightness is a quantitative measure, whiteness a subjective judgment. There are no standards dictating either brightness or whiteness for specific printed products. Papers with high gloss can measure very bright but not appear as white as less glossy sheets.

Brightness affects readability. Type on a sheet with low brightness lacks contrast, but type on a very bright sheet can cause eyestrain. Papers for books, technical manuals and the financial sections of annual reports need less brightness than papers for magazines and brochures.

Recycled papers appear slightly less white and bright than comparable virgin stock because of variations in raw materials and difficulty of removing 100 percent of ink and dye.

Opacity

Printing on one side of the paper should not interfere with printing on the other, nor should images on a sheet underneath the one being viewed. Good opacity prevents unwanted images from showing through.

Paper mills rate opacity on a scale of 1 to 100, with 100 being completely opaque. Most printing papers fall in the 80 to 98 percent opacity range.

Opacity increases with basis weight and bulk and is affected by coatings, colors, chemicals, ink color and coverage, and impurities. Because of its residue of ink, recycled paper is slightly more opaque than comparable virgin stock. The average difference is about 2 percent.

Opacity affects readability. High opacity helps readers concentrate and reduces confusion and eyestrain. Opacity also prevents photos, screen tints or reverses on one side of a sheet from showing through to the other side.

Use Visual 6-5 to compare the opacities of papers and decide which papers have adequate opacity for a specific printed product.

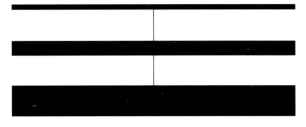

6-5 Opacity comparison bars *The opacity of paper determines the extent to which printing on one side interferes with printing on the other. To compare the opacity of two pieces of paper, lay the sheets so that their edges meet at the center line of the pattern above. The sheet that makes the bars most difficult to see is the more opaque.*

HOW PAPER FEELS

In addition to the way paper looks, it has many physical traits that affect the way it performs on press and in the printed product.

Surface

As mills turn pulp into paper, they adjust its surface for look, feel and printability. Each grade has its own set of terms that describe surfaces for that grade. Surfaces for each grade are listed on the chart in Visual 6-11.

Rollers at the mill press paper to make it smooth. Paper becomes smoother as it passes between each set of rollers, a process called calendering. Uncoated paper may or may not be calendered; all coated paper is calendered to some degree. With uncoated paper, the process yields vellum, antique, wove and smooth finishes. With coated papers, minimum calendering yields matte finish, medium calendering results in dull finish, and extensive calendering creates gloss and ultragloss.

The process of calendering affects paper in several ways. As the degree of calendering increases, paper becomes smoother and more glossy and has better ink holdout. The heat and pressure of calendering also makes paper thinner, less bulky and opaque, and often less bright.

Embossing is done off the papermaking machine by steel rollers that press patterns into paper surfaces. Embossed finishes have special names, such as stipple and canvas.

A paper's surface determines how easily it accepts ink, how rapidly the press can run while maintaining uniform ink coverage, and other elusive factors affecting printability. If a printer grumbles about the printability of a particular sheet, listen.

Recycled and tree-free papers are available in most of the surfaces made using virgin fibers.

Grain

During papermaking, fibers become aligned in one direction. The result is grain. When fibers run parallel to the length of a sheet, the stock is grain long; when fibers run crosswise, the sheet is grain short.

Mills have several ways of indicating grain direction on labels and in swatch books and price books: They print "grain long" or "grain short." They underline the dimension parallel to the grain; for example, 11″ × 17″ means grain short. They write "M" for "machine direction" after the dimension parallel to the grain; for example, 23″ × 35″ (M) means grain long.

If you have a sheet with unknown grain direction, you can determine the grain by moistening one side of the sheet. It curls parallel to the grain. You can moisten a piece of letterhead enough by placing it on a surface that has been wiped with a damp cloth.

Grain direction affects printing because moisture in the air and in dampening solutions causes the fibers in paper to expand slightly. Fibers become wider (fatter), but not longer; a sheet expands against the grain, but not with the grain. Printing that requires tight register is done on grain long paper so that fibers lie parallel to the length of the cylinder, giving press operators maximum control over register as sheets expand.

Knowing grain direction helps design for folding and strength. Heavy stock folds most smoothly with the grain. Folds against the grain may need scoring first. Grain long book pages turn more easily than grain short; grain long letterheads and counter displays are more rigid than grain short.

Recycled paper has relatively short fibers, so it scores, folds and embosses more easily than comparable virgin stock.

HOW PAPER IS MEASURED

Paper has physical characteristics that influence cost and suitability for particular printing equipment. Understanding these traits adds to your control over the cost and helps printers meet your service expectations.

Weight

Each grade of paper, such as bond and offset, has one basic size used to determine basis weight. Visual 6-11 shows basic sizes for the various grades. Note that basic size is only one of the many standard sizes for each grade.

Basis weight is expressed in pounds and is figured using one ream (five hundred sheets) as a standard quantity. To see how this works in practice, take five hundred sheets of paper at the basic size for its grade, then weigh the pile. The result is the basis weight of the paper in the pile. Visual 6-6 illustrates this concept.

When writing basis weight, the word "pound" is abbreviated with the symbol #. Fifty-pound coated is written 50# coated. You may also see it written as BS 50 meaning basis 50 pound.

Sometimes paper is designated in substance weights, as in "sub 24." Substance weight and basis weight are identical concepts. Both refer to the weight of five hundred sheets of the basic size.

Often packages of paper identify both the basis weight of the contents and basic size of the grade. For example, a carton of 17½″×22½″ 80# text might be marked "80# (25″×38″)." The figures in parentheses refer to the basic size used when computing the basis weight.

To help understand the concept of basis weight, consider pulp that yields eighty pounds of paper. The mill could make the pulp into five hundred sheets of 25″×38″ book paper or into five hundred sheets of 20″×26″ cover grade. Both reams would weigh the same and both would consist of 80# paper. The cover paper would measure almost twice as thick as the book paper, and its sheets would only be about half the size (520 square inches vs. 950 square inches). In this example, each individual sheet of book grade and cover grade would weigh the same; therefore, each sheet would have the same basis weight.

Some grades of paper have more weights available than others. In practice, the differences are as follows.

Bond. The majority of bond is either 16# for forms, 20# for photocopying and quick printing, or 24# for stationery. You can get other weights, such as 13#, 28# and 32#, but rarely need them.

Text. Text papers come only in relatively heavy weights required to carry the texture of the paper. Most jobs using text run on 70# or 80#. A few use 60# or 100#.

Uncoated book. You can get offset in many weights, but 50#, 60# and 70# are most common. More printing jobs run on 60# commodity offset than on any other paper.

Coated book. Print buyers specify a greater range of weights in coated than in other grades. Sheetfed jobs use weights from 60# to 110#; web jobs use weights from 30# to 70#.

Cover. Most cover is specified as 60#, 65#, 80# or 100# or in calipers of 8 pt, 10 pt or 12 pt (see "Caliper"). A few mills paste sheets together to make "cover plus" in 88#, 110# or 130#.

Understanding paper weight increases cost control because paper is sold by the pound. For example, 70# book costs about 15 percent more per sheet than 60#. If you plan twenty-five thousand copies of an 8½″×11″, sixteen-page brochure, the cost difference of the paper might be four hundred dollars. You might save even more when considering postage. If the brochure on 70# stock takes you over a per-piece weight limit at the post office, you might pay more to mail than to print.

Equivalent weights. Often you have to compare papers whose basis weights are computed using different basic sizes. For example, you might consider printing an invitation on either bond or text. In such situations, knowing equivalent basis weights helps you decide.

The relationships between book and bond basis weights:

grammage	basis weight
34	9# manifold
44	30# book
45	12# manifold
59	40# book
60	16# bond
67	45# book
74	50# book
75	20# bond
81	55# book
89	60# book
90	24#bond
104	70# book/text
105	28#ledger
118	80# book/text
120	32#ledger
135	36# ledger
147	67#bristol
148	100# book/text
150	40# ledger
162	60# cover
163	90# index
163	100# tag
176	65# cover
199	110# index
216	80# cover
218	125# tag
219	100# bristol
270	100#cover
352	130# cover

comparison guide to
common basis weights

500 sheets of 20 x 26
80# cover paper

500 sheets of 25 x 38
80# book or text paper

500 sheets of 17 x 22
28# bond

500 sheets of 24 x 36
28# newsprint

90 gsm
paper

270 gsm
paper

basic size and basis weight

6-6 Basic size and basis weight *Papers can have different basic sizes but the same basis weights. The top scales each hold one ream (five hundred sheets) of 80# paper, one book grade and one cover grade. The basic size of the cover paper is smaller than the basic size of the book paper. The cover paper, however, is thicker than the book, so the two piles weigh exactly the same. The middle pair of scales shows the same* concept for bond and newsprint.

Graphic arts professionals outside of North America refer to the weight of paper in grams per square meter (gsm), called "grammage." The bottom pair of scales shows that using the metric system eliminates the concept of basic size and makes it easy to compare weights among different grades.

40# book equivalent to 16# bond
50# book equivalent to 20# bond
60# book equivalent to 24# bond
70# book equivalent to 28# bond

The relationships between book and cover basis weights:

90# book equivalent to 50# cover
100# book equivalent to 55# cover
110# book equivalent to 60# cover
120# book equivalent to 65# cover

When using equivalent weights to design printed pieces, keep in mind that book weights apply to uncoated book, coated book and text, all of which have the same basic size. You may also hear book weights called text weights.

Laser printers and photocopy machines can run heavier paper than most users realize. Using your knowledge of equivalent weights, you can find book and cover papers that work fine in office machines. For example, you could use 100# text, equivalent to 55# cover, to print report covers. Running this stock through your laser printer means you could add individualized information, such as a personal name, to each cover.

Caliper

Paper thickness is defined as caliper. It is measured in thousandths of an inch and expressed as point size. One point equals .001 inch. Stock called 7 point is .007 inches thick and abbreviated "7 pt."

Note that points describing caliper of paper are not the same as points describing size of type. Paper points refer to thickness; type points to height. A type point is $1/72$ inch, almost fourteen times larger than a point describing paper.

Buyers often specify cover stock and other thick paper by point size. The most common calipers for cover paper are 8 pt, 10 pt and 12 pt. The typical telephone directory has a 10-pt cover. If you want paper thicker than 12 pt, look for stock called tag, blanks or board.

The U.S. Postal Service requires that postcards and business-reply cards measure at least 7 pt. Any paper merchant carries a supply.

Publishers often express caliper in pages per inch (ppi). Knowing ppi is important when specifying type sizes for printing book spines. Visual 6-7 shows how pages per inch can affect the thickness of a book.

When thinking about pages per inch, remember that one sheet of paper equals two pages.

Bulk

Bulk refers to thickness of paper relative to its basis weight. An uncalendered sheet is relatively bulky compared to a calendered sheet of the

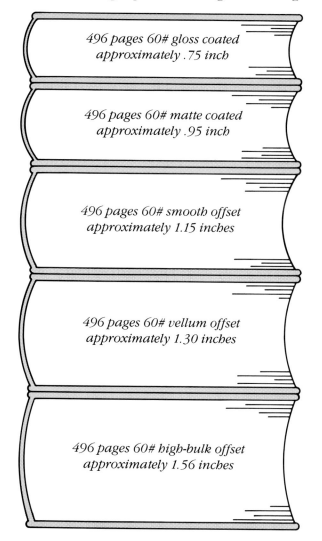

496 pages 60# gloss coated
approximately .75 inch

496 pages 60# matte coated
approximately .95 inch

496 pages 60# smooth offset
approximately 1.15 inches

496 pages 60# vellum offset
approximately 1.30 inches

496 pages 60# high-bulk offset
approximately 1.56 inches

6-7 Comparing caliper *Paper caliper determines thickness of the printed piece, an important consideration with products such as books, catalogs and directories. This chart represents books made from 248 sheets (496 pages) of typical 60# papers.*

When imagining the books represented in this chart, keep in mind that all five have identical weights. Although some are thinner than others, all contain 496 pages of paper with the same basis weight.

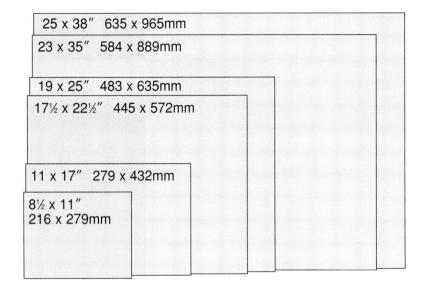

North American sheet sizes

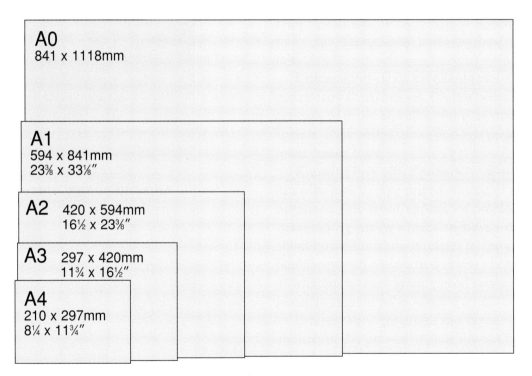

ISO sheet sizes

6-8 Common sheet sizes *Printers in North America use sheets measured in inches. Many sheets are multiples of 8½″ × 11″. Outside of North America, printers use sheets measured in millimeters. Metric dimensions are called ISO sizes because they are supported by the International Standards Organization.*

The starting point for ISO sizes is the A0 sheet containing one square meter. Each smaller size is a fraction of the A0 size. *For example, A4 means that the A0 sheet has been cut into four smaller sheets, each containing .25 square meters. The A4 size is used for letterhead. When folded, it fits a standard DL envelope just as 8½″ × 11″ letterhead fits a standard #10 envelope. If you produce jobs using ISO paper sizes, keep in mind the same sizes for envelopes, folders, binders and other coordinated products.*

same basis weight. Gloss-coated paper has low bulk; uncoated paper has moderate bulk; reply-card paper has high bulk.

Caliper and bulk are not related to basis weight. One paper may be thicker or bulkier than another but have the same basis weight.

Size

The graphic arts industry in the United States and Canada measures paper in inches. A $25'' \times 38''$ sheet is 25 inches wide and 38 inches long. Paper comes in the standard sizes shown in Visual 6-8. Throughout the rest of the world, printing paper is measured using the metric system, also shown in Visual 6-8.

Efficient design reduces waste by coordinating paper and press size. You pay for the paper in your printer's dumpster; keep waste to a minimum.

Using paper economically requires knowing the most common sheet sizes. Quick printers use two cut sizes, $8\frac{1}{2}'' \times 11''$, or A4, and $11'' \times 17''$, or A3; commercial printers may also run cut sizes, but generally use larger sizes, often called parent sheets.

Knowing how many products come out of one press sheet and designing with paper sizes in mind increases control over production times and costs. Often you can design your product to fit available paper rather than choosing paper after finishing design. Visual 6-9 shows the variety of printed pieces that might be cut from one parent sheet.

Paper mills ship sheets in a variety of sizes. Large pieces, called parent sheets, are usually printed to fold into smaller pages or to cut into smaller products. For example, a $17'' \times 22''$ sheet could fold into a sixteen-page booklet measuring $5\frac{1}{2}'' \times 8\frac{1}{2}''$ or could cut into four $8\frac{1}{2}'' \times 11''$ sheets of stationery. Both the booklet and the stationery are standard sizes. Often, however, products are made to a nonstandard size. The $17'' \times 22''$ sheet, for example, might cut into twelve handouts each five inches square.

Letterhead building block. The graphic arts industry in the United States and Canada, from making paper to using it, revolves around the $8\frac{1}{2}'' \times 11''$ sheet. Laser printers, small presses, photocopy machines, fax machines, typewriters and file drawers are designed for $8\frac{1}{2}'' \times 11''$ sheets. So are binders, file folders, envelopes and other products related to paper.

Large sheet sizes are multiples of $8\frac{1}{2}'' \times 11''$. Some multiples, such as $17'' \times 22''$, are exact; others, such as $23'' \times 35''$, are slightly oversized to allow for grippers and trimming. Still others, such as $25'' \times 38''$, are even more oversized to allow for bleeds and color bars. Visual 6-8 shows common sheet sizes; Visual 7-3 explains how printers create bleeds.

The most common multiples of $8\frac{1}{2}'' \times 11''$:

• $11'' \times 17''$ sheets, used to print jobs such as letterhead two up, four-page newsletters and saddle stitch covers for $8\frac{1}{2}'' \times 11''$ booklets

• $17'' \times 22''$ sheets, used to print jobs such as letterhead four up, brochures and eight-page newsletters

• $23'' \times 35''$ sheets, used to print jobs such as sixteen-page signatures requiring no bleeds, small trims and narrow color bars

• $25'' \times 38''$ sheets, used to print sixteen-page signatures and other products requiring bleeds, large trims, wide color bars and bindery laps

You can plan printing jobs most effectively when you keep in mind the letterhead building block.

Quantities

Reams consist of five hundred sheets. "Ream wrapped" means sheets are packaged in bundles of five hundred.

Cartons of paper weigh approximately 150 pounds, but may contain any number of sheets depending on the size and basis weight of the paper they contain. For example, a carton of $25'' \times 38''$ 70# paper holds one thousand sheets. Paper of the same size in 100# comes eight hundred sheets per carton. Page 56 of Mark Beach's book *Papers for Printing* contains a chart showing carton contents for various combinations of sheet size and basis weight.

Paper distributors use cartons as units of sales. Ordering less than a full carton means

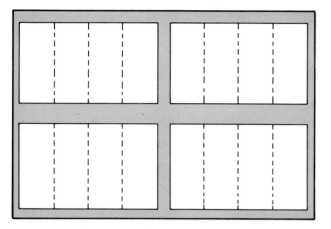

*four 8-panel 4″ × 9′ rack brochures
printed four up and four out*

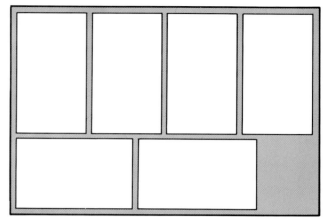

*six 8½″ × 14″ newsletters
printed six up and six out*

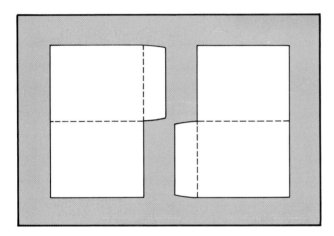

*two 9″ × 12″ pocket folders
printed two up and one out*

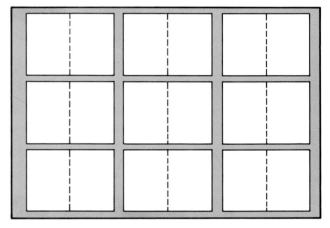

*nine 4½″ × 6¼″ greeting cards
printed nine up*

6-9 Products from a 23″ × 35″ sheet *Understanding how paper in standard sizes cuts to yield printed pieces leads to more efficient use of paper. Above, solid lines represent trims and dotted lines, folds. Shading represents areas of the paper that become waste.*

Up and out. *When printers plan press sheets, they refer to how many products print up and how many cut out."Up" refers to the total number of products on the sheet, regardless of format or imaging."Out" refers to a specific product. For example, a press sheet might print business cards nine up. If* each card shows the name of a different person, then each card prints only one out.

Ganging. *You can reduce the costs of paper, prepress and press time by printing more than one product on the same sheet. For example, the pocket folders illustrated above might print on 10-point cover stock. The press sheet has plenty of room to print business cards or post cards along with the folders. With the sheet printed as illustrated, almost half the paper goes into the waste pile when it's trimmed from the folders.*

increased packing and inventory costs, so the price per ream or pound goes up.

Skids are wooden platforms loaded with ream-marked sheets, then covered to keep out moisture. Paper that is bulk packed on skids costs slightly less per sheet than paper in cartons. A full skid of paper normally weighs about 2,500 pounds. As with cartons, the number of sheets on a skid depends on size and basis weight.

CWT means hundred weight. In paper parlance, cost per CWT means dollars per 100 pounds. CWT prices apply to all mill orders and roll stock for web presses. Paper not bought by the CWT is purchased by the thousand sheets. Pages from price books give prices per one thousand sheets and per CWT.

Carloads weigh anywhere from 20,000 to 100,000 pounds, depending on the mill or merchant using the term.

BOND AND WRITING

Mills make bond paper for individual correspondence, such as letters and forms. Bond lacks the opacity of book and text paper. Because it is designed to carry ink only on one side, show-through may be a problem. Duplex photocopy on bond works better than duplex printing on bond because paper doesn't absorb toner as it does ink.

Bond paper is made as either sulphite or rag. Sulphite refers to chemicals used to create paper from wood fiber; rag denotes paper with high cotton content.

Mills distinguish rag bond according to percentage of cotton; 25 percent and 100 percent are most common. Both are usually watermarked and are available in the same variety of finishes as #1 sulphite. Rag bonds are for prestige stationery or materials that must be extremely durable. The rag content comes from cotton fabric trimmings left over in clothing manufacture. U.S. currency is printed on 100 percent rag (75 percent cotton and 25 percent linen).

Bond without cotton fibers is called sulphite bond and comes in two common quality levels, #1 and #4. The first level, #1 sulphite, is used for routine business stationery. It may have a

❝ *Why are people always so fussy about using exactly the right color or finish of paper? With some jobs I'm real particular, but with others I'll use almost anything the printer has gathering dust on a shelf. Like our newsletter. Each member of our club only gets one copy, so who cares if the whole batch was printed on three different papers? My printer always feels happy to get rid of odd quantities of paper left over from other jobs and practically gives it to me free when I use it.* **❞**

watermark and texture and is whiter and more opaque than #4. The everyday stock for typing, mimeograph, photocopy and quick printing is #4 sulphite, which costs about 35 percent less than #1.

Mills make bonds in a variety of finishes and textures. Laid bond has a handmade look and dates back to Chinese methods of making paper in bamboo molds. Mills make linen finishes by embossing dry paper. Because embossing compresses fibers, linen bond is slightly calendered and has better ink holdout than laid. Bond with a visible finish should be printed on the pattern side.

To ensure stock best suited to each application, mills make bond in the following varieties.

Writing. Writing has extra sizing to make its surface accept handwriting and printing well. It comes in 20# and 24#. Writing has shorter fibers than standard bond, making the sheets slightly softer and more able to accept ink.

Onionskin. Also called manifold, this is used to make carbon copies. It comes in weights of 7#, 9# and 10#.

Ledger. Ledger is used for bookkeeping and account books. It comes in 28#, 32# and 36#.

Laser. Laser is extra smooth and has higher moisture content to run well in laser printers. It comes in 20# and 24#.

Xerographic. Also called copier paper, this is smooth and made for photocopy machines. It comes in 20# and 24#.

Dual-purpose. Dual-purpose bond, labeled DP, is smooth and uniform and is made for printing using either ink or toner. It comes in 20# and 24#.

Form bond. Also called register bond, this is made for business forms and computer paper. It comes in 16# and 20# and is available in rolls for web presses or continuous forms (fanfolds) for computer printers. Form bond comes in a variety of colors to make easily distinguishable snap-out sheets.

Bond must stand up to abuse and be versatile. Products printed on bond may get folded, stapled, collated, filed, mailed and handed around at meetings. Sheets might be embossed, engraved or die cut and printed offset, letterpress or photocopy. Bond may also pass through office machines using ink-jet, photocopy or laser printing.

If you plan to run preprinted bond through a laser printer, keep in mind the way the machine may affect the previous printing. The heat and pressure of a laser printer may damage thermography, engraving, foil-stamping or embossing.

Mills place watermarks on some bond to identify brand and sometimes cotton content. In addition to enhancing image, custom watermarks guarantee that stationery is from a particular organization, an important feature for prestige legal and financial documents.

Make sure to load watermarked bond into presses, photocopy machines and laser printers so the machine places the image on the correct side of the sheet. When you can read the watermark, you are looking at the correct side.

If papers are part of a package including letterheads, cards, envelopes and other coordinated materials, try to choose sheets with matched characteristics in several grades. Many mills make grades, such as text and cover, in colors and weights to complement their bond, although slight color variations may occur between batches. If you want a perfect match and are

❝ I thought I was pretty smart designing a rack brochure 9¼" high to stick out above the others. I realized my mistake when it was time to mail to last year's visitors. My oversized brochures were too big to put into #10 envelopes. ❞

buying in large quantities, have envelopes made from the same mill run as letterhead. Remember that colors and finishes on matching cover grades for business cards may seem different from bonds. For example, a laid-finish business card may feel smooth on one side and rough on the other, while the side-to-side difference of its matching letterhead may be more subtle.

GENERAL-PURPOSE OFFSET

Offset paper, also known as uncoated book paper, is for general printing of all types. This paper comes in several shades of white plus six or eight standard colors, depending upon the mill. Some sheets are more opaque than others, and mills may add the word "opaque" to the name of their products to indicate extra opacity.

You can find offset paper that works in copy machines and laser printers and looks fine with halftones that are specified with appropriate screen rulings. It's the general-purpose, workhorse paper.

Offset paper comes in three quality groups:
Group one: #1 opaque and #1
Group two: #2 opaque and #2
Group three: #3 and commodity
Price and quality differences among sheets within each group are small, so further rating categories aren't needed.

Printers often refer to offset as #1 or #3. The first is brightest, most opaque, comes in the greatest variety of colors and finishes and is most costly. For example, one mill makes #1 offset in twenty colors and seven finishes. In contrast, #3 offset offers more limited choices, lacks the high-grade feel of the premium version and costs less.

Offset paper comes in a vast array of colors, although mills don't keep offset colors as up-to-date or fashionable as colors available in text papers.

Most offset papers are available in two categories of surface: rough and smooth. Finishes within categories have many names, but differences are so subtle that few people can tell which is which.

rough/low finish	*smooth/high finish*
antique	smooth
vellum	lustre
eggshell	satin
machine	wove
high-bulk	English

Rough finishes are relatively absorbent, allowing ink to dry quickly. Experts refer to rough surfaces, such as vellum, antique and high-bulk, as toothy finishes because they feel coarse.

Smooth finishes do not absorb ink as quickly as rough finishes and consequently have better ink holdout. Mills use words such as "satin" and "silk" to make their papers seem smoother than the competition. To choose between brands, compare samples and decide which you like.

Lightweight versions of uncoated book paper run well on web presses and are popular for large books, catalogs and direct-mail items. Although lightweight stock costs more per pound than medium weight, you might save the extra money several times over at the post office. Many mills make lightweight papers with good bulk and opacity. Most of these papers come only in rolls because the long print runs required by high-volume direct mailers and catalogs typically go on web presses. Finding a printer who can do your job on lightweight stock might save you thousands of dollars.

Make dummies before deciding on a specific paper. Lightweight papers are often hard to run through sheetfed presses and folding machines. Both setup time and paper waste may be higher than when using medium-weight stocks.

LUXURIOUS TEXT

Text (short for texture) paper, an uncoated stock, looks impressive even in the unprinted areas of a brochure or announcement. Light striking textured surfaces gives added depth by making printing seem three-dimensional. Specific finishes have special characteristics.

The name "text" comes from the deeply textured look and feel of most sheets in this grade. The term "text paper" has no relationship to textbooks or to the text portion of publications. Mills use the word "text" to help sell papers they want you to consider first class. The word means almost the same as premium.

Offset printing works best for papers with surface patterns because offset presses put ink on paper from a soft blanket, not a hard plate. The blanket pushes ink into the patterns, ensuring uniform coverage. Printing by photocopy, laser printing and gravure looks best on very smooth paper.

Some mills rate texts using categories such as #1 and #2. Others do not assign numeric ratings, assuming that all text is premium.

Ratings are less important for text than for other grades because design decisions involving text rely more on appeal of the surface rather than on quality differences. Their wide range of colors and surface patterns make text papers difficult to compare.

Price books often organize text papers by surface. Categories include felt, laid, vellum, linen and flocked fiber (also called tinted fiber).

Felt text. Felt text is made by rollers applying the pattern to paper that is still wet. The process requires little pressure, thus yields stock with high bulk and stiffness. Because fibers have not been compressed, felt text is ideal for embossing.

Laid text. Laid text is made the same way as laid bond. Mills occasionally put both laid and felt patterns on the same sheet, yielding a very distinctive surface.

Vellum text. Vellum text has passed through calendering rollers just enough to make its surface uniform but not smooth. The result is good bulk and stiffness with a somewhat dull surface well suited to printing soft illustrations.

Rollers create embossed finishes after the stock dries, yielding paper with good ink holdout due to slight calendering. Linen and canvas are common names for embossed finishes.

Text comes in a wider range of colors than other grades. Colors include whatever hues are currently in fashion as well as standard shades. Moreover, mills make a good selection of cover stocks in the same shades as their text so, for example, invitations made from cover will match envelopes made from text. Whether white or colored, text often looks brighter than book or bond papers because mills add fluorescent dyes to the pulp.

Because of its high quality, text runs well on press and handles easily in the bindery. It works well in operations like die cutting, foil-stamping and folding. Top-of-the-line text has some cotton fiber for long life.

Text papers bring combinations of color and finish to jobs that otherwise might seem flat. Photographs of materials such as carpeting, which itself has texture, have good depth. Illustrations that feature high or wide objects look more vivid when printed on a text surface with pattern lines running the same direction as the art. Text makes a good choice for products such as quarterly reports, programs, posters, invitations and greeting cards.

Not all papers called text have surface patterns. You can find very smooth sheets, both coated and uncoated, that mills call text papers.

Mills make many text papers (and a few uncoated book papers) without using acids in the pulp. Acid-free papers keep their color and structural integrity for many years, so they are popular for art prints, limited-edition books and archival products.

SOPHISTICATED COATED

Mills apply clay coatings to uncoated paper to created coated papers. Coatings come in a range of thicknesses. Take the concept of coated paper literally. Mills start with uncoated paper, then apply coatings. They refer to the uncoated stock as the base sheet.

Wash coat. Also called film coat, this gives just enough clay to improve ink holdout. Think of wash coating as something like priming raw wood—enough to seal, but that's all. Wash coat papers are good for publications such as club directories that include pictures of members.

Matte coat. This has more clay than wash coat and offers good bulk. It works well with body copy and multicolor printing, but may not look good enough with color photos. Matte coat tends to appear mottled in areas of heavy coverage of dark ink.

Dull coat. Also known as suede or velvet, this is heavily coated and moderately calendered, yielding good contrast between paper and high-gloss inks or varnish. Like matte, dull is well suited to materials with extensive type because its low glare minimizes eye fatigue.

Gloss coat. Gloss coat has the same amount of clay as dull, but sheets are more highly calendered and polished. Colors reflect well and dull inks and varnishes give good contrast. Color photographs look crisp. Gloss papers cost slightly less than dulls and tend to run a little less white than dulls of the same name. The heat required to polish gloss stock also slightly browns it.

Mills rate coated papers according to brightness and opacity. Ultrapremium rates highest and costs the most, followed by premium, #1, #2, #3, #4 and #5. Paper with the highest ratings is available only as sheets; #4 and #5 coated is used for catalogs and magazines and is available only in rolls.

Coatings hide flaws and impurities, so the lowest-rated coated papers include some groundwood pulp. You can use #4 or #5 for directories, programs and other products with minimal quality requirements and short lifetimes.

Coated papers come in shades of white identified by terms such as balanced, warm and cold. Be sure to view samples of each before specifying. Cream and natural tones are also popular. Stronger colors are rare because coated stock is often used to show off color printing and thus doesn't need to have color itself. Customers using premium coated papers typically have premium or showcase printing in mind.

Coated paper enhances ink gloss. Ink includes varnish and other chemicals to make it glossy. The sheen stays on the surface of coated

Ink holdout   **Light reflectance**

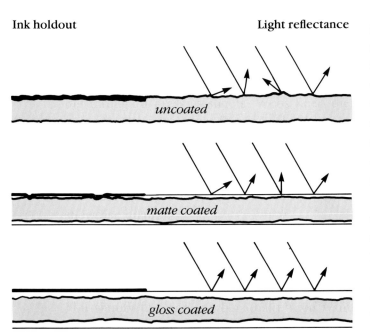

6-10 Ink holdout and light reflectance *This edge view of paper illustrates how coatings affect ink. The left side shows the amount of ink that sheets absorb, the right side the way they reflect light. Uncoated paper absorbs ink quickly and has a rough surface that scatters light, reducing image brightness. Matte paper holds more ink on its surface and is smoother and brighter. Gloss paper has superior holdout and is very smooth and bright, yielding sharp dots and vivid colors.*

stock better than on uncoated. Coated paper is also smoother than uncoated, which shows hills and valleys around the fibers when magnified. Coating gives a flat surface ready for uniform ink coverage.

Mills coat papers to improve ink holdout, which is the ability of ink to dry on the surface of the paper rather than being absorbed. When ink dries on the surface, images stay sharp; when paper absorbs ink, images become fuzzy as the liquid feathers into fibers. Holdout also affects color saturation, drying time and many other printing factors.

Uncoated paper absorbs fine-screen dots so much that they may touch because they are too close to each other. Shadows become gray or fill in solidly, losing detail. Generally speaking, absorbent sheets call for coarse screen rulings. As holdout improves, you can specify finer screens.

Because paper surface affects dot gain, design and page makeup, software allows users to specify coated or uncoated paper before outputting halftones or separations. This simple choice does not, however, allow precise control of image quality on press. Dot gain on uncoated stock can range from 15 to 40 percent and on coated stock from 10 to 30 percent. The amount of gain depends on the specific paper surface, method of printing and many other factors.

If you wish to compensate for dot gain, consult with your printer first. Take your printer's advice about the proper adjustment. Visual 5-4 illustrates dot gain.

Coating and calendering increase gloss and holdout but reduce bulk and opacity. Using coated stock may also result in a product that seems surprisingly heavy. For example, 60# uncoated has about the same bulk and opacity as 70# matte coat. A book printed on the 60# premium uncoated may look just as good but weighs 15 percent less than one printed on 70# matte coat.

You don't necessarily pay more for coated papers than for uncoated. Relative costs depend on the quality of each sheet in each category. It's true that the best coated costs more than the best uncoated (but far less than the best text or bond), but there are plenty of economical coated sheets whose cost equals uncoated options.

Most readers find type on glossy paper hard to concentrate on for more than a few minutes because of glare. If you need coated stock in a book or manual, use matte or dull. The National Geographic Society prints its magazine on 60# gloss but its maps on 50# matte. Gloss gives better fidelity with photos, but matte is easier on the eyes.

In addition to any conventional coatings, papers for on-demand presses require special coatings to make them receptive to proprietary inks and toners. Manufacturers of on-demand presses, such as Agfa and Indigo, work with paper mills and distributors to certify papers for specific technologies.

Grade and Basic Size	Common Names	Features	Surfaces
Bond 17 x 22	bond, ditto, erasable, forms, ledger, mimeo, onionskin, photocopy, rag, writing	lightweight, matching envelopes, pastels, light colors, watermarked	cockle, laid, linen, parchment, ripple, wove
Uncoated Book 25 x 38	book, offset, opaque	easy folding, wide range of colors	antique, smooth, vellum, wove
Text 25 x 38	text	deckle edged, textured, wide range of colors	antique, embossed, felt, laid, linen, vellum
Coated Book 25 x 38	coated offset, dull, enamel, gloss, matte, slick	good ink holdout, ink gloss, smooth surfaces, usually white only	cast, dull, embossed, gloss, matte
Cover 20 x 26	bristol, CIS, C2S, cast coat, cover, text cover	durable, stiff, strong	*uncoated:* antique, embossed, felt, laid, linen smooth, vellum, wove; *coated:* cast, dull, embossed, gloss, matte
Board	blanks, bristol, board, card, chip, index, plate railroad, sulphite, tag	stiff, strong, thick, variety of colors and surfaces	coated, embossed, plate, vellum, water resistant
Specialty	carbonless	standard colors	wove
	kraft	brown or manila, opaque, strong	vellum
	gummed, label, presure sensitive, self-adhesive	variety of colors, glues, and surfaces	*uncoated:* English finish, vellum; *coated:* dull, gloss: *synthetic:* acetate, Mylar, vinyl
	newsprint	inexpensive, lightweight	vellum
	synthetic	durable, tearproof, water resistant	smooth, textured

6-11 Guide to printing papers This chart summarizes the characteristics and uses of printing papers. Use it to stimulate ideas and inquiries, not as an exclusive guide to ordering paper. Keep in mind that not all paper in a grade comes in every combination of size, weight, color and finish. Most merchants, however, can supply paper of each grade in the most common sizes, weights and calipers.

Standard Sizes	Weights	Thickness Range	Uses
8½ x 11, 8½ x 14, 11 x 17, 17 x 22, 17 x 28, 19 x 24, 19 x 28, 22 x 34, rolls	9, 12, 16, 20, 24, 28	.002-.006	certificates, directories, fliers, forms, handbills, letterheads, newsletters, photocopy, quick printing, resumes
17½ x 22½, 23 x 29, 23 x 35, 25 x 38, 35 x 45, 38 x 50, rolls	30, 32, 35, 40, 45, 50, 60, 70, 80	.003-.006	books, brochures, calendars, catalogs, direct mail, fliers, manuals, newsletters, programs, rate books
17½ x 22½, 23 x 35, 25 x 38, 26 x 40	70, 75, 80, 100	.005-.008	annual reports, announcements, art reproductions, books, brochures, calendards, posters, self-mailers
19 x 25, 23 x 29, 23 x 35, 25 x 38, 35 x 45, 38 x 50, rolls	*sheets:* 60, 70, 80, 100, *rolls:* 40, 45, 50, 60, 70, 80, 100	.003-.007	annual reports, books, brochures, calendards, catalogs, directories, direct mail, magazines, newsletters, newspaper inserts, posters
20 x 26, 23 x 35, 25 x 38, 26 x 40	56, 80, 100; *calipers:* .007, .008, .010, .012, .015	.006-.015	business cards, calendars, covers for annual reports, books, catalogs, and directories, folders, greeting cards, invitations, menus, point-of-purchase displays, postcards, posters, table tents, tickets
22 x 28, 22½ x 28½, 23 x 29, 23 x 35, 24 x 36, 25½ x 30½, 28 x 44	67, 90, 100, 110, 125, 140, 150, 175; *ply:* 4, 6, 8, 10, 14	.006-.050	business-reply cards, covers, displays, file folders, paper boxes, signs, screen-printed posters, tags, tickets
bond sizes	12½ – 38	.003-.007	forms
rolls	30, 40, 50	.003-.006	bags, envelopes, fliers
17 x 22, 20 x 26, 24 x 30, rolls	60, 70	various	labels, signs, stickers
rolls	30	.003	directories, fliers, newspapers, tabloids
23 x 35, 25 x 38, 35 x 45, rolls	various	.003-.010	banners games, maps, tags

....

STURDY COVER

Cover sheets are usually just extraheavy bond, book or text papers. Printers use cover stock to cover books and catalogs, make folders and run brochures and cards.

Mills identify some cover stocks by caliper rather than basis weight. Cover that is ten point measures .010 inches thick. The most common thicknesses are 8, 10, and 12pt. Small paperback books typically have 8-pt C1S covers, meaning that stock measures .008 inches thick with clay on the printed side only.

Mills integrate cover papers with other grades so that printed products coordinate. One example is letterhead and envelopes made from bond and matching business cards made from cover. Another example is a booklet whose cover matches its inside pages that are printed on text paper.

Some mills consider the match between text and cover papers so important that their swatch books showcase papers from both grades. They refer to their papers as text/cover papers, meaning that the papers are identical in surface and color even though they have different basis weights and calipers. Other mills put similar emphasis on matches between bond and cover.

You find cover coated on one side or both sides. C1S (coated one side) is for the book cover or folder that prints only on the coated side.

Stock coated on two sides is called C2S. For additional protection and gloss, printers often coat the sheet again with varnish, plastic or laminating film after printing.

Mills also make cover papers not linked to other grades. At the premium level, cast-coated cover papers have a very thick coating dried slowly over a chrome drum to achieve almost a mirror finish. Cast-coated stock comes in several colors and is ideal for fine postcards, presentation folders and covers of prestige annual reports. Cover paper at the commodity level is coated only on one side (C1S) because it's normally printed only on one side.

Not all covers are made from cover paper. For many products, such as consumer catalogs, any paper more sturdy than the inside will work. Covers for other products, such as direct mailers, can be made from the same sheet as the inside pages. Such products are known as self-covers.

MISCELLANEOUS GRADES

Mills make a wide range of papers that have special sizes and uses, such as index, bristol, tag, board and newsprint. Many are used in both the packaging and printing industries. Several manufacturers produce specialty papers that resist tearing and moisture. You've seen them as envelopes, labels, maps, menus and textbook covers.

The paper industry refers to heavyweight, bulky stock as board. The material is rigid, strong, hard and durable. Names such as index, bristol and tag are common in addition to the general term "board." Sometimes an additional name gives a clue to intended use. For example, weatherproof bristol makes good lawn signs; plate bristol has a hard surface for business cards; vellum bristol is soft with good bulk for direct-mail cards.

Because there is no consensus about basic sizes for board stock, basis weights vary greatly. Furthermore, some boards are described in caliper and others in ply. Ten-ply board, for example, consists of ten sheets of paper laminated like plywood. Ply board, also called railroad board or posterboard, comes in many colors and may be weatherized for outdoor use.

Mills make chipboard from mill waste without concern for strength or printability. This inexpensive material is used for light-duty boxes and backings on notepads. Chipboard may be designated by caliper or by number of sheets in a fifty-pound bundle.

Board paper. This is very thick and used primarily for posters and signs. It's usually coated on one side and is available in traditional sizes for advertising inside buses and trains. Board is printed in a variety of ways depending upon its thickness. Thinner board runs satisfactorily on sheetfed offset presses; board over 20 pt is generally printed letterpress or silkscreen.

Bristols. These come in various finishes. Vellum bristol is used for business-reply cards and self-mailers. Bulky and very porous, it runs well on quick print presses. Index bristol is used for file and index cards as well as direct-mail pieces. Its hard surface gives good ink holdout. Tag is a heavily calendered, dense, hard paper for products such as labels, scoresheets and notecards.

Bristols, tags and similar grades seldom carry numerical ratings. That does not mean, however, that all sheets are equally good. As with most papers, price is a good guide to quality.

Newsprint. This comes from groundwood pulp and usually runs on open web presses. It can be sheetfed, but runs slowly due to lack of body and impurities that lead to frequent cleanings of plates and blankets. The impurities also make this very inexpensive stock opaque but likely to yellow with age.

Kraft. This is a cousin to newsprint made for wrappings and bags. It costs very little, may be hard to find for commercial printing, prints slowly and comes only in the familiar brown and manila. Because of its distinctive color and feel, kraft works well to give an old-fashioned look to mailings, newspaper inserts and menus.

Dry gum. This paper has glue on the back ready to activate with either moisture or heat. Mills apply water soluble glues to stock for

> **" We worked much better with printers after we wrote a profile of our printing needs. We described the jobs we need printed and explained how often, how many, how good and how fast we need them. Instead of printers sending samples to us, we sent samples to them. The shops that we work with understand us much better now than before. "**

stamps, shipping labels and sealing tape. Heat-sensitive glues are used for labels in retail applications such as meat packing.

Pressure-sensitive papers. Often called stickyback, these are printed to make the popular peel-off label. Adhesives can be either temporary or permanent. Almost any kind of paper is available with a self-adhesive backing.

Carbonless. These papers have chemical coatings that duplicate writing or typing on an undersheet. The stock is used primarily for multipart business forms. Sheets come in three types: CF (coated front), CB (coated back) and CFB (coated front and back). A four-part carbonless form would have a CB top sheet, CFB second and third sheets and a CF bottom sheet. Special glues adhere to the coatings but not to the papers. Glue applied along the edge of a large stack of carbonless sheets assembled in proper sequence pads them into sets, each having the correct number of sheets.

Synthetic. These papers are petroleum products with smooth, durable surfaces. They are very strong, as anyone knows who has tried to tear a synthetic envelope. Synthetics make fine maps, covers for field guides, game boards and other products that must withstand weather, water and hard use. Synthetics cost about three times more than comparable premium-coated book papers.

Specialty papers include metallic paper coated with either mylar or powdered metals, and synthetic paper, which is actually not paper at all, but plastic film. These papers are expensive and may require special inks and printing techniques. If your design calls for using a specialty paper, discuss it with an experienced printer first.

SPECIFYING PAPER

After deciding what paper you want, you must describe it clearly to your printer or paper distributor. The description is short, but must be accurate and complete to prevent confusion.

Good paper specifications deal with eight characteristics. If you are buying paper yourself, you must handle all eight; if your printer is buying for you, you need only deal with the first five. Visual 6-12 shows properly written paper specifications using all eight characteristics.

Quantity. How many sheets or pounds?

Size. Describe sheet or roll size in inches.

Grain direction. Grain long or short? Show grain direction by underlining the correct numeral. A sheet 25″ × 38″ is grain long—grain running parallel to the 38-inch edge.

Weight. Use the basis or sub weight as listed in the sample book or price page.

Color. Write the exact name the mill uses for the color.

Brand name. Usually this is the name for an entire line of paper made by a specific mill.

Texture or finish. If the finish isn't part of the brand name, be specific.

Grade. State whether you want bond, book, text or cover, or use the name of a specialty paper.

PRINTING INKS

Of all the factors to consider when managing print jobs, ink seems least complicated. After choosing a color, most customers give it little thought. That's appropriate. Let your printer choose inks that perform well on press. Your printer does, however, need to know if you want paper with an unusual surface or have a special need such as fade resistance.

Most printing inks are glossy when dry. Darker colors look more glossy than lighter ones; heavy layers of ink increase gloss.

Paper influences ink gloss more than ink itself. Uncoated stock absorbs ink rapidly, making

> **Some printers seem to regard a press check as automatic conflict between printer and client. I don't see it that way. If everyone doesn't focus on both, neither the printer nor the client can stay profitable.**

it appear dull. Coated and heavily calendered sheets absorb ink more slowly, allowing more to dry on the surface and bringing out luster. Presses with heaters enhance ink gloss. After heat evaporates solvents, the printed paper runs through chill rollers, which set the glossy ink surface.

Matte images are easy to achieve—in fact, hard to avoid—with ordinary inks on uncoated stock. If you want a matte look on coated stock, specify dull or matte ink or varnish. Such inks and varnishes cost a bit more and may be harder to run on press.

Ink for offset printing has the consistency of thick honey. To change colors, printers must thoroughly clean presses of one color before a new color goes on. Press operators wipe every trace of ink from the fountain, blanket and rollers. Wash-up may take ten minutes on a small press or an hour on a large one.

If your job requires changing colors, you pay for wash-up. Presses run black ink most of the time. Almost every time you use a color other than black, you pay for at least one wash-up.

Ink is a relatively small part of the cost of most print jobs, especially large ones, but special inks for short runs may drive up costs. Printers buy ink by the pound, which is far more than needed for a few hundred letterheads or fliers. The price of a pound of ink for the letterhead job may represent 10 percent of the total invoice, while the same pound of ink entirely used up printing a forty-eight-page magazine may represent only 1 percent of total costs.

After black, the most common and least costly inks are the basic colors used by color matching systems and the three process colors

6-12 SAMPLE PAPER SPECIFICATIONS

The following nine orders for paper show how to specify quantity, size, grain, weight, color, name, surface and grade. Sometimes grade is omitted when the name is so specific that misunderstanding is impossible.

- 62,500 sheets, 23″×35″, 100# white, Lustro dull-coated book
- 5,000 sheets, 26″×40″, 65# Del Monte Red, Beau Brilliant cover
- 78,525 lbs, 35-inch, 80# Lustro dull web-coated book
- 5,000 sheets (10 reams), 8½″×11″, 24# Chiaro Gray, Filare Script bond
- 2,500 sets, four-part 8½″×11″, pre-collated sets NCR, black print bond
- 1,000 sheets, 20″×26″, 60# white, Fasson Satin Litho Crack 'n Peel Plus label
- 1 skid (approximately 16,000 sheets), 25″×38″, 60# blue white, Halopaque Satin uncoated book
- 1 carton, 23″×35″, 105# blue-white, Halopaque Satin reply card
- 16 cartons, 17½″×22½″, 35# white, Flecopake #1 opaque offset

cyan, magenta and yellow. As with black inks, printers like certain brands and plan press chemistry to conform. Basic and process colors are standard mixes, and every printer doing color work has a supply on hand.

Ink formulas change according to printing method and substrate. Flexography, gravure, engraving and other forms of printing have individual standards for viscosity and tack. Formulas also differ according to end use. For example, offset inks used for products that will pass through laser printers don't contain waxes that react to the heat of the printer. Laser-friendly inks are especially important on products destined for high-speed, commercial laser printers as compared to desktop printers.

Soy inks

Ink contains pigments suspended in fluid that must vanish the instant that ink meets paper. Inks based on petroleum fluids release volatile organic compounds (VOCs) when the fluids evaporate. VOCs help cause air pollution.

Inks using soybean oil dry onto the paper instead of evaporating. Soy inks also make paper easier to recycle than petroleum inks. Recycling mills can remove the inks more easily, causing less damage to fibers and leaving a brighter recycled paper. Finally, soy oil is biodegradable, so it disappears more quickly when it finally reaches a landfill.

Inks with labels such as "soy" or "soy based" still contain some petroleum. The amount of soy oil varies according to the printing process (offset or flexo), type of press (sheetfed or web), ink color (more in black, less in other colors) and other conditions, such as cold vs. heatset web.

Soy oil boils at higher temperature than petroleum, so soy inks withstand the heat of laser printers and copiers better. Images stay uniform and keep their colors as they pass through machines using toner.

Some printing buyers claim that inks containing soy oils do not yield colors as dense or clean as petroleum inks. Get samples printed on your favorite papers so you can judge for yourself.

Special inks

Digital presses and offset presses using waterless plates require ink formulas different from the formula of inks for conventional offset. In some cases, the inks are proprietary to the specific brand of press. Color matching systems and proofing materials, however, work best with conventional, nonproprietary inks. You may find that colors are harder to predict and control when printing with processes that require special inks.

> **"** *We designed a fantastic calendar that all our outlets could imprint and mail to their customers, then went crazy trying to find square envelopes to match. Finally we had to have the envelopes custom made. It cost us two fortunes—one for the custom making and one for rush service. Next time we'll design envelopes at the same time that we plan calendars, not as an afterthought.* **"**

....

Waterless and digital presses don't require fountain solutions, partly because their special inks contain more oils than conventional inks. More oily inks mean less dot gain. Less dot gain allows for finer screen rulings. More important from the standpoint of cost, less dot gain yields vivid colors on less costly papers whose surfaces might not be satisfactory for conventional inks.

Metallic inks in gold, silver and bronze hues come from a mixture of varnish and metal dust or flakes. They tend to tarnish and scuff when dry, so they should have a coating of varnish or plastic.

Metallic inks show off best on coated paper. Even stock with good ink holdout, however, may require two layers of metallic ink for satisfactory coverage of large solids. Although printers can't mix metallic inks from basic colors, several swatch books show standard colors.

Fluorescent inks seem extra bright because they absorb ultraviolet light and come in many colors. They must appear on white paper to achieve full effect. Because fluorescents have more opacity than standard inks, they overprint other colors effectively.

Use fade-resistant and sunfast inks for window displays and other materials exposed to strong sunlight. Formulas are easy to make and print but cost a bit more than standard inks. Cool colors, such as blues and greens, resist fading better than warm colors, such as reds and yellows. Even these special inks, however, fade in just a few weeks when subjected to direct sunlight.

Packaging, book covers and other products exposed to a lot of handling call for scuff-resistant inks. They work best when coated with scuff-resistant varnish or plastic. Scuff-resistant inks must pass rub tests by a machine that rubs printed surfaces against each other at a pressure of three pounds per square inch. Normal inks show significant scuffing after a few rubs; scuff-resistant inks stand up to one hundred or more rubs.

Printers can get many other specialty inks. The U.S. Food and Drug Administration approves nontoxic inks for printing items that contact foods. Scented inks are made to smell like just about anything: strawberries, chocolate, roses or sweat socks. They work best when printed on highly absorbent, uncoated paper. Use scratch-off inks for contest forms and lottery tickets. Magnetic inks allow machines to read numbers on checks. Sublimated inks are heat sensitive so they transfer from printed paper to polyester items such as T-shirts.

Special inks cost more, may take extra time to obtain and may require special handling on press. Consult with your printer well beforehand whenever considering a job using special inks.

PROTECTIVE COATINGS

All dried inks show fingerprints, scuffing and other blemishes from handling, especially in dark solids. Readers can ruin a beautiful report cover in only a few minutes. The answer is some form of protective coating.

Printers think of coatings in two categories: coatings applied like ink on press and coatings applied during finishing or binding. Press coatings are thinner and cost less than bindery coatings, which are applied over dry ink at relatively slow speeds.

Pens, rubber stamps and glue don't work very well on most coatings. If you plan to write or stamp on a product such as a catalog, leave an uncoated window to accept the individual message. Foils stamped over coatings may bubble from trapped gas. Coating should be the final step in production.

Coatings tend to deepen the color of the underlying ink, slightly discolor white paper, and yellow with age. Printers not skilled with coating on press may use too much anti-offset powder, resulting in sheets that feel like fine sandpaper. The coarseness comes from powder trapped in the coating.

Coating is supposed to protect your product from abrasion. Insufficient coating may mean an incompatibility with ink or fountain solution or insufficient curing. Poor packing means products rubbed against each other in transit, causing coatings to scuff.

Varnish

Varnish costs about the same as another ink color and comes in either glossy or dull finishes. It can also be lightly tinted, thereby achieving both color and protection for the cost of only one. For a deeply matte effect, print dull varnish over dull ink. Varnish works best on coated papers and, in fact, may absorb so completely into uncoated stock that it neither protects nor beautifies.

Printers either flood or spot varnish. Flood varnishing means covering the entire sheet; spot varnishing refers to hitting only certain areas, such as photographs. Gloss varnish adds sheen to highlight and protect. Spot-varnished photos on glossy paper can appear as glossy as original prints.

Aqueous

The very glossy coating you often see on magazines is an acrylic mixture of polymers and water. It has better holdout than varnish and doesn't crack or scuff easily. Printers can apply aqueous coating as gloss, dull or primer (very thin).

A press can apply aqueous coating inline only when equipped with a special coating unit. For this reason, aqueous costs about double the cost of varnish.

Ultraviolet

For even more protection and sheen than varnish or aqueous, some printers can coat with a plastic that dries under ultraviolet light. These products give tough surfaces for book covers, record jackets and table tents. As with varnish, you can ask for dull or gloss finishes and flood or spot coverage. Spot coverage is done using screen printing and yields an exceptionally thick covering.

Some web printers can apply ultraviolet coating in line with printing, but the task is most commonly performed as a separate finishing operation.

Because plastic liquid coatings are cured by light instead of heat, they have no solvents to enter the atmosphere. They are, however, sometimes brittle, so they may crack when scored or folded. ■

7. OFFSET PRINTING

To keep up-to-date about offset printing, visit our Web site (www.gettingitprinted.com).

Offset lithography is the most popular commercial printing method because printers using it produce results quickly and inexpensively. Other processes work better in specific situations, but lithography performs best for most jobs.

Lithography yields excellent results because plates carry sharp images. It's fast because plates are easy to make and allow for long runs at high speeds. Easy platemaking and fast press speeds mean lower costs.

Knowing how offset presses work means you can plan jobs to take full advantage of different machines and avoid expensive problems. Understanding presses leads to sound decisions about quality and how it relates to costs. Finally, familiarity with presses makes you a better judge of whether you are getting good service and are likely to stay on schedule.

Printers vary greatly in the types, sizes and abilities of the presses in their shops. Customers who understand the limitations and advantages of various presses make good choices between printers to ensure economy and quality.

In this chapter you learn about offset plates and presses. You discover what quality levels you can reasonably anticipate from printers using presses of different sizes and complexity. Using concepts such as register, ink density and ink trapping, you identify what to expect of jobs printed at the four quality categories introduced in chapter one. Finally, you learn how to conduct a successful press check.

The information about quality in this chapter guides you through most offset printing jobs. Consult Visual 9-10 for guidelines about quality in binding.

BEST FOR MOST JOBS

Lithography literally means "writing with stones." The technique began as a way of manufacturing art prints. Artisans inscribed images on flat stone, then used the stone as a printing plate.

From its beginning, lithography was based on the chemical principle that water and oil repel each other. Ink is oily. Images were carried on the stones by keeping water on the nonimage area, thereby forcing ink to stay only on the image area.

Modern lithographic plates function on the same chemical principle. The ink-receptive coating on plates is activated only in the image area. Most modern plates prevent ink from invading nonimage areas by coating them with water. Other plates use a technique called waterless printing in which the nonimage areas are coated with an ink-repelling substance, such as silicone.

Waterless plates yield images with lower dot gain and higher ink densities than plates using water. The technique also reduces makeready, makes presses easier to control and permits screen rulings up to 500 lpi. Advantages also bring disadvantages. Plates cost more and wear out faster. Many proofing systems are designed for plates using water, so proofs may not predict press outcome.

The original lithographers printed images by pressing paper directly against the inked surface of the stone. Modern presses transfer images from an inked plate to a rubber blanket. It's the blanket, not the plate, that comes in contact with the paper and actually prints the image. The image offsets from plate to blanket, then offsets again from blanket to paper. Because all lithographic presses use the offset principle, the method is simply called offset printing.

PRESS COMPONENTS

All offset presses have five basic components: Feeding units deliver paper into the machine. Register units assure paper arrives under the printing units in the same place each time an image is made. Inking units convey liquids to

---

7-1 SHEETFED OR WEB?

No formula establishes the type of press best suited to a specific printing job. Compare printers based on the cost, quality and schedule of your jobs, not on the machines used to produce them.

Although we cannot supply a formula to determine sheetfed or web press, we can offer some rules of thumb. Generally speaking, web presses print long runs more economically than sheetfed presses do. The point at which one type of press becomes more economical than the other, however, varies greatly from job to job and shop to shop. Use estimates based on identical specifications to compare costs among printers.

Web may work best when:
• paper basis weight is under 50#
• paper is relatively inexpensive
• stock is newsprint
• number of impressions is over twenty-five thousand
• the job can print both sides at once

Sheetfed may work best when:
• paper basis weight is over 70#
• you need showcase quality
• paper is relatively expensive
  Remember that folding and binding requirements may influence cost and speed as much as printing.

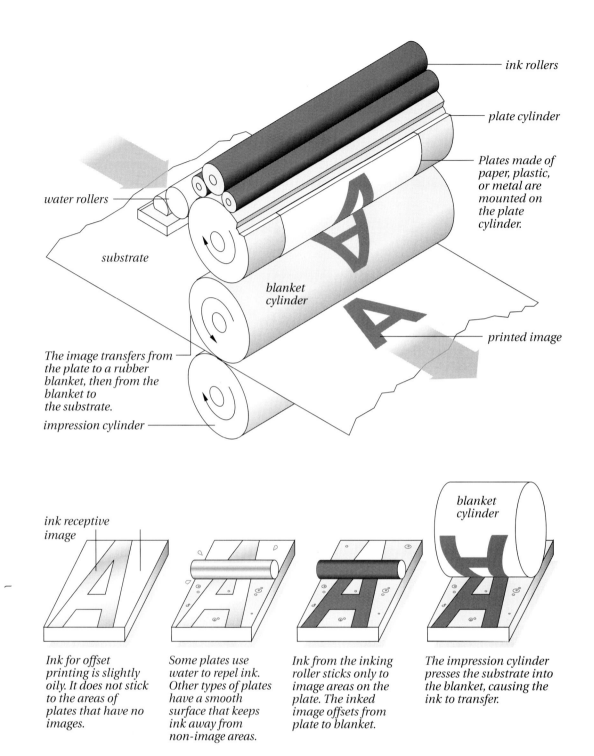

ink rollers

plate cylinder

Plates made of paper, plastic, or metal are mounted on the plate cylinder.

water rollers

substrate

blanket cylinder

printed image

The image transfers from the plate to a rubber blanket, then from the blanket to the substrate.

impression cylinder

ink receptive image

blanket cylinder

Ink for offset printing is slightly oily. It does not stick to the areas of plates that have no images.

Some plates use water to repel ink. Other types of plates have a smooth surface that keeps ink away from non-image areas.

Ink from the inking roller sticks only to image areas on the plate. The inked image offsets from plate to blanket.

The impression cylinder presses the substrate into the blanket, causing the ink to transfer.

7-2 Offset printing Offset printing produces a sharper image than printing directly from plate to paper because the rubber blanket conforms to the tiny surface variations of paper. In addition, offset plates are right-reading. If images went di-rectly from plate to paper, they would have to appear backward on the plate. You could read them in a mirror but not on the plate itself. Right-reading plates are easy to inspect because the image reads exactly as it should on the printed product.

plates. Printing units transfer images to the paper. Delivery units remove the printed paper. Most presses also have a water unit that brings dampening fluid to the plate.

Feeding and register units. The feeding and register units of a sheetfed press take one sheet of paper at a time and position it ready for printing. Good register requires that each sheet enter the printing unit from precisely the same position. Guides on one side and at the leading edge hold the sheet in place while it waits for grippers to draw it under the rotating cylinder holding the blanket.

The feeding and register units of small, inexpensive presses may vary the position of each sheet by as much as $1/16$ inch. Large, costly presses may have register tolerances close to $1/1000$ inch. Perfect register is difficult for a machine running three sheets per second.

After the sheet comes into position, grippers, like metal fingers, pull it into the printing unit. There the impression cylinder presses the sheet against the blanket cylinder, transferring ink from blanket to paper. While the press actually prints, operators register the images by adjusting plate cylinders.

When printers talk about the gripper edge of paper, they mean the leading edge that enters the printing unit first. Paper for small presses goes in shortest dimension first. On an $8\frac{1}{2}'' \times 11''$ sheet, the $8\frac{1}{2}$-inch side is the gripper edge. Large presses take paper the wide way. A 35-inch press takes a $23'' \times 35''$ sheet, with the 35-inch side providing the gripper edge.

Grippers hold tightly to about $3/8$ inch of paper, forming a strip that cannot receive ink. With large presses, the gripper edge is usually no problem because paper is almost always trimmed or cut up after printing. Small presses, however, usually run stock cut exactly to $8\frac{1}{2}'' \times 11''$ or $11'' \times 17''$.

When planning jobs that run on stock already cut to final trim size, plan carefully so that grippers don't run into the image area. Designs for pieces printed on small presses should avoid image within $3/8$ inch of the leading edge of the sheet.

Grippers also affect planning for bleeds. A bleed is any image that goes directly to the edge of the paper, seeming to run off (bleed from) the sheet. Printers create the illusion of a bleed by trimming the edge of the paper into the inked area, as shown in Visual 7-3. Designs calling for bleeds always require using more paper (larger sheet size) and sometimes mean using a larger press, both of which may increase costs.

Inking units. Ink is a pasty liquid held on press in a trough serving as a reservoir or in plastic bottles tipped upside down. Press operators control ink flow onto the rollers. Operators can increase or decrease the flow to control the amount of ink applied to specific sections of the plate.

A small press has only one ink fountain with ten or twelve outlets. A very large press may have eight ink fountains, each having fifty or sixty outlets.

Ink rollers transfer ink from fountain to plate. The number of rollers varies with press size. Small presses have four or five rollers per plate while large presses have eighteen or twenty. Rollers work together to smooth the ink and spread it evenly across the plate to help achieve uniform density.

Presses that use dampening fluids to protect nonimage areas of plates keep the fluids in a water fountain. The fluids contain ingredients such as acid, gum arabic and alcohol in a base of water. Dampening units transfer fluids to the plate via a system of rollers similar to the system of inking rollers.

Plates using water must receive just enough fluid to prevent ink from adhering to nonimage areas, but not enough to transfer water to either blanket or paper. The fountain solution, also called dampening solution, must evaporate instantly from the plate, leaving only a thin film

❝ Even after approving a press sheet I feel nervous. I always take a sheet back to my studio so I can be sure the rest of the job matches the press sheet I signed. ❞

of ink on the image areas. The craft of offset printing depends heavily on proper balance between ink and dampening solution.

Printing units. A printing unit consists of the series of rollers and cylinders that transfers the inked image to paper. Presses may have one or more printing units. Printers describe the number of printing units a press has by referring to how many colors it can print. A press with four printing units is known as a four-color press.

Delivery units. Once a sheet has been printed, the delivery unit removes it from the last printing unit and deposits it in a pile. This simple task becomes complicated as the amount of ink on a newly printed sheet increases. Exit wheels and guides must not mark areas of heavy coverage.

Delivery units normally include a system for spraying fine powder over the sheets to inhibit wet ink from transferring from the front of one sheet to the back of another. The unwanted ink transfer is called offsetting and is especially likely to occur when using gloss-coated paper with good ink holdout. The dust is known as anti-offset powder. A heatset web press passes printed paper through an oven to dry the ink before cutting the web into sheets.

Quick print presses are not equipped with

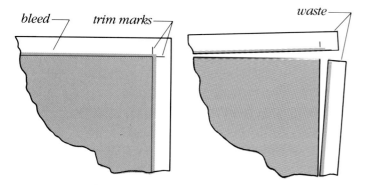

7-3 Bleeds *Press operators produce bleeds by printing on sheets larger than the trim size of the final piece then cutting away edges. Trims for bleeds cut into the inked image to create the illusion that the press printed to the edge of the sheet.*

Producing jobs with bleeds requires either increasing size of paper or reducing the number of printed products cut from each sheet. Make sure you specify bleeds before your printer orders paper for your job, and remember that bleeds increase cost because they increase the amount of paper needed.

anti-offset units and don't usually run coated paper.

PRESS TYPES, SIZES AND FEATURES

Printers think of offset presses in categories according to format of paper, size of paper and number of printing units. Each category can have many special features.

Format of paper

Offset presses are either sheetfed or web. Paper feeding into a web press comes off a roll and is cut into sheets after printing. Paper feeding into a sheetfed press has already been cut. Visual 7-2 shows a typical sheetfed press, and Visual 7-4 illustrates paper for web presses.

Size of paper

Press size is identified according to the widest sheet or roll of paper the machine can handle. A 40-inch press can run a sheet or roll up to 40 inches wide.

Small sheetfed presses print sheets 18 inches or less. That size includes most presses at quick and in-plant shops whose maximum is typically 11″×17″. Printers use these machines to run letterheads, business cards, fliers, envelopes, newsletters and forms.

Small presses run solid ink on uncoated paper 90 percent of the time, but many are capable of much more. Look for shops that display samples of multicolor printing or pieces on matte-coated stock.

Large sheetfed presses can run stock anywhere from 12″×18″ up to 55″×78″, although few printers have machines larger than 40 inches. Most commercial printers consider 19″×25″ and 25″×38″ sheet sizes versatile enough to handle almost any job.

Large presses prove highly efficient for many jobs because they gang images. An 8½″×11″ flier prints eight-up (eight copies of the flier) on one 23″×35″ sheet, so a press able to run eight thousand sheets an hour can print sixty-four thousand fliers in sixty minutes. Sheets from large presses yield signatures with more

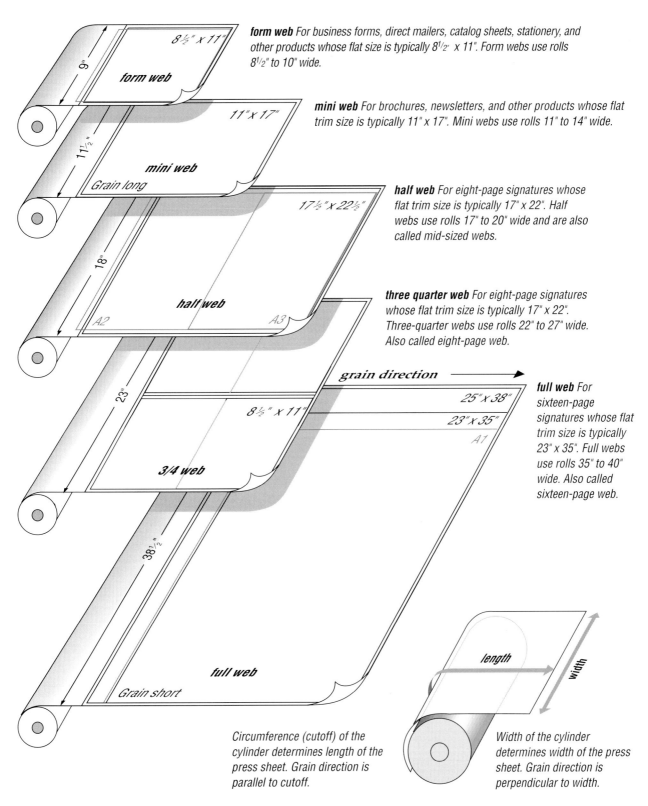

form web *For business forms, direct mailers, catalog sheets, stationery, and other products whose flat size is typically 8¹/₂" x 11". Form webs use rolls 8¹/₂" to 10" wide.*

mini web *For brochures, newsletters, and other products whose flat trim size is typically 11" x 17". Mini webs use rolls 11" to 14" wide.*

half web *For eight-page signatures whose flat trim size is typically 17" x 22". Half webs use rolls 17" to 20" wide and are also called mid-sized webs.*

three quarter web *For eight-page signatures whose flat trim size is typically 17" x 22". Three-quarter webs use rolls 22" to 27" wide. Also called eight-page web.*

full web *For sixteen-page signatures whose flat trim size is typically 23" x 35". Full webs use rolls 35" to 40" wide. Also called sixteen-page web.*

grain direction →

8½" x 11"
form web
9"

11" x 17"
mini web
11½"
Grain long

17½" x 22½"
half web
18"
A2   A3

23"
3/4 web
8½" x 11"

25" x 38"
23" x 35"
A1

38½"
full web
Grain short

length
width

Circumference (cutoff) of the cylinder determines length of the press sheet. Grain direction is parallel to cutoff.

Width of the cylinder determines width of the press sheet. Grain direction is perpendicular to width.

7-4 Web presses *Sizes of printed sheets produced on a web press are the same as sizes for sheetfed presses. The range of common finish sizes for printed products is the same whether the products are printed sheetfed or web.*

pages than sheets from small presses, reducing time and expense in binding.

Web presses come in five general sizes described in Visual 7-4. Printers refer to paper going through a web press simply as "the web." If the paper tears coming off the roll or while passing through the press, it's called a web break. Operators must shut down the press and thread paper all over again.

The circumference of the impression cylinder on a web press is its cutoff and determines the maximum length of the image area. A web press with a 23-inch cutoff and running a roll 35 inches wide would print images imposed similarly to a sheetfed press running $23'' \times 35''$ stock. On most web presses, cutoff is not adjustable.

Knowing cutoffs for specific presses helps plan for efficient use of paper. For example, a 9-inch rack brochure produces efficiently on a press with an 18-inch cutoff, but a press with a 23-inch cutoff would waste 5 inches of paper on every impression. This translates into wasting 22 percent of the paper.

Printing units

Most large sheetfed presses and many small ones can print more than one color at once. Sheets pass under two, four or as many as eight blanket cylinders, each adding a different ink or varnish.

Although presses could have any number of printing units, the typical configurations are one-color, two-color, four-color, six-color and eight-color. A four-color job run on a six-color press leaves two printing units idle. Many four-color jobs, however, use a fifth unit for flat ink (hence the term "fifth color") and a sixth unit for varnish.

Each time a sheet passes through a sheetfed

....

❝ No, it's not only your printing jobs that always seem to have something wrong. Everyone's jobs have something wrong. It's just that you know your jobs intimately. You recognize flaws in your jobs instantly and flaws in other jobs rarely. **❞**

press, it's called one impression. During one pass, a four-color press prints a sheet having four ink colors. Note that "impression" refers to press sheets, not final products. One sheet of paper or one web cutoff equals one impression regardless of how many products it yields after being cut into pieces.

Press speeds are measured in number of impressions per hour (iph). A sheetfed press might run at 12,000 iph, meaning that it prints 12,000 sheets in one hour. A two-color press running at 10,000 iph yields 10,000 press sheets in one hour. You may also express web speeds as iph, referring to the number of cutoffs per hour.

Perfecting presses print both sides of the paper during the same pass through the machine. Some sheetfed and most web presses are perfectors. Some perfecting presses print both sides simultaneously as paper goes between two blankets; others automatically turn paper over to print the other side.

Presses that print more than one color on both sides during one pass through the press are multicolor perfectors. A large web press, for example, might have eight printing units, four for each side of the paper.

Special features

Web presses are categorized not only by size but according to their ability to dry inks. Open webs allow the paper to dry unaided. Heatset webs speed the drying process by passing the printed paper through ovens before cutting it into sheets.

To achieve high ink gloss on coated stock, heatset webs also have chill rollers that harden ink and return the paper to room temperature. In contrast, open web presses can only print uncoated stock. Open webs work economically for products such as newspapers, telephone directories and direct-mail inserts. Forms presses are usually open webs.

Web presses can often fold and bind in sequence with printing. Paper enters the first folding unit immediately after being printed and before being cut into sheets. In-line finishing saves time and money because of efficient manufacturing. Materials move quickly through the printing process.

Web presses can also print relatively light stock. Paper less than 50# tends to wrinkle passing through a press as sheets. Webs keep the paper under tension, so they commonly print 40# and even 30# paper.

Sheetfed and web presses perform equally well for basic, good and premium printing. Only the best web presses, however, can produce showcase quality.

QUALITY EXPECTATIONS

You make the most important decisions about quality when you plan jobs and select printers. You signify to printers what quality you want by the appearance of mock-ups and files, by how well you specify and preflight your work, by how precisely you identify features you consider critical to success, and by how expertly you examine samples and proofs. Printers use these signs to infer how much quality you recognize and demand.

Many printers refer to a job in terms of the effort they believe it requires. Some jobs are routine; others call for the shop's best effort. You need to know the difference between routine and superior work at an individual shop and to tell the printer which you want. When the printer knows which level of effort you want, staff produces and prices your job accordingly.

An individual print shop can produce different printing categories for different kinds of jobs. For example, a shop might produce showcase single-color work but only premium four-color process printing.

Basic quality printing doesn't receive a great deal of attention at any stage of the job. Speed and legibility count for more than dense color or premium paper. Good quality jobs get more attention to preparation and proofs, and more care in press operation. With good quality, printers show more concern for pleasing and consistent appearance.

Attention increases significantly with premium quality printing. Pressroom and bindery

7-5 DEFECTS NOT RANDOM

Quality problems that originate in prepress occur consistently throughout the job, but variations that originate on press or in bindery usually occur in clusters. For example, if you spot washout halftones, it's likely that a press operator saw the same problem and corrected it. The press operator may have considered the problem minor, however, and allowed the sheets to stay with the production run.

When you identify a problem, examine other sheets produced in sequence with the sheet showing the problem. Examining sheets or final products at random tends to hide the true extent of the problem.

operators are especially trained in quality control. Customers buying premium quality printing are more sophisticated and more likely to be graphic arts professionals than those buying basic and good quality. With showcase quality jobs, everybody involved strives for perfection.

Quality-conscious printers regard printing as a craft, not merely a manufacturing process. Press operators must watch constantly for dozens of variables and make frequent adjustments, often while machines are running at high speeds. Mistakes can cost thousands of dollars in wasted paper and time.

As quality expectations increase, demands on press operators become intense. Operators at all quality levels, but especially for premium and showcase jobs, must have a distinctive mix of physical and mental attributes. They must feel confident controlling complicated machinery, pay meticulous attention to detail, and work easily as members of a production team.

Controlling printing costs while achieving quality means matching individual printing jobs with individual printers. Too many customers take good and even basic quality jobs to premium and showcase quality printers. They waste money on quality control that they don't need.

Correct register

Register means that printed images appear where they were planned to appear. Properly registered images are correctly placed in relationship to each other and to the edges of the paper. If a file shows a headline to begin 1 inch from the left edge of the paper, but the finished product has the headline only $^{11}/_{16}$ inch from the edge, the headline is not registered correctly.

Factors such as the quality of prepress work, the press and paper being used, and the objectives of the printed piece all define what register is close enough. For example, art reproductions, sales brochures and newspapers each have totally different requirements for register.

Register on one-color jobs simply requires getting the image onto the sheet correctly positioned and aligned to the edges. Two-color jobs are more difficult to register because two images must align to each other as well as to the edges of the paper. Each color requires paper to pass under a separate blanket inked by a separate plate. Variations of $^1/_{64}$ inch can ruin image trapping.

With multicolor work and especially with four-color process printing, register becomes critical. Good quality four-color process work calls for register tolerances of .010 inch; showcase separations must register with no variations.

Register affects chokes and spreads. Guidelines about image trapping assume precise register. Most jobs, however, show a slight variation in register throughout the run. For example, if you design a .010 inch trap for a job that prints .015 inch out of register, you lose your trap on one side of the image. When you plan traps, keep in mind all factors that affect register as well as trapping estimates for common screen rulings.

Register also affects color with four-color process printing. Even one color slightly out of register can cause a hue to shift or produce a cast across the entire sheet, especially if that color is magenta or cyan. For that reason, verify register before checking color when doing a press check.

Plates and presses vary greatly in their ability to register. Equipment at quick printers should get one-color jobs properly aligned to the edges of the paper with variation no more than $^1/_{16}$ inch. Those machines can handle two-color register where the colors need not align precisely. Presses found at most commercial printers should handle tight, multicolor register easily. A good operator should get pleasing four-color process work from most medium and large presses.

Problems with register often begin long before a job goes on press: Laser printers and many imagesetters output images whose placement varies from one printout to another; paper and film as surfaces that carry images can stretch or warp; film may be stripped out of register.

To determime whether operators can solve a problem with register on press or must return the job to prepress, examine every edge of the press sheet. If images appear uniformly out of register, the press operator can probably make corrections. If register varies from one portion of the sheet to another, the problem lies in prepress.

Paper that absorbs moisture on press can affect register. As its moisture content increases, paper can expand across the grain by as much as .5 percent. That much expansion would hardly affect simple jobs on small sheets, but could cause major problems with four-color process jobs on large sheets intended to print premium or showcase quality.

....

66 People ask me how we can stay so profitable when we spend so much money on training employees and customers. I say that we get our profit because of training, not in spite of it. Training means that we prevent most mistakes before they happen. We hardly ever do a rerun because of poor quality. Some printers eat hours of press time every month because they didn't do a job right the first time. When we run a press, a customer pays for it. 99

Backups and crossovers. The concept of register includes backups and crossovers. Backups refer to images on opposite sides of the sheet. Crossovers are type, rules, art or photographs planned to line up at the gutter after sheets are folded, trimmed and bound. Crossovers require precision stripping, printing and folding. Even keeping a line of headline type properly aligned across the gutter can prove difficult and expensive. Expect perfect crossovers only with showcase printing.

Technically speaking, any images that do not appear precisely where they are intended are out of register. As a practical matter, however, many printing jobs are slightly out of register. Printers and customers approve those jobs because precise register is difficult to achieve on every sheet—and the untrained eye doesn't notice or care.

Hairline register. Terms such as "hairline register" and "commercial register" have no standard meaning. Regarding four-color process printing, hairline register may mean register within one row of dots or half a row of dots, depending on the size of the dots. Regarding reverses or traps, commerical register may refer to a choke or spread made extra large.

You should expect the best register that equipment at the print shop can provide. Your printer has a corresponding expectation that you design jobs appropriate to the machinery in that specific shop. You and your printer should agree before contracting for the job that the shop is capable of the register you want.

Ink density

Getting the right amount of ink onto paper requires controlling density. Proper density means that line copy looks vivid and has sharp edges. Halftones have contrast without losing shadow detail. Separations show satisfactory detail and strong, vibrant colors.

Too little ink produces washed-out images: Type looks thin and pale; colors seem weak; photos look flat; dots in highlights of halftones and separations may drop out.

Too much ink makes type appear fat and

> **❝ When I show a printer an example of what I want, I don't worry about what the example says. I pay attention to physical features such as color, paper and folding. I pick up samples of what I like everywhere from trade shows to hotel lobbies, then ask my printer how I can make my jobs more like those good examples. ❞**

fuzzy. Large dots in screens and halftones may run into each other, plugging up shadows. Plugged-up shadows lose detail.

Proper ink density is more than a matter of aesthetics. Legibility requires good contrast between type and paper. Washed-out type lowers contrast and makes your message difficult to understand.

Problems with ink density are most common with jobs printed in the basic and good quality categories, especially those run on small presses. Small presses deliver ink less efficiently than larger presses.

Press operators are responsible for achieving satisfactory density and then maintaining it. In quick print shops, operators are often hurried and typically judge density only by watching sheets as they come from the press. In commercial shops, operators have more training and time to set up jobs and should use a densitometer to measure density.

Density readings are the printer's responsibility, not yours. You should inspect a sheet for satisfactory results and let the printer worry about how to achieve them. Specify densities only when you feel certain that your target numbers yield the results you want on the specific paper and press used for the job.

Putting appearances first doesn't mean ignoring density readings. On the contrary, approval sheets that you file with other materials for the job should have densities written along their color bars. That information permits faster makeready during reprints and may save you

> **" People come in here every day wanting to use process inks to match this color or that color. They must think I'm a magician. And they don't even think about how paper affects color. I explain how easily we could run a fifth or sixth flat color instead of fussing all day with process. "**

another press check. And you can use density requirements to specify quality in measurable terms.

Density expectations. Different printers have different ideas about proper density. Some shops think yellow at 1.05 is about right, but others think .80 gives best results. Magenta varies from .95 to 1.50. Cyan and black also have wide ranges.

In addition to variations because of opinions about color, densities vary according to kind of paper. Coated papers yield higher density readings than uncoated sheets, and premium papers yield higher readings than commodity. For example, you might like magenta at 1.50 on a #1 dull coat, 1.40 on a #5 groundwood, 1.15 on a DP bond and only .90 on newsprint.

Adding ink on press requires less time than taking it away. In other words, increasing density is easier than decreasing it. Furthermore, printing at maximun densities leaves no margin for error. For those reasons, many press operators like to run jobs at the lowest densities that yield satisfactory results. On basic and good jobs, that technique works. On premium and showcase jobs, however, a little extra time at a press check may bring much better results.

After you have approved a press sheet, a printer needs to know what densities satisfied you. Satisfactory ink density should measure across the sheet. In some cases, satisfactory means the density is uniform across the entire sheet. In other cases, it means varying density to achieve specific results in certain areas of a sheet. For example, achieving satisfactory skin tones might call for slightly less magenta in one

separation than in another. If the adjustment wasn't made quite well enough during prepress, operators might make it on press.

Consistency from one press run to the next is harder to achieve than consistency during one run. Brochures printed in March may look different from those reprinted in July; logos on envelopes may look different from those on stationery done at another shop. Big jobs such as magazines, books and catalogs often have consistency problems page to page because one signature may print today, another tomorrow or the front of one sheet today and the back tomorrow.

Density in solids. Large solids often look washed out. As a rule of thumb, small presses have problems with areas larger than about $3'' \times 3''$ square and with type larger than 72 points. Large presses can easily handle solids $9'' \times 9''$, but bigger solids than that may require special attention. On very large solids, especially with metallic or opaque inks, the printer may need to print two layers of ink to eliminate streaks and spots. When seeking a uniform, dense black, a printer may suggest an underlying layer of dark blue to increase the density of the black ink and reduce the risk of hickies (see "Hickies" this chapter).

Large screen tint areas, like large solids, are tougher to print than small ones, as the slightest density variation across the image makes the tint appear uneven. Producing tints that are consistent from page to page is very difficult, even for large presses.

Mottled images appear blotchy and uneven. The problem stems from either press conditions or paper. Poor ink transfer or worn blankets can cause mottled images. Inadequate paper coating, formation, calendering or sizing can also cause mottling when ink absorbs unevenly. Paper with coarse fibers tends to mottle more readily than stock with more delicate strands. Uncoated or lightly coated sheets mottle more easily than fully coated stock.

Mottling is especially noticeable in large solids, halftones and screen tints printed in dark colors. All require premium presswork and materials to ensure uniform coverage.

If you see what appears as mottling in a duo-tone, color separation or overlapped tint, double-check that it's not a moiré pattern. Moirés are caused by screens that overlap at incorrect angles and thus are consistent. Mottling is caused by uneven paper formation or poor trapping and thus is random.

Ink trapping

Ink trapping refers to the ability of one ink to capture a second ink printed over it. If the second color adheres to the first, drying uniformly, it is well trapped. Poorly trapped second colors look mottled. Trapping is not difficult with good, premium and showcase printing, so mottling is unacceptable at those quality levels.

MISCELLANEOUS QUALITY PROBLEMS

Although most quality problems occur with register, ink density or ink trapping, several other problems sometimes develop.

Conscientious press operators check every fiftieth or hundredth sheet throughout a run to confirm that the press consistently delivers its best work. Basic quality print shops let more marginal sheets remain than do other shops. The refuse containers at premium and showcase quality printers are full of sheets that, at first glance, may seem acceptable. Good press operators instantly see flaws that come to the attention of most customers only after careful inspection.

Basic quality jobs should have at least 75 percent of the sheets printed satisfactorily; good quality should have at least 95 percent; premium and showcase quality should have 100 percent.

Ghosting

When an unplanned image appears within areas of heavy ink coverage, it's called a ghost. The phantom image is always a pattern of something else on the plate. As the name implies, the image looks faint and elusive.

Ghosts begin with layouts that have not taken the potential problem into consideration. You need to recognize layouts that are prone to ghosting. Printing salespeople and production planners should also help spot layouts with potential

" When I was only doing small printing jobs, I could miss a press date and the printer would always work me in a few days later. I figured that I was a regular customer and that's how everyone in the printing industry scheduled time. When I started doing web press work, I had to learn that a missed press date might cost me five or six weeks. Time on those huge presses is scheduled that far in advance. "

ghosts, but often they don't. The job may get past the production department and pressroom supervisor before the problem finally shows up on press.

Ink starvation can lead to ghosts of two kinds: a light pattern within a solid or a dark pattern within a lightly screened area, such as a 20 percent tint. Eliminating either kind requires running the job on a larger press or changing the layout.

Ghosts are most likely to appear with layouts having large solids. Large, bold headlines, clusters of halftones, large tints and reverses are all possible problems. Whenever you plan large solids and want premium or showcase quality printing, consult with your printer to ensure that no spirits haunt your job.

Hickies

Dirt and fibers from paper can lead to hickies and other flaws. Conscientious printers keep their presses clean and well adjusted during the press run.

Hickies look like tiny white doughnuts with a spot of ink as the doughnut hole. They come from specs of dirt or dust on the plate or blanket that prevent ink from transferring properly. The particles can be dirt from the press itself, imperfections in the ink, or flecks of coating or fiber from the paper. When sticky ink pulls off particles of paper or coating, printers call it picking. Good paper resists picking.

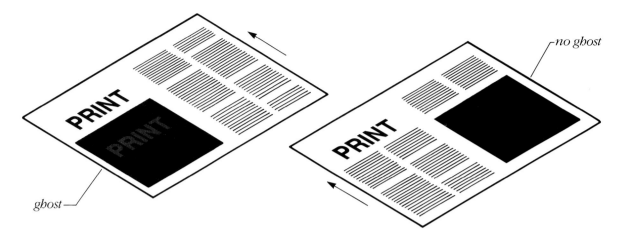

7-6 Ghosts *Ghosting usually results from poor coverage of a solid, tint or halftone that follows a heavily inked image on a press sheet. The ghost represents an ink-starved version of the preceeding image. To cure the problem, you can change the layout or print on a larger press.*

Although hickies may appear in type and halftones, they show most commonly in large solids. Because hickies are caused by loose particles, they wander around the sheet and come and go during the run. They are difficult to prevent. Good printers spot the large hickies, but a few small ones are inevitable on most jobs.

Setoff

As printed sheets are delivered into a pile, the accumulating weight of sheets falling on top of each other while the ink is wet may transfer the image from the top of one sheet to the bottom of another. Printers call the phenomenon setoff or offsetting and prevent it by spraying a fine powder over the wet sheet to separate it from the next one falling on top.

Customers sometimes incorrectly identify setoff as show-through. It is rare that a sheet is printed so heavily that ink from one side soaks through to the other.

Freshly printed sheets should sit a few hours or even overnight before handling. Some papers have setoff if trimmed too soon after printing because paper cutting machines hold piles of paper under heavy pressure to make sure sheets don't move while being cut. Ink setoff can also occur if sheets are folded too soon. Give your printer plenty of time to allow ink to dry between press runs and before trimming or folding.

Web pull

Heatset web presses may yield sheets with a slight waviness, especially when there's heavy ink coverage. Experienced operators believe that paper going through a web press under tension ripples as it wets with ink. Drying units bake in the distortion. Some presses and papers ripple more than others, but web pull may happen with almost any job.

Doubling and slurring

Doubling happens when dots or type blur because of a slight second contact between paper and blanket. When dots double, each shows a tiny shadow. Slurring makes dots appear oblong instead of round. The problem shows as smears on trailing edges and comes from poor blanket pressures or ink tack. Slurring is especially difficult to prevent on a perfecting press but is rarely a problem when using uncoated paper.

Printers use quality control images, such as the test patterns shown in Visual 3-11, to detect doubling or slurring.

Scumming

Presses often have a problem with scumming. It may appear as a streak or tinge of ink running the length of the sheet or show up as fat or fuzzy type. Scumming occurs when the plate receives too little water, leading ink to stray into nonimage areas. Often scumming looks so faint that you hardly notice. Scummed sheets, however, show poor presswork and don't belong in your job.

SUCCESSFUL PRESS CHECKS

No proof substitutes for examining first sheets from the press. Furthermore, no proof from the same file or film can predict results at different printers. At a press check you confirm that your job prints as you planned.

During a press check you meet with the press operator for your job and one or two other people from design and production. The meeting takes place at the print shop when the production run is about to begin. Some printers do press checks at the delivery end of the press. Others meet with customers in special proofing rooms.

Keep your schedule flexible on the day of a press check. Your printer tells you when production has scheduled your job, but that time is a goal, not a promise. You can't predict whether the check will last fifteen minutes (routine) or two hours (nightmare). In addition, many jobs require several press checks. You might hang around the plant or return after lunch to inspect another signature, then return tomorrow to check the second sides of signatures you approve today.

Many printers work two or three shifts, so

....

❝ *Press checks can be crazy experiences. Once I wandered over next to another press and noticed that skin tones in all the separations looked red, like all the models were sunburned. I couldn't believe that's what the customer wanted, but no one was there to evaluate color. I didn't say anything, but I've often wondered how the customer reacted to that job.* **❞**

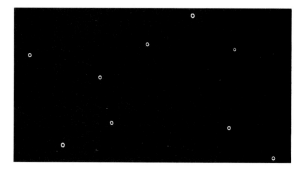

7-7 Hickies Hickies may appear as small, white doughnuts anywhere that ink covers paper. They are most obvious in large solids and the shadows of halftones. The dust or bits of paper that cause hickies can come from many sources, so it's almost impossible to produce a printing job totally free from this common problem.

you may have a press check at 8:00 P.M. or 4:00 A.M. Production tries to avoid causing you inconvenience but must juggle the schedule of many other customers at the same time.

Press time may cost your printer several hundred dollars an hour. Arrive promptly for a press check, pay close attention and help get the job moving quickly. If you ask to correct a mistake that was not your printer's fault, expect to pay for press downtime.

Your printer builds the cost of an average press check into the price of your job. If you take longer than average, you probably don't get charged extra. You may, however, get quoted higher prices on future jobs.

Asking for a press check does not signal mistrust. On the contrary, a press check means that you continue your close working relationship with your printer through the final stages of production. A production manager or graphic designer may do several press checks per month, sometimes traveling thousands of miles to show up at press time.

When to do a press check. Do a press check whenever you produce a job that has any of the following characteristics:
- premium or showcase quality
- uses a paper or process unfamiliar to you
- at a print shop you haven't used before
- when you feel even the slightest uncertainty about how it may turn out

7-8 GUIDE TO PRINTING QUALITY

Register

basic	Variation limit ± .015 inch (0.38 mm)
good	Variation limit ± .010 inch (0.25 mm)
premium	Variation limit ± .005inch (0.13 mm)
showcase	Precise register; no variation

Density

basic	Variation limit ± 7%
good	Variation limit ± 5%
premium	Variation limit ± 3%
showcase	Variation limit ± 1%

Screen percentages

basic	Variation limit ± 10%
good	Variation limit ± 5%
premium	Variation limit ± 2%
showcase	No variation

Dot gain

basic	Variation limit ± 10%
good	Variation limit ± 5%
premium	Variation limit ± 3%
showcase	Variation limit ± 1%

Halftones

basic	No shadow detail, slightly fuzzy
good	Some shadow detail, sharp
premium	Full shadow detail, very sharp
showcase	Almost match originals

Separations

basic	Not applicable
good	Pleasing color
premium	Almost match originals
showcase	Almost match product or scene

Color match

basic	Slight perceptible differences
good	Just noticable differences
premium	No perceptible differences
showcase	No measurable differences

Minor flaws

basic	On maximum 10% of sheets
good	On maximum 5% of sheets
premium	On maximum 2% of sheets
showcase	On 0% of sheets

Coatings

basic	Not applicable
good	Uniform, slight cast & flaws
premium	Uniform, no cast or flaws
showcase	Uniform, no cast or flaws

Finishing

basic	Variation limit ± 1/16 inch (1.6 mm)
good	Variation limit ± 1/32 inch (0.8 mm)
premium	Variation limit ± 1/64 inch (0.4 mm)
showcase	Variation limit ± 1/64 inch (0.4 mm)

To learn more about guidelines for printing quality, visit our Web site at www.gettingitprinted.com.

The chart at the left identifies ten features of printed products and spells out standards they should meet to fall within one of the four quality categories. Information on the chart uses concepts also found in the text. The chart helps you select the quality category appropriate for a specific job and evaluate work that a printer claims is within one of the categories.

Register. Use inches or millimeters to specify register, not subjective terms such as "tight" or "hairline." Even the term "rows of dots" means little because it doesn't tell dot size. One row of dots equals .02 inch on a 150-line screen, but is twice that size on an 85-line screen.

Density. Appropriate ink density depends on the job. Once established, however, you can record densitometer readings and measure percent of variation from the approval sheet. Percents apply to:
- the same sheet throughout the run
- signature to signature throughout the job
- exact reprints on identical paper

Screen percentages. If you specify 20 percent screens for good quality printing, you shouldn't get 26 percent on one sheet and 17 percent on the next. Most color control bars include tint patches so you can keep track of screen percentages.

Dot gain. Appropriate dot gain depends on the job. Once established, however, you can record dot gain and percent variations from the approval sheet. Percents apply to:
- the same sheet throughout the run
- signature to signature throughout the job
- exact reprints on identical paper

Halftones. Guidelines assume that photos have been taken with reproduction in mind. Density ranges of originals should lie within the ability of a press to reproduce. Premium highlights should include 5 percent dots; showcase highlights, 3 percent dots. Premium shadows should run to 90 percent; showcase shadows, to 95 percent.

Separations. Guidelines assume that photos have been taken with reproduction in mind. Density ranges of originals should lie within the ability of a press to reproduce. Good color should match proofs. Premium color should match original photos. Showcase color should match original products or scenes.

Color match. Match applies to both flat and process colors. Compare the swatch or proof color with color on the press sheet. Do not compare color on a computer screen to color on a press sheet. Use standard lighting conditions. Keep in mind that register, density and dot gain all affect color. After achieving satisfactory color, variation should stay within limits for each quality level.

Minor flaws. Flaws include scumming, setoff, hickies, smudges, wrinkles, doubling, slurring, smudges, streaks, smears, scratches, nicks, gear and roller marks—a long list that includes any visual defects that could be eliminated in prepress or on press.

Coatings. Varnish, ultraviolet and aqueous should not crack, blister, peel or cause curling. They should cover uniformly.

Finishing. The accuracy of finishing includes die cuts, drills, folds, trims, scores and perfs. Remember that trims occur during binding, so apply to saddle stitching, perfect binding and other binding methods. For additional quality guidelines in bindery, see Visual 9-10.

7-9 STEPS TO A SUCCESSFUL PRESS CHECK

Before you start evaluating press sheets, do the following:

• Introduce yourself. Try to help everyone feel comfortable.

• Confirm that the session takes place under proper lighting conditions and that production people have a densitometer.

• Make sure you have available your original specifications and all alterations in writing, the printer's job ticket, all final proofs and any color matching swatches used while planning the job.

• Remind yourself not to look for errors or flaws that you should have caught on a proof. It's too late!

Evaluate press sheets *in the following sequence*:

1. Determine that the paper is what you specified. Verify grade, basis weight, color, finish and grain direction. The information is all on the label on the carton, skid or roll near the feed end of the press.

2. Ask someone to trim and fold the press sheet while you continue with the next steps.

3. Check for physical flaws, such as scratches or multiple hickies.

4. Check register. Especially with four-color process printing, verify that separations register within tolerances appropriate to the quality level of the job.

5. Assess overall color. Does it seem too weak, too strong or about right? Is it consistent across the sheet?

6. Examine critical color. Study features that most affect the success of this job.

7. Compare the press sheet to proofs to confirm that prepress made all the corrections you indicated.

8. Examine the trimmed and folded sheet to verify features such as page sequence, bleeds and adjustment for creep. Measure the trim size.

Any time you identify a problem, if it's a Critical flaw that means you cannot accept the job, stop the press run and go back to prepress. This takes guts.

Major error that detracts from the value of the job, consult with others on the scene to decide how to fix the problem, how much time and money it would take and whether to do it. This takes leadership.

Minor problem that most readers won't notice, call it to someone's attention but approve the sheet anyway. This takes common sense.

When you feel satisfied with a press sheet

• Ask to see three more sheets to verify that they match the one you like.

• Ask the press operator to write density values along the color control bars of all four sheets.

• Sign and date two sheets for the printer's records and keep two for your files.

• Thank everyone for their efforts and say how much you look forward to seeing the final product. Don't forget the assistant press operator who loads the paper.

Press checks, also called press OKs, sometimes make people feel tense. The press operator and your sales representative wait for your reactions. The room may sound noisy, you may feel rushed, and responsibility for final approval may make you feel nervous. You focus on a successful product while the printer focuses on efficient production. Use the checklist in Visual 7-9 to calm your nerves and help you manage your part of the event.

Checking jobs on web presses causes more headaches than checking sheetfed jobs. Operators can run a sheetfed press slowly during a press check, but must keep a web almost at full speed. Makeready from a web can double makeready running sheetfed. When you press

> **When I first learned about web presses, I started specifying web or sheetfed for each job. I thought I was very sophisticated, but I really didn't know what I was doing. One time I'm sure that I paid too much for a rerun that the printer had to restrip for web. Now I just pay attention to how much the job costs and when I can have delivery. I let the printer worry about what kind of press to use while I worry about getting copy and files ready on time.**

check a web job, skip the small talk and move quickly through your checklist.

Unless you have lots of experience in print production, speak to technical people in plain English. Say, "Overall color looks a little weak," instead of, "Black is not running dense enough." Let the press operator deal with color bars and densitometers while you decide whether your job looks right.

Slight adjustments in density or register often result in significant color changes. Adjustments are easy to make. After the third or fourth adjustment, however, press sheets look about as good as they're going to get. Unless you're checking a showcase job, sign off and go celebrate another job well done.

Most press checks are positive experiences with competent printers hosting satisfied customers. Occasionally things go wrong. Press problems force long delays, dirty paper causes hickies, or the perfect halftone prints too light. These rare situations call for an extra measure of understanding from both you and your printer as you strive to keep quality up, costs down and schedule intact.

Treat signing a press sheet as you would signing any other proof. If it has a hickie or other minor flaw, circle it before signing. Don't insist on waiting for a perfect sheet. If the sheet has a major defect or critical error, however, you can refuse to sign. Whether you sign, wait for a new sheet, or return for another check depends on the nature of the problems and your faith in the printer to solve them. ∎

8. OTHER PRINTING METHODS

To keep up-to-date about other printing methods, visit our Web site (www.gettingitprinted.com).

Although offset lithography is the most popular method of commercial printing, many purposes and products require other methods. In this chapter you learn about these other processes and ways to locate printers who use them.

Some printers using nonoffset methods focus on particular products, such as labels, clothing, magazines or boxes. You can buy these products through an offset printer, but usually at a substantial markup. Going directly to a specialty printer saves money and speeds production. Knowing about nonoffset printers also increases options in design and management because offset simply cannot print many items.

Printing is any mechanized process that repeatedly transfers an image from a master, such as a plate, die, negative, stencil or electronic memory, to a substrate, such as paper or cloth. All of the following methods fit that definition.

In this chapter we refer only occasionally to the four quality categories for offset printing defined in chapters one and seven. Although concepts such as register, density and dot gain remain the same, reasonable quality standards vary widely from one printing method to the next.

Some printers using flexography and screen are not accustomed to meeting the exacting quality standards common with offset and gravure printing. For example, ink density may vary throughout the run causing reversed type to block up or making bar codes unreadable. You can specify parameters for density and other measurable aspects of quality just as you would for offset, then use a press check to verify that the printer meets your requirements.

Planning and prepress. The process of planning and preparing a print job stays essentially the same regardless of which printing method you use. You need answers to questions about quantity, cost and schedule. Prepress services familiar with the requirements of specific printing methods can work with files in common formats, such as PostScript, TIFF/IT and PDF.

In addition to variations caused by different substrates and quality expectations, each printing process has specific guidelines for screen rulings, image trapping, dot gain and ink densities. Dialog boxes in commonly used design software, however, refer to offset printing, not to one of the other methods. Furthermore, platemaking for other processes that require plates—which is most of them—is relatively slow and expensive.

8-1 PROS AND CONS OF ON-DEMAND PRINTING

Machines made for on-demand printing are designed for efficient production of short runs: one hundred to five thousand copies. They offer both advantages and disadvantages when compared to conventional offset printing.

Advantages

• **Fast turnaround.** All-digital pathway from computer to press. Machines ready to print within minutes of receiving RIPed data. Sheets dry, ready for finishing when delivered from press.

• **No film or plate.** No disposable supplies cut costs and reduce wastes.

• **Precise quantities.** Print only what you need.

• **Low makeready.** Presses up to contract color in ten or fifteen sheets.

• **Lower unit costs on short runs.** Fast prepress and makeready compared to other printing methods.

• **Variable message.** Printing controlled by database can change the image—personalize—individual sheets.

• **Uniform quality.** Fixed and variable data printed at the same time using the same technology.

• **Up-to-date message.** Fast turnaround and eliminating inventory means products carry no obsolete information.

• **Easy adjustments on press.** Machines respond quickly to computer commands to change color and density.

• **Improved cash flow.** Dollars not tied up in inventory and the costs of storage.

• **Easy archiving.** Jobs are stored as digital files, not hard copy or film.

• **Useful for imprinting.** Many on-demand presses accept stock previously printed by another method.

Disadvantages

• **Higher unit costs for long runs.** Processes require highly skilled operators and proprietary supplies.

• **Less accurate prepress proofs.** Digital proofing systems integrated with conventional inks, not toners and proprietary inks.

• **Less accurate color matches.** Systems based on toners and proprietary inks yield colors that may not match colors developed for conventional printing inks.

• **Extensive testing and partnering.** Workflow management requires careful interfacing and constant preflighting.

• **Reduced paper choices.** Machines have maximum sheet size approximately 13″ × 18″ (340mm × 460mm) and limited to a handful of paper weights and surfaces.

• **Reduced quality options.** Resolutions of 600–800 dpi limit screen rulings.

• **Fixed press speeds.** Operators cannot run machines slowly for press checks and then change to high speeds for production runs.

Only offset offers dependable computer-to-plate technology. For these reasons, you need to work closely with prepress experts when preparing files for any printing method other than offset.

PRINT ON DEMAND

Printing on demand at a commercial or in-house shop is similar to using a desktop printer. Writing, design and prepress are part of the customer's digital workflow. Files go electronically to a printing machine. There is no film or plates.

8-2 PERSONALIZING WITH ON-DEMAND AND INK-JET

In addition to applying addresses and postal bar codes from databases, on-demand and ink-jet printing can personalize products in many ways. Following are just a few examples:

• newsletters with articles written for specific departments or neighborhoods

• magazines with ads and inserts for readers with specific interests

• bid specifications and requests for proposals

• catalogs with local maps and pricing

• direct mailers whose product mix and drop dates are based on customer demographics

• sales letters with coupons for recipient's favorite products

• review copies of books and liners for CDs and videos

• invoices and statements with charts and graphs showing usage

• proposals edited for specific agencies and review sessions

• financial reports with charts showing the status of individual accounts

• operator manuals and training guides tailored to individual system configurations and workflows

• textbooks with illustrations and reading difficulty specific to grade level

---

Customers use printing on demand to produce short runs of documents such as textbooks, technical manuals and impact statements. The processes are also useful for short runs of products such as fliers, brochures and inserts that need pleasing color and instant turnaround.

To locate printers with on-demand capability, check retail quick printers and copy centers. You may also get leads by asking the textbook manager at the bookstore of a large university, the documentation production manager for a software publisher, or sales reps for companies that provide the hardware, such as Agfa, IBM, Indigo, Tektronix, Xeikon and Xerox.

Many customers who use on-demand printers have icons for printing companies, and sometimes even specific presses, on their computer desktops. They finish designs or update information and then click their mice to send files to the printing company. Products from files ready to print are produced in a few hours.

On-demand devices operate at one uniform speed, so they have an entirely different economy from presses that operate at variable speeds. With presses, unit costs drop as print runs increase. With on-demand printing, unit costs stay the same throughout the run. Copy number one thousand costs the same as copy number one.

Most on-demand systems use toner, a powder that sticks to the charged areas of a belt or drum. The toner transfers to paper as it passes through the machine. Heated rollers fuse the toner to the paper. The generic name for this process is xerography.

Like offset presses, some on-demand machines operate sheetfed and some operate as web presses. In addition, many on-demand presses can print on one side (simplex) or both sides (duplex).

The largest on-demand presses have imaging areas about 20 inches wide, considerably smaller than the largest offset, flexo and gravure presses. Relatively small imaging areas, combined with relatively slow press speeds, make on-demand printing most economical for very short runs.

Machines based on xerography produce four-color jobs using toners that simulate process inks. A few machines, however, use inks. Like toner-based machines, these machines create images using lasers controlled by digital files. Images transfer to a blanket cylinder that picks up ink and passes it to an impression cylinder for printing on paper. This offset process is similar to presses that use plates.

Conventional offset printing creates an identical image on each sheet, but on-demand printing creates a new image for each impression. The "new" image might be identical to the previous image, or the new image might involve a slight change, such as the name of a different reader or a different color on the cover.

Causing a new image on each press sheet requires that all ink transfer from the blanket with each impression. This feat requires proprietary inks with special formulas, not generic to any brand of offset press. Proprietary inks drive up costs and may not create colors that integrate with common color matching systems.

The ink-based machines also require papers with special coatings to ensure good holdout and 100 percent ink transfer. The need for special papers adds to costs and limits choices of substrates.

INK-JET

Another form of computer-controlled printing uses equipment with tiny nozzles that release ink droplets through an electrostatic charging unit onto paper. The charge shapes droplets into letters.

Ink-jet printing is quiet and fast. Nothing mechanical strikes paper. One nozzle might generate sixty-six thousand drops a second and print a business letter in two seconds. Because ink-jet systems have few moving parts, these setups are highly reliable and easily maintained.

Ink-jet as a commercial process is used for printing addresses and personal messages at mailing services. Messages can change in a microsecond. Moreover, inking nozzles are mounted in line with collating and addressing equipment. Most periodicals and catalogs are addressed using ink-jet. A printer making catalogs might have six nozzles to print individual

❝ *Our printer did compatability testing for our platforms and software for a long book project. All went smoothly until blueline stage when I noticed odd fraction characters that popped up for no apparent reason. The culprit turned out to be a minor upgrade in their page layout application that recognized certain keystrokes in my older software as something quite different. They just assumed that I had upgraded too.* **❞**

sales messages on bound-in order forms and another six nozzles for a different message plus address and bar codes on the cover.

While ink-jet is most useful for direct mailings, its speed and economy make it practical for personalizing business forms, coding document entry systems and numbering tickets. The process also works well with rough and uneven surfaces.

Most printers and lettershops using ink-jet offer one color only. Color work, however, is available. Using the three process colors plus black, color ink-jet systems can produce anywhere from eight to five thousand shades, depending on software.

Large-format printers. If you need very shorts runs—or even single copies—of banners, displays, maps or other large items, look for a large-format printer. These devices use ink-jet and similar technologies to print directly from computer files.

Large-format devices operate like desktop printers on steroids. Preparing files requires similar skills and software, but the devices print on wide rolls instead of office-size sheets. Substrates can include films for backlit displays and plastics for outdoor ads as well as a variety of paper.

You can find large-format devices at quick print and sign shops, reprographic and blueprint companies, and photo developing and prepress services. Some screen and flexography printers use the devices to make proofs as well as produce end products.

FLEXOGRAPHY

Printing on substrates that don't work well in offset presses often calls for flexography. The process uses soft plastic plates on a web press. Water-based inks dry almost instantly, allowing fast press speeds on substrates that do not absorb moisture.

Flexo is popular in the packaging industry because presses can run so many different substrates, from 10-mil plastic for bags to double-wall corrugated cardboard for cartons. Printing buyers familiar with converting boxes and envelopes routinely use flexo printers.

You see flexo printing in everyday products, such as milk cartons, bread and candy wrappers, gift wrapping, cereal boxes, corrugated cartons, priority mailing envelopes, grocery bags (paper and plastic) and labels on cans and bottles.

Plates for flexo are made from film or files, are available in a variety of thicknesses and cost about 25 percent more than offset plates to make. Prepress services choose and image plates according to requirements of specific substrates and presses. Flexo printers typically leave prepress to outside services. Digital platemaking on press for flexo is common only in the newspaper industry with standardized substrates and press adjustments.

Flexography doesn't give the fine screen rulings of offset, so images may not seem sharp. Furthermore, the soft plates stretch and bend on press, giving flexography standards of dot gain and register lower than those of offset. Minimum highlight dots are about 10 percent, compared to about 3 percent for offset and gravure. On the other hand, flexo can lay down dense layers of ink on some substrates, creating opacity approaching screen printing.

The wide variety of substrates and inks used in flexography make color management more difficult than with offset or gravure. Quality expectations vary widely according to substrates ranging from metallic labels to absorbent paperboard. Flexo printers and customers often consider any color good enough, so they print without proofing.

You can see flexo color control images, small squares called eye markers, printed on the inside flaps of packages containing consumer goods, such as food or cosmetics. Eye markers are used for automatic control of density and register and may be used to guide slitting and trimming machines.

Printers using flexography specialize in specific products, such as wallpaper or shrink-wrapping, and often perform finishing operations in-line with printing. For example, package printers die cut, label printers semi-slit, and envelope converters score, fold and glue.

To locate flexographic printers, look in classified directories under "Packaging" and under products such as boxes, labels and bags, or inquire at a local prepress service.

LETTERPRESS

For centuries, printing meant letterpress. Asian artisans invented the technique, using individual letters made of clay. Gutenberg developed the process in Germany, using characters molded from lead. He assembled the characters into wooden trays, inked their surfaces, then pressed paper against them to transfer the image.

Letterpress is a form of relief printing, meaning that characters on the plate are higher than the material surrounding them. Rubber stamps work on the same principle. Type printed on a letterpress may feel indented because of its direct contact with the paper.

In addition to setting letters by hand, printers can mold letterpress plates from a variety of materials, including plastic, and can etch plates with chemicals or lasers.

Etchings are called cuts, a term applied to all letterpress art. The process of etching removes the nonimage area from the plate, leaving raised lines, halftone dots or other matter to print. Before the day of camera-ready art, printers maintained a supply of standing cuts to use much like today's clip art. Information set in type under the cut was called the cutline, a term still used as a synonym for caption.

Fine letterpress printing is cloaked in five centuries of graphic tradition that, for some hobbyists, lends its products an ancient mystique. Artistic letterpress printing is often produced on

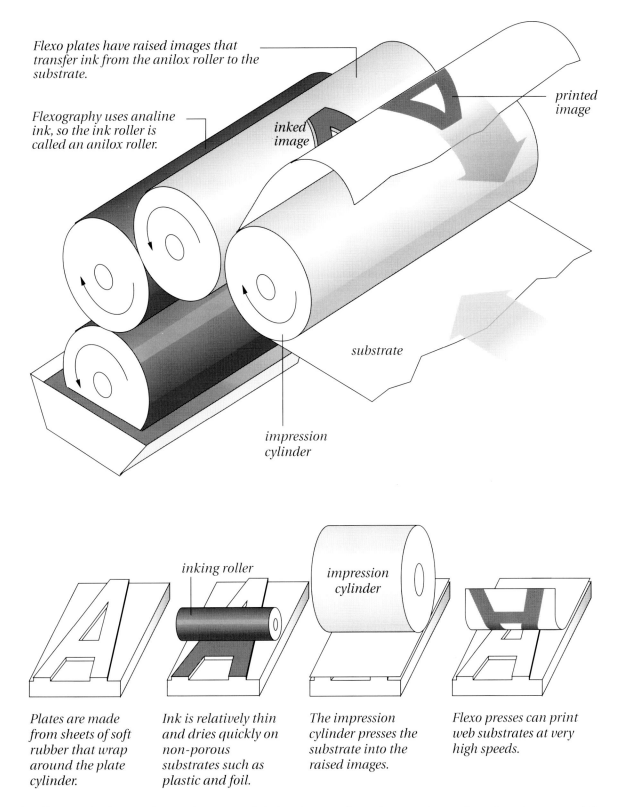

Flexo plates have raised images that transfer ink from the anilox roller to the substrate.

Flexography uses analine ink, so the ink roller is called an anilox roller.

inked image

printed image

substrate

impression cylinder

inking roller

impression cylinder

Plates are made from sheets of soft rubber that wrap around the plate cylinder.

Ink is relatively thin and dries quickly on non-porous substrates such as plastic and foil.

The impression cylinder presses the substrate into the raised images.

Flexo presses can print web substrates at very high speeds.

8-3 Flexography *Because flexography uses a relatively soft plate and prints plate to surface (not offset), it works for rough materials, such as fabric, wallpaper, corrugated cardboard and paneling, where quantity requirements make screen printing prohibitive. Flexo is also useful for printing labels and decals because the same plate that prints can also kiss die cut.*

handmade paper and enhanced with gilding and other flourishes.

To locate a printer or hobbyist who can print using a letterpress, ask owners of art and photo galleries. Letterpress printers may also be known to engravers, die cutters and officials of your regional trade association of printers.

SCREEN

Screen printing is the most simple of all printing processes. A printer needs only a screen stencil, ink and squeegee. The screen fabric is wire or polyester, not silk. Ink forced through the screen prints in the stencil's pattern.

Printers use the screen method for products such as T-shirts, signs and bottles. Most products are printed after manufacture. Ring binders, for example, don't go through an offset press but can easily be screen printed. Plastic comb bindings have screen printed titles on the spine.

Stencils for screen printing are cut by hand, stamped by machine or made photographically. Photographic stencils are made by exposing light through a negative onto light-sensitive emulsion spread on the screen.

Commercial screen printing may be done by hand using only simple equipment or on automatic presses of varying size and complexity. Large commercial presses use the same technology you can use to print a few T-shirts for your softball team.

Halftones can be screen printed. On smooth surfaces, such as bottles, 80-line screens work fine. On fabrics, halftone dots must be large enough to adhere to the mesh of clothing. Ideally, one dot prints at the intersection of at least four threads. Fabric mesh counts should be about four times the line count of halftone screens. Screen-printed halftones tend to look better on synthetic rather than natural fibers because monofilament threads give sharper images and better register.

Screen printers make stencils from hard copy or files, so you need to consult a printer for details. The shop may prefer larger traps than needed for offset printing or want film emulsion up instead of down. Screen printers vary widely in their preferences for halftone dot sizes, especially for billboards and other large signs.

Screen printing has several advantages over other methods in specific situations.

Short runs. If you need twenty lawn signs, fifty posters or two hundred bumper stickers, think of screen printing.

Heavy ink coverage. Screen printing lays down ink up to thirty times thicker than lithography and five times heavier than gravure. Furthermore, inks are opaque. Colors are more dense and durable than from other processes. Screen works perfectly for outdoor advertising, such as billboards.

Ink variety. Screen printing lends itself to ink with satin, gloss or fluorescent finishes and to ink that accepts flocks or other decorative substances. There are special inks to print on glass, metal, cardboard and other substrates. The electronics industry uses screen printing to etch circuits on copper-plated boards. Acid-resisting ink covers image areas, allowing acid to etch away the nonimage copper surfaces.

Large images. Because the screen process is so simple, frames holding stencils can be larger than the largest offset presses. Screen printers make huge posters and banners.

Versatility. Advocates call screen printing the print-anything process. In addition to printing clothing and dishware, the process works well for menu covers, greeting cards and posters. Wallpaper, paneling, metal signs, glass and other materials that cannot be printed with lithography are easily screen printed. Inks go on so heavily they adhere to almost any surface.

Screen printing does have limitations. It's slow both in printing and drying. Register on some substrates can be difficult and dot gain unpredictable, especially with fabrics whose absorbency varies.

Screen printers have their own classification in most directories. They are also listed under the products they make, such as outdoor advertising, book and catalog covers and loose-leaf binders.

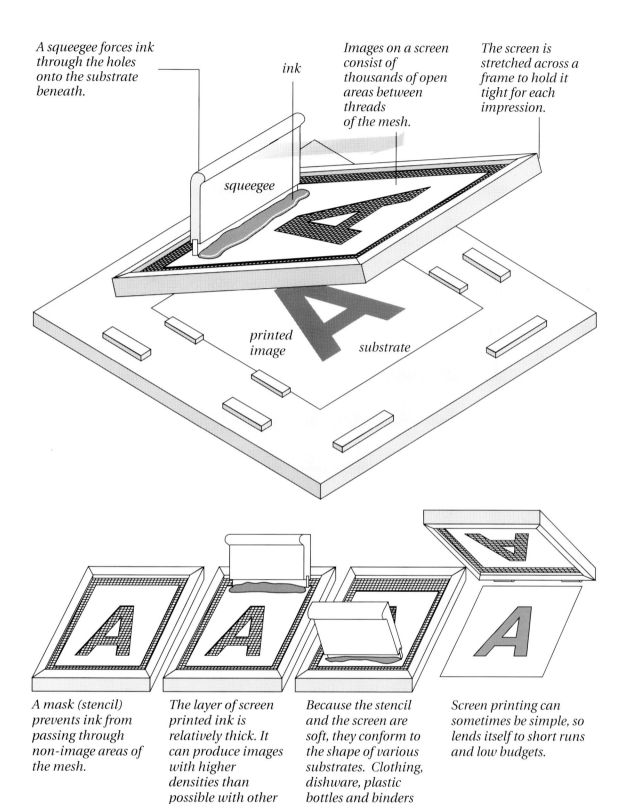

A squeegee forces ink through the holes onto the substrate beneath.

ink

Images on a screen consist of thousands of open areas between threads of the mesh.

The screen is stretched across a frame to hold it tight for each impression.

squeegee

printed image

substrate

A mask (stencil) prevents ink from passing through non-image areas of the mesh.

The layer of screen printed ink is relatively thick. It can produce images with higher densities than possible with other forms of printing.

Because the stencil and the screen are soft, they conform to the shape of various substrates. Clothing, dishware, plastic bottles and binders are screen printed.

Screen printing can sometimes be simple, so lends itself to short runs and low budgets.

8-4 Screen printing You can use your computer to design for screen printing, but you may need to output as positive prints, not negative film. Keep screen rulings very coarse—85 lpi for smooth substrates, 65 or even 55 lpi for rough surfaces.

GRAVURE

Gravure plates are cylinders that carry images consisting of millions of tiny cells filled with ink. The cells vary in depth and width, so some hold more ink than others. Mounted on web presses, the cylinders transfer ink directly to paper. Presses have no blankets. Printers use gravure for long runs (millions) of magazines and catalogs.

The size of a gravure press is expressed by the width of paper it can print. And compared to offset webs, gravure presses are huge, running rolls anywhere from 70 inches to 118 inches wide with cutoffs from 50 to 75 inches. Large widths mean that gravure commonly produces signatures of forty-eight or sixty-four pages.

Paper for gravure is relatively soft and extremely smooth. Stock with even minor irregularities tends to miss contact with some of the tiny wells carrying ink. But stock doesn't have to cost lots of money. In fact, gravure is attractive for jobs such as direct-mail catalogs because it works well on relatively low-grade paper. To ensure that it releases from the wells onto paper, ink has almost no tack. Picking doesn't happen.

The ability to cut portions of the image to various depths into the plate gives gravure the ability to print a wide range of tones because the plate can deliver different amounts of ink to various parts of an image. Dense and varying ink coverage yields superior color, even on inexpensive papers. And inking remains constant throughout the run.

Printers use a diamond stylus to engrave a gravure cylinder (plate). The stylus is guided by lasers scanning halftone positives or by digital files.

Cylinders for gravure printing cost about four times more than offset plates to make, so gravure works best for runs of over a million impressions. The typical customer of a gravure printer is a publisher with a magazine or catalog on press ten or twelve times per year. Each issue might require a week or more of press time. Buyers who work with gravure printers are experienced and specialized.

Gravure has specifications for film- and plate-making different from the specs for offset. For example, a printer may ask for film positives developed to density standards that you find unfamiliar.

To compare gravure with lithography, examine any copy of *National Geographic* published since 1975. The editorial matter, both text and photographs, is printed gravure at 175 lpi, while the advertising and cover are printed web offset.

Classified directories for major cities list gravure printers under "Rotogravure." Many gravure printers advertise in trade journals aimed at printing buyers for catalogs and national magazines, and are known to printing buyers at companies that mail millions of consumer catalogs.

ENGRAVING

For years, commercial printers were called "printers and engravers." Printing used letterpresses; engraving involved images cut (engraved) into thick metal plates. Currency and most stock certificates are still engraved because engraving yields the sharpest image of any printing method.

Images for engraving are cut into the metal plate rather than raised above plate surfaces as in letterpress. The surface of the plate is covered with ink, then wiped clean, leaving the engravings full of ink. The press then forces paper into the inked recesses, transferring the image to the surface of the paper.

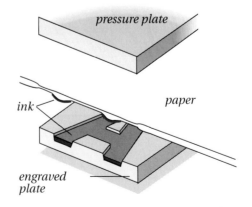

8-5 Engraving The intense pressure of an engraving press forces paper into recesses etched into the plate. Engraving ink is very thick, making the raised image even more distinct.

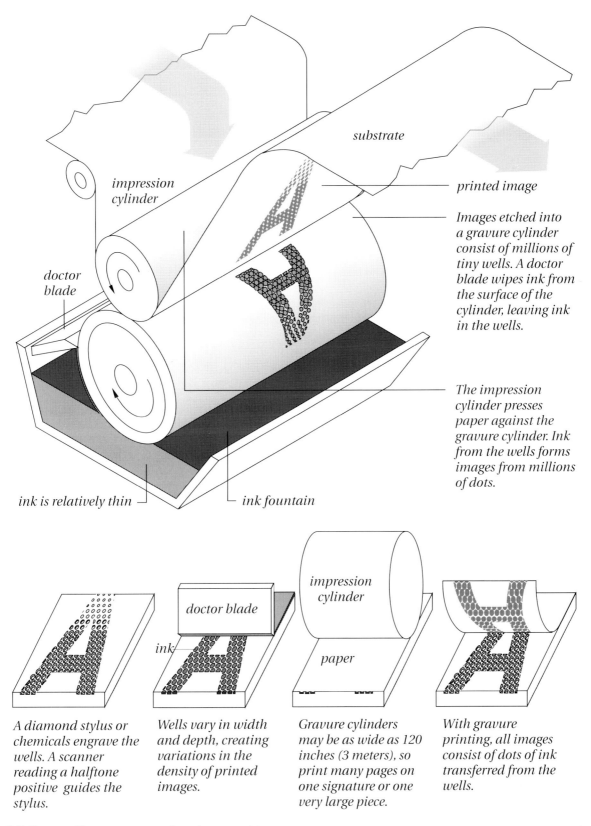

substrate

printed image

impression cylinder

Images etched into a gravure cylinder consist of millions of tiny wells. A doctor blade wipes ink from the surface of the cylinder, leaving ink in the wells.

doctor blade

The impression cylinder presses paper against the gravure cylinder. Ink from the wells forms images from millions of dots.

ink is relatively thin

ink fountain

A diamond stylus or chemicals engrave the wells. A scanner reading a halftone positive guides the stylus.

Wells vary in width and depth, creating variations in the density of printed images.

doctor blade

ink

impression cylinder

paper

Gravure cylinders may be as wide as 120 inches (3 meters), so print many pages on one signature or one very large piece.

With gravure printing, all images consist of dots of ink transferred from the wells.

8-6 Gravure The gravure process has a large appeal for magazines and catalogs because it can print on lightweight paper. Many publications appear on 35# or even 30# stock, saving many dollars on postage as well as paper. The method competes with flexography for printing packaging materials and special products, such as floor coverings. It rivals lithography for long-run publications, such as advertising supplements to Sunday newspapers.

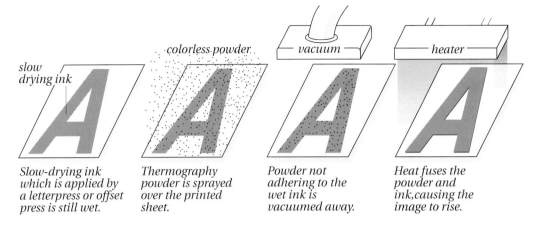

slow drying ink

colorless powder

vacuum

heater

Slow-drying ink which is applied by a letterpress or offset press is still wet.

Thermography powder is sprayed over the printed sheet.

Powder not adhering to the wet ink is vacuumed away.

Heat fuses the powder and ink, causing the image to rise.

8-7 Thermography *While slow-drying ink is still wet, a nozzle sprays thermography powder over the printed sheet. Powder that doesn't adhere to the ink is vacuumed away. Heat melts the remaining powder, making it rise. The powder has no color itself, so, as it melts, it takes on the color of the underlying ink.*

Engraved paper feels slightly indented behind its image areas. The process uses thick, opaque inks available in both gloss and dull finishes. Gloss inks may appear metallic. When planning engraved letterhead destined for a laser printer, verify that inks are heat resistant.

Presses for engraving apply high pressures over small areas and tend to be small. Images larger than approximately 4″×8″ require dividing. To get engraved images at both top and bottom of a letterhead, for example, requires two impressions.

Engraving takes special presses and techniques and costs more than offset. Operators cut dies by hand, chemically etch them from mechanicals or laser-burn them from electronic files. Hand-cut dies are made of steel; etched and burned dies are made of copper.

Whether to use engraving steel or copper dies depends on needs for quality, variety and quantity. Steel dies give the highest quality and the longest press runs, but engravers making them may be limited to only a few typefaces. Copper dies are limited to press runs up to about five thousand impressions.

People who appreciate engraved printing also recognize fine paper. Using anything less than the best reduces engraving's exquisite impact.

THERMOGRAPHY

Also known as raised printing, thermography costs less than engraving, can be produced more quickly and, to the untrained consumer, looks and feels similar.

Thermography is a four-stage process that begins with offset printing using ink that dries slowly. Printed sheets exit from the press onto a conveyor belt taking them through the next three stages. First, sheets are sprayed with a fine resin powder. Powder sticks to the wet ink. Second, a vacuum unit collects all powder not adhering to ink. Third, a heating unit melts the remaining powder into the ink. The powder swells as it melts, so the printing rises above the surface of the paper.

Powder used for thermography may be fine, medium or coarse. The choice of powder depends on the image being thermographed. Very little powder can adhere to the wet ink of fine lines and small dots, but larger type and solids hold powder easily. Medium powder works well in most situations, but fine lines require fine powder for best results.

Thermography powder takes on the color of the underlying ink, but may not match perfectly. If your job needs precise color match, experiment with inks and papers before beginning production.

How much rise a thermographed image has depends on how much powder adheres to its ink when wet. Control over inks, powders and heat also determines whether the outcome looks uniformly glossy or has a stippled, orange-peel effect.

Thermographed images may scratch. Abrasion is no problem with lightly handled products, such as announcements, but can make images on catalog covers appear dull after heavy use. And thermography doesn't stand up well to heat, such as from laser printers. The powder may melt, losing its rise and luster.

Although thermography is used mainly for business cards, invitations and letterheads, the method is applicable to many other products. You could use thermography on the covers of booklets and directories, on greeting cards of all

" Scheduling used to be the most difficult topic I dealt with. People in marketing just could not accept how long it really took to plan and produce printed materials. Now we produce all our materials on-demand using digital presses. Nobody calls me the last minute witch woman anymore. "

kinds and on small fliers and posters. But avoid thermography across folds, where it can crack, and in large solids, where it can blister.

Thermography can use several ink colors and even works with screen tints having coarse rulings. The melting powder may, however, plug up finely ruled tints and fine lines in reverses. ∎

9. FINISHING AND BINDING

To keep up-to-date about finishing and binding, visit our Web site (www.gettingitprinted.com).

After printing, most jobs require more work to convert them into the final product. Products may need images created by die cutting, embossing or foil stamping. Large sheets may need cutting into individual pieces or folding to become parts of books. Printed sheets may need drilling, punching, stitching or some combination of a dozen possible ending steps.

Printers lump everything that happens to paper after actual printing under the general category of bindery work. The category includes a process as simple as letterfolding fliers and as complicated as case binding books.

Bindery operations take place in binderies that are either departments of a print shop or separate businesses. When they are separate businesses, they are known as trade binderies and are listed in classified directories under "Binderies" or "Bookbinderies." In addition to having all the basic equipment, many trade binderies offer less common services, such as tab sealing and calendar tinning.

Binderies may have only a few machines in a back room or be multimillion dollar plants handling truckloads of printing per day. Large trade binderies serve printers throughout their region, and printers send many jobs to a trade bindery instead of operating their own bindery departments. When complicated work goes to a trade bindery, it pays to consult directly with its staff as well as with the printer who sends it.

Mistakes in the bindery can prove disastrous. A short trim or crooked fold can ruin a job that has been expertly managed and produced from design through preparation and presswork. It is imperative to take bindery needs into account while planning the job.

Machines that perform bindery operations are the least accurate of graphic arts equipment. Even an average press can register to .010 inch. In contrast, folding, trimming and binding are seldom done to tolerances greater than 1/32 of an inch. Good design includes a clear understanding of what happens to the job in the bindery.

Bindery operations are also relatively slow compared to speeds in prepress and on press. For that reason, bindery may threaten a tight schedule, especially with short-run jobs. Learning about finishing and binding helps you prevent bindery from becoming a bottleneck.

In this chapter, you learn about common finishing and binding operations and the implications of decisions about packaging, final counts, shipping and storage.

IMAGING IN BINDERY

When paper moves from pressroom to bindery, it often requires additional imaging before cutting, folding or binding. Machines in binderies create images by cutting shapes (die cutting), pressing shapes (embossing) and covering shapes with foils (foil-stamping) and labels (holography).

Die cutting

Letterpresses can cut paper using thin metal strips embedded in wood. The dies are pressed into the paper to cut the desired shape, just as a cookie cutter produces shapes from dough. Die cutting can make irregular shapes, such as pocket flaps on presentation folders, and large holes, such as in door hangers.

Printers use die cutting to produce decals and labels, and outlines with tabs and slots that fold into packaging. Often they keep a supply of standard dies for common items, such as door hangers and table tents. Custom dies, however, require using special tools and skills.

Dies are made from metal strips soft enough to bend into desired shapes. After being shaped and sharpened, strips are pressed into grooves

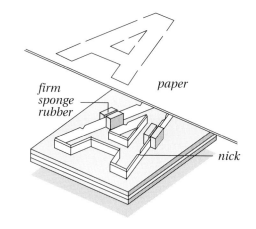

9-1 Die cutting Die makers use thin metal strips with sharp edges to make dies for cutting. After shaping the strips into patterns, they mount them on a wooden base. A press forces the cutting edge into paper. After cutting, rubber pads push the paper away from the die, allowing the sheet to continue through the press.

in wooden blocks. The metal strips, called rules, are higher than the wooden backings, creating cutting edges. Dies are heat tempered to withstand the pressure on press.

Metal rules for scoring and perforating can also be mounted into wood. In fact, the three functions—scoring, perforating and die cutting—can all take place in one impression.

Because die cutting is a press operation, it costs about the same as running one ink color. Costs depend on complexity of the die and length of the run. To reduce waste and keep the process simple, avoid intricate shapes. Also avoid too many cuts that can weaken the overall sheet.

Kiss die cutting. Labels and decals are made by kiss die cutting on a letterpress or, for longer runs, on a flexographic press. Cuts are made through the printed paper, but not through the release paper on which the label is mounted. Sheets of peel-off address labels are examples of kiss die cutting.

Complicated shapes not practical to cut using metal dies may be cut using lasers because pinpoints of laser light can burn away paper in intricate patterns. To locate a laser die-cutting service, inquire at a trade bindery or at a company that produces products such as place mats.

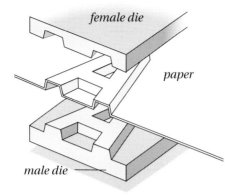

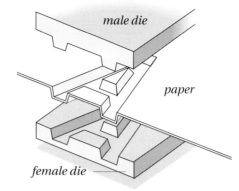

9-2 Embossing and debossing *Embossing and debossing each require two matched dies, one of which is heated. Pressing paper between the dies creates the image. The techniques give* *best results on text and uncoated cover papers and not very good results on coated papers.*

Embossing and debossing

Embossing and debossing take printing into a third dimension: depth. Paper is pressed between two molds, called a die, that sculpt its fibers by as much as ⅛ of an inch. Printers use the process for stationery, presentation folders and covers for books and annual reports.

Images higher than the rest of the paper are embossed; images lower are debossed. Both are produced under heat to assure fine detail. Heat also makes the images smooth and shiny.

Embossing and debossing have identical requirements for type and graphics, skills in die making and press operations, and have similar considerations for paper.

Embossed impressions made without having to register over a previously printed image are said to be blind embossed. Blind impressions cost less than impressions over ink because press operators don't have to register dies precisely.

Dies are made from either magnesium or brass. Magnesium is easy to engrave using chemical processes, so it can be made into dies photographically from camera-ready mechanicals. Engravers cut brass embossing dies by hand.

Some printers do multilevel embossing. Chemicals etch dies in stages, each deeper than the last, to achieve a layered effect. Diemakers also make multilevel dies by hand. The craft is complicated because the design being cut is

backward, yielding a right-reading image when embossed or debossed.

Regardless of how embossing dies are made, designs should not call for lines so fine that paper doesn't press into them. Deep dies need beveled edges to avoid cutting the paper. And beveled edges optically reduce the size of images, so prepare original art slightly oversized.

Soft paper, such as felt text, takes impressions more easily than hard paper, such as laid bond, and textures may become smooth under pressure. Most customers using heavily textured paper view smoothness as an advantage because of its contrast with the surrounding texture. Ask experienced embossers for their advice before specifying paper and the depth of dies.

Foil stamping

In foil stamping, hot dies with raised images press a thin plastic film carrying colored pigments against the paper. The pigments transfer from backing film to paper, bonding under heat and pressure. Printers use the process for presentation folders and covers for books and annual reports.

Any product that can stand up under heat and pressure can be foil stamped. Designers use it on pencils, toys and picture frames as well as on paper products. Foil adheres especially well to the cloth on case-bound books.

Foil stamping is done on letterpresses. The

size of the foil image is limited only by the size of the roll of foil and the intense pressure required to transfer the image. Operators suggest keeping the image area of one impression within 8 square inches.

Foil comes in over two hundred colors and patterns. The most common colors are bright metallics that take advantage of foil's shine, but foil is also available in dull, pastel, clear, matte and patterns, such as wood grain and cobblestone.

Images that are foil stamped are so opaque that they completely cover any underlying color. For example, white foil stamped onto dark paper prints sharp and dense, whereas white ink for the same image might require two or even three impressions.

Because most foil is opaque, offset printers don't have to reverse out areas in halftones or solids that the foil covers. Foil, however, may blister when applied over inks or varnishes containing silicones or waxes. Also when applied over coated paper. The blisters come from trapped gas released by heat. Gas trapping can also occur if the image area of foil is too large.

When designing for foil stamping, allow adequate space between letters or lines or the foil may not pull away from nonimage areas. How much space is needed depends on the material being stamped.

Foil stretches, so foil stamping mixes well with embossing for dramatic results. The process is called foil embossing—foil applied first, then embossed—and looks best on high-grade text, cover and bond papers. Foil embossing is appropriate for portfolio covers and annual reports as well as letterheads. Successful foil embossing demands the right blend of paper, design and printer. Get advice and samples before going ahead.

Holography
Holograms offer three-dimensional visual impact that no other form of printing can. You see holographic images on book covers, credit cards, sports trading cards and labels for compact discs and beverages.

Holograms can originate from the same variety of artwork as used for other forms of printing or from photos made with special laser lighting. Starting with conventional art, the three-dimensional effect is simulated by dividing the image into layers. Laser-lit photos have the third dimension embedded in the original image. In either case, image size should not exceed approximately 7″ × 8″.

Preparing a holographic plate, called a shim, involves lasers that etch the image onto a metal surface. The laser beams scribe lines one millionth of an inch apart. These microlines refract light, giving the image depth. Refraction also breaks the light into colors in the same way as a prism.

After making the shim, operators mount it on a press that uses a thin sheet of plastic as a substrate. Images are transferred when the plate presses into the plastic, a process called holographic embossing. The plastic holds the hologram as an embossed image.

After image transfer, the hologram is combined with other elements to become peel-off labels, laminating film or material for foil stamping, depending on the printing method used for other parts of the job.

Holography is a highly specialized process performed by only a handful of creative services and printers. To locate one, ask the production manager for a printed product that includes a hologram or call Printing Industries of America.

Costs and availability
Die cutting, foil stamping, engraving, embossing and thermography are all options to dress up

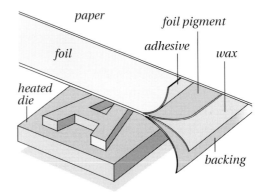

9-3 Foil stamping *A heated die sticks foil to paper in the shape of its raised image. For best results, avoid designs with fine lines and intricate shapes.*

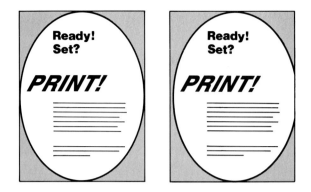

9-4 Trimming *Good design takes into account the relative lack of precision of bindery equipment. A trim only slightly off ruins the above design. Consult Visual 7-8 for reasonable trim tolerances for the quality level of your job.*

products. The first four of these processes require dies. Single-level dies cost about the same regardless of how they print. Dies cost more as they get more complex. Thermography doesn't require a die, thus takes less time and money to get on press.

Despite the virtually equal cost of making dies, engraving costs almost twice as much as embossing and about 75 percent more than foil stamping. The difference lies in press make-ready and running times. Engraving presses may run as slowly as one thousand pieces an hour.

Presses used for foil stamping set up relatively quickly. Operators simply install the dies and rolls of foil; there's no ink to wash up. Once ready, letterpresses with foil run at moderate speeds of about two thousand impressions an hour—slow compared to other printing methods but twice as fast as engraving. Embossing goes even faster than stamping once dies are on press. There's no ink to let dry and no foil to keep adjusted. A job that takes two hours of press time for engraving and one hour for foil stamping might take about forty-five minutes for embossing.

Many trade binderies do foil stamping, embossing and die cutting, but the dies themselves are most likely made by independent diemakers. Engraving and thermography are usually services performed at dedicated companies.

Because die cutting, embossing, engraving, foil stamping and thermography are so often coupled with offset printing, they are frequently subcontracted by the lithographer. In many cases, it's easier and may not cost any more simply to let the offset printer buy out the additional work.

Classified directories help you locate printers able to use most of the methods described in the last few pages. Engravers are listed separately as "Engravers—Metal." If you need a thermographer, ask a printer or trade bindery to refer you. Another option is to look for display ads for raised printing in the general "Printers" section of a classified directory.

CUTTING AND TRIMMING

Most press runs use paper slightly larger than the finished piece or print several items on one large sheet. Waste must be cut away and items cut apart from each other.

All straight line cuts are called trims. Job specifications should include trim size as exact measurements of the final product, and mechanicals, whether paper or electronic, should include trim marks. The trim size of this book is 8½″ × 11″.

Printers usually have a paper cutter at least large enough to handle sheets from the largest press in the shop. Cutters all work on the same principle: With the paper held tightly under pressure to assure an even cut, a guillotine blade slices down and across, cutting anywhere from one sheet to a stack three inches thick.

Some slight variations in trim size are inevitable, but not ragged edges or cuts that are out of square. The ragged look comes from dull blades or stacks not held under sufficient pressure. Jobs out of square are simply sloppy work.

The stack of paper on a cutter is known as a lift. Although the lift is held under pressure during cutting, some movement of the sheets is inevitable. The movement is called draw and leads to variations in trim size within the stack. Draw is held to a minimum by keeping blades sharp and lifts small. If specifications on mechanicals are clear, production trims should conform to the tolerances shown in Visual 7-8.

Printed sheets that are trimmed before their ink is completely dry may smear or offset while in the cutter. Your printer should insist on ample drying time, depending on ink coverage and type of paper, and warn you if your schedule is too rushed.

Round cornering is a variation on trimming available at most trade binderies. The process itself is fairly slow and may require extra production time. Corners may be cut in a variety of standard sizes specified in radius from edge to edge. Round cornering prevents items such as membership cards from becoming dog-eared.

DRILLING AND PUNCHING

Drilling holes for ring or post binding is as common and easy as trimming and almost as easy to specify. Hole diameters between ⅛″ and ¼″ are commonly available. State what size holes you want and how far they should be from each other and the edge of the paper. Better yet, give your printer an example of the binder the sheets must fit. Your printer may know sizes for a standard three-ring binder but may not understand drilling for five-ring binders or other less familiar formats.

Holes that are not round or are too small to die cut must be punched. Punching for binding methods such as plastic combs and wire spirals costs quite a bit more than simple drilling.

Some binderies have equipment to reinforce holes in sheets that must stand up to hard use. Round holes can have protective metal eyelets. As an alternative, areas of the sheet to be punched or drilled can first be reinforced with mylar strips. Binderies can also lay strips of Mylar or other plastic along the tabs of file folders and binder dividers.

It's easy to forget about drilling and punching during design. Do not start copy so close to an edge that holes pierce headlines or puncture borders. Avoid problems by giving the printer a drilled or punched dummy that shows exact placement. Specify sizes in fractions of inches. If the size or shape of the holes you need has a name unique to your industry, verify that your printer knows the correct pattern.

SCORING AND PERFORATING

Scoring means to crease a printed piece so that it folds more easily. The procedure is necessary whenever paper thicker than .005 inches folds by machine or when sheets need precise folding.

Scoring is done by equipment that presses paper against the metal edge of either a rule or a wheel. Coated stock, especially if printed with large solids of a dark color, may require the softer touch of string scoring to assure that paper doesn't appear cracked.

Perforating is simply punching a line of holes to make tearing easier. Most bindery machines can perforate in only one direction and only in straight lines. Perforating in more than one direction or in curved lines is normally done on press.

Specify scores and perforations on mechanicals by drawing a black line similar to a trim

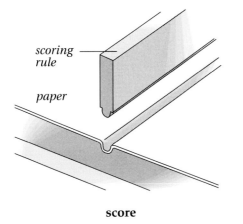

score

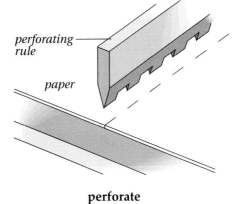

perforate

9-5 Scoring and perforating *Binderies should score thick paper before folding, especially if it's coated stock, has heavy* ink coverage across the fold or must fold against the grain.

mark outside image areas. Label the line "score here" or "perforate here."

Scoring and perforating can each be done on offset and letterpresses as well as specialized bindery equipment. When done as part of offset printing, they require attaching metal strips to the impression cylinder. The procedure saves time on long runs because it happens simultaneously with printing, but it ruins blankets (cost charged to you) and may adversely affect printing.

When done on a letterpress, scoring and perforating can be done simultaneously with printing or die cutting.

FOLDING

The number of ways paper can fold seems endless. Most printers have equipment to make common folds using sheets as large as their largest presses. Trade binderies typically have machines with six or eight folding stations to accommodate complicated work.

Folding is not precise. Most folding machines can work within a tolerance of ⅟32 inch per fold, but even that is not close enough for perfect crossovers. Plan your design to allow for tiny variations in folds just as you would for variations in trims.

On a large sheet that must fold several times, the accuracy of the first fold affects all subsequent folds. A ⅟32″ variation on the first fold may shift the second fold ⅟16″ and the third ⅛″. Even the thickness of the paper causes a variation. Rollover folds, for example, require that panel widths increase by at least ⅟16 of an inch each as they move from inside panels to outside. To plan accurately for folds, make a dummy folded from paper specified for your job.

Folding requires careful design. Poor positioning of copy means products may not read correctly when folded or a fold might run through important visuals.

Paper less than 50# may be difficult to feed into the folder and may wrinkle going through; paper more than 80#, especially coated stock, often needs scoring before folding. Designing for printing on medium and heavy stock should anticipate folding by assuring that most folds run with the grain of the paper. Folding with the grain is especially important with gate and accordion folds.

Signatures created from three, four or more folds may develop a gusset wrinkle, a crease running down from the head of the signature. Gusset wrinkles are especially likely to occur with thick papers or when several sheets are folded at once. When they run into the image area, gusset wrinkles distract readers and may be a symptom of weak binding.

Although folding in a specific style may be easy for the bindery, it may lead to problems elsewhere. For example, machines that stuff envelopes for mass mailings may not handle items with accordion folds.

Grain direction. Paper folds better with the grain than against it. When designing multiple folds, plan the final fold grain long so your piece lies flat and opens easily.

Grain direction affects binding as well as folding. Signatures in perfect-bound books often pucker at the spine and develop waves at the face when bound grain short.

COLLATING

Almost everyone has made endless trips around a table to assemble sheets for a book or report. Even for a printer or bindery, hand-collating sometimes works best for small jobs.

Collating can be done automatically by equipment that holds stacks of sheets in pockets and then presents one sheet from each pocket for assembly. Machines have highly specific tolerances and capabilities. For example, they have a specific number of pockets, such as thirty-two or forty. If your job has more sheets than pockets on the machine, collating requires additional runs. Paper weight is also a factor. Machines may miss sheets that are too thick or glossy and wrinkle sheets that are too thin.

Products such as cookbooks with mechanical bindings (comb or wire) look like assemblies of loose pages, but in fact were probably printed and folded into signatures having several pages on each large sheet. After folding, the sheets

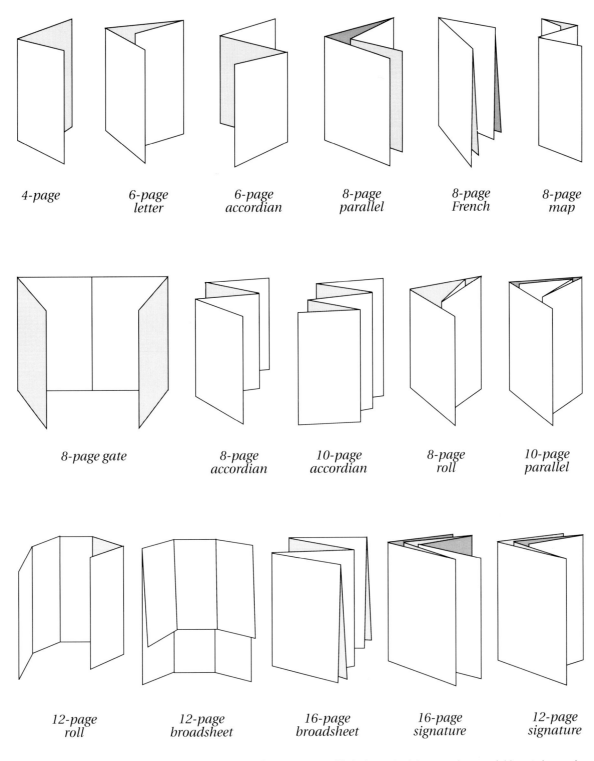

4-page

6-page
letter

6-page
accordian

8-page
parallel

8-page
French

8-page
map

8-page gate

8-page
accordian

10-page
accordian

8-page
roll

10-page
parallel

12-page
roll

12-page
broadsheet

16-page
broadsheet

16-page
signature

12-page
signature

9-6 Common folds *Referring to folds by their standard names helps you communicate clearly. But provide a folding dummy as well. A folding dummy also helps you find a vendor able to produce your product quickly and within budget.*

Binderies and printers can do many folds not shown above, although they may have problems with especially light or heavy paper.

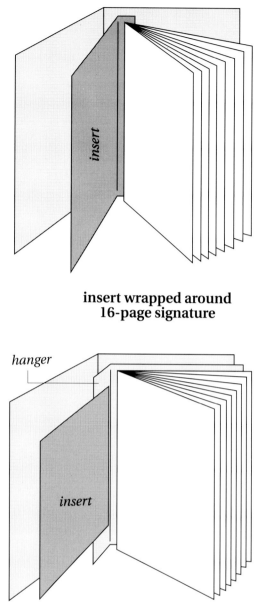

**insert wrapped around
16-page signature**

hanger

insert

insert tipped onto hanger

9-7 Inserts *A bindery can wrap an insert around a signature or tip it onto a hanger page. The insert can appear at any place in the publication with a break between signatures. This illustration shows inserts for saddle stitching, but you could plan inserts for any binding method. Keep in mind that each insert requires its own pocket in the bindery line.*

were trimmed on four sides to cut away folds and leave a pile of collated, individual pages.

Signatures for publications must be collated so that, after they are trimmed, pages are in proper sequence. Nested signatures go inside of each other for saddle stitching. Gathered signatures go on top of each other for binding with square spines. Nesting and gathering, shown in Visual 9-8, take place on highly automated equipment that may also bind and trim in one operation.

Equipment for nesting and gathering holds signatures in pockets, taking one signature from each pocket to assemble one copy of the publication. Machines have a specific number of pockets, such as twelve or sixteen. Each unit of a publication, including order forms or inserts that might be two- or four-page signatures, occupies a pocket. Part of the charge for binding depends on how many pockets the publication requires.

Printers specializing in publications produced on web presses may print, fold, trim and bind all in one machine sequence. Unit costs can be far lower than when working with printers who must set up new equipment for each stage of the job or who must send jobs to trade binderies.

LAMINATING

The toughest coatings cover paper with a thin layer of polyester applied on one side or both sides. Laminating is a relatively simple operation available from many binderies and special services. Although slow and costly, it yields an exceptionally strong surface that is also washable.

Laminates are available in thicknesses from .001 inch to .010 inch and with either gloss or dull finishes. Specify thinner films on products such as book jackets and counter displays and thicker films on products such as menus and name tags.

Some film used for lamination prevents moisture from reaching or leaving the underlying paper. The product can curl when atmospheric conditions are different from those present during manufacture. To prevent curling, ask for porous laminating film made to lie flat.

ADHESIVE BINDINGS

There are several ways to glue loose sheets, folded sheets or signatures to each other. Each

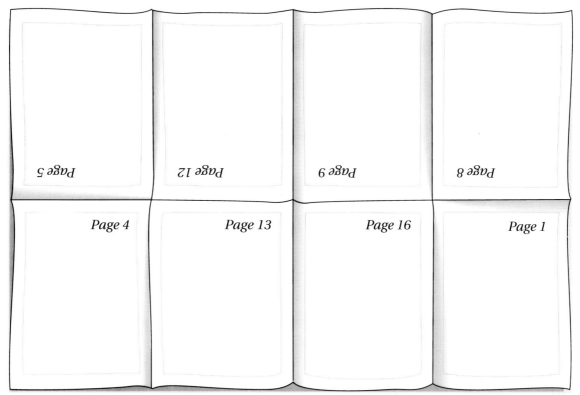

This press sheet with 8 pages printed on each side is a 16-page signature. Other common signature sizes are 4 pages, 8 pages, 12 pages, 24 pages, and 32 pages.

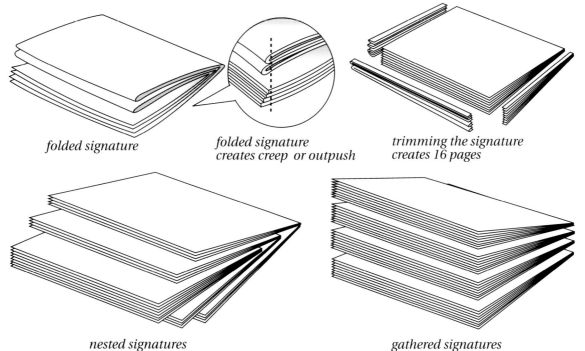

folded signature

folded signature creates creep or outpush

trimming the signature creates 16 pages

nested signatures

gathered signatures

9-8 Signatures Prepress must plan press sheets that fold into signatures so that pages appear in correct sequence after folding and collating. Saddle stitching calls for nested signatures. Bindings with squared spines, such as perfect binding and case binding, require gathered signatures. Binding method influences imposition as much as folding sequence and sheet size. The concept of imposition is further illustrated in Visual 5-5.

The effects of creep are most apparent with thick paper, many folds, or many signatures nested into each other. Folding and binding dummies made from the paper that you plan for the job reveal whether the product has too much creep.

method offers a different mix of aesthetics, permanence, convenience and cost.

Padding

Almost every printer can make pads from stacks of loose sheets, the most simple binding operation. For most printers it's a hand operation with brush and glue pot.

Gluing

Binderies and envelope makers can apply adhesives in strips for individual sealing by the user. They are available as either remoistenable glue or a sticky surface protected by peel-off paper.

Remoistenable glue strips cost little to apply and can be wet and sealed by machinery when necessary. Peel-off strips are handy for large envelopes and products to assemble by hand.

Tipping

When one sheet is glued to another sheet or to a signature, it's referred to as tipping. Most trade binderies have machines that do tipping.

Inserts, such as maps or special advertising sections, are often tipped onto an adjacent signature. Visual 9-7 shows a typical example.

Sealing

Often binderies have machines for sealing folded items ready to mail. Binderies that do tab sealing apply an adhesive circle or short strip of tape to the face of a booklet or self-mailer. Tab sealing is relatively inexpensive and helps products go through the mail in good condition.

Paste binding

Booklets with just a few pages of paper less than 80# can be paste bound as an alternative to saddle stitching. With paste binding, a web press or folder lays thin strips of glue along fold lines. When the sheet is folded, glued creases meet glued folds to form the bond. After trimming, glue along the creased spine is the only binding. Some photocopiers paste bind in line by laying glue along the edge of single sheets, adhering them as they fall on top of each other.

Paste binding is much more economical than

stitching for booklets of eight, twelve or sixteen pages. The upper limit for the number of paste-bound pages depends on bulk of paper and capabilities of press or folder. High-bulk paper may be too thick to paste bind more than sixteen pages.

Perfect binding

Perfect-bound books are made from gathered signatures. The left side of the stack, the spine, is trimmed to get rid of the folds and expose the edge of each page. The stack is then roughened and notched along the spine to assure maximum surface for glue adhesion.

The familiar paperback book is perfect-bound. So are most annual reports and technical manuals and many magazines, such as *Reader's Digest*.

Glue for perfect binding is applied along the spine. When the cover is pressed against the surface wet with glue, it adheres to the pad as well as forces some glue between the sheets. After the glue is dry, the assembled book is trimmed on the remaining three sides.

Perfect binding works for publications with a wide range of thicknesses and trim sizes. Paper should be not more than 80# and—very important—should run grain parallel to the spine. Grain short bindings are weaker than grain long bindings, and pages may become wavy along the face as they absorb moisture.

The glue for perfect binding should be even, free from lumps and not forced too deeply between the sheets. Glues used for perfect binding must remain flexible when dry, allowing books to open easily and without cracking. Some printers caution against perfect binding coated cover papers because coatings prevent glues from adhering strongly to fibers. If you're concerned about adhesion to coated cover stock, specify C1S cover grade so that the uncoated side may face inward.

Binderies that do burst perfect binding make slits along the spines of signatures so glue is forced toward the inside pages. Burst perfect signatures look similar to sewn signatures because they are not trimmed and roughened along

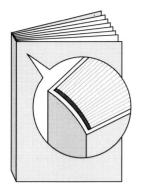
perfect

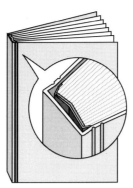
lie flat perfect

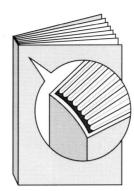
burst perfect

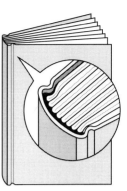
case

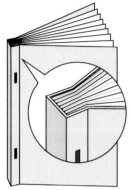
side stitch

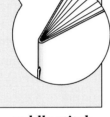
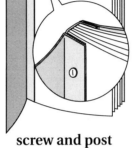
saddle stitch

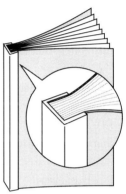
screw and post

plastic grip

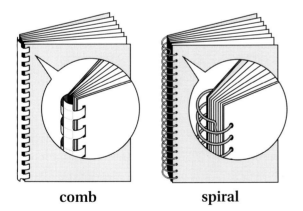
comb

spiral

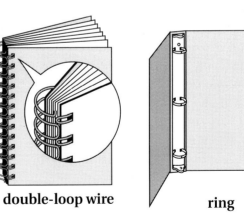
double-loop wire

ring

9-9 Common binding methods *These twelve binding methods are commonly available at binderies and from printing companies. Each has pros and cons, depending on page count, kind of paper and how readers use your product.*

the spine. They are almost as strong as sewn signatures and cost much less.

Paper covers may also be glued over sewn signatures, a cross between perfect and case binding that yields a very strong and—compared to case binding—inexpensive product.

Lay-flat binding

The cover of a perfect-bound book attaches to the spine across its full width. The spine is stiff and the book doesn't lie flat. When the cover attaches only at the corners of the spine and is loose across its width, as shown in Visual 9-9, the book can lie fully open.

Lay-flat binding is an alternative to mechanical binding for technical manuals, music books, cookbooks and directories. It costs more than perfect binding but less than comb or wire and isn't as durable or versatile. Paper weights and coatings are limited for both cover and text and paper must run grain long to the spine. As with perfect binding, coated papers can be bound lay-flat by sewing signatures before gluing.

The key to successful lay-flat binding lies in water-based glue, also known as cold or polyurethane reactive (PUR) glue, that stays flexible for the life of the product. As an additional advantage, cold glues aid recycling because pulp mills can separate them easily from paper. Cold glues do require special machinery and twenty-four hours to cure, so production schedules should take additional costs and curing times into account.

Hot glue bonds mechanically with the fibers in paper, but PUR glue bonds chemically. For that reason, some binderies will perfect bind books printed on coated stock for customers willing to pay the premium for PUR glue.

MECHANICAL BINDINGS

There are several ways to attach loose sheets, folded sheets or signatures to each other using plastic or metal. As with adhesive bindings, each method offers a different mix of aesthetics, permanence, convenience and cost.

Stitching

Stitch bindings are done with wire staples either through the crease of the spine or near one edge of the sheets.

Saddle stitching. This means staples go through the crease of the spine, as shown in Visual 9-9, allowing pages to lie nearly flat. Most magazines are saddle stitched. So are many brochures, catalogs, presentation folders and calendars. The method is fast and inexpensive but does not yield a flat outer spine that can show printing.

Any product up to about twenty sheets (eighty pages at four pages per sheet) of 60# or 70# paper lends itself to saddle stitching. How well the stitching holds depends on thickness of the sheets and length of the staples. Products having more than about twenty sheets (eighty pages) or thicker than ⅜″ need some other kind of binding.

Saddle stitched products can easily accommodate special inserts, such as envelopes, membership forms or order blanks. Such inserts must fold into signatures and have a binding lip. Saddle stitching also accommodates a wide range of paper weights and surfaces.

Because of the bulkiness of paper, saddle stitched products printed on heavy stock and/or using many pages need to allow for the effects of creep, especially when the products have narrow outside margins. Pages must be shingled to take creep into account to assure equal margins throughout the printed piece. Shingling may be more trouble than it's worth if readers hardly notice slight variations in the margins. Make an untrimmed paper dummy to show whether and how much to shingle pages.

Loop stitching. This is a variant of saddle stitching where each staple has enough play outside the crease to go over the rings of a ring binder. The method is an alternative to drilling for catalogs that insert into ring binders.

Side stitching. This puts staples through an entire stack of sheets near its edge. The method results in a strong bind but means pages do not lie flat. Staples use some margin, so plan copy to start well in from the edge. Heavy-duty equipment can side stitch products up to an inch and a half thick, but the result may look and feel cumbersome.

Stacks of paper that have been side stitched can have a wraparound cover applied with glue, thereby yielding a square spine on which to print copy.

Comb and wire

Cookbooks and technical manuals needing to lie flat when open can be bound with plastic or wire shaped into either a spiral or comb, as shown in Visual 9-9. Two of these bindings are commonly referred to by the brand names GBC (plastic comb) and Wire-O (double-loop wire).

Mechanical bindings cost more per unit than other binding methods except case. Spiral binding costs least and double wire the most, with plastic comb somewhere in the middle. The cost differences among all forms of mechanical bindings are not very large, and cost relationships change with high quantities.

The most important differences among mechanical bindings concern how they function. Spirals may be either plastic or wire. They allow the product not merely to lie flat but to double over, a useful feature for technical manuals, notebooks and calendars. Spiral-bound products have lots of play between individual pages and cannot have pages added to them. Furthermore, the spirals may get crushed.

Comb bindings. These are less subject to damage than spirals and allow for less play in the pages. They are relatively easy to install, thus can be done at many small printers and in-plant shops. Plastic combs come in a variety of colors and can be screen printed on the spine. They bend open to insert additional pages in the product. Combs have the greatest thickness capacity of any mechanical bindings, some allowing for products up to 3 inches thick.

Plastic comb bindings have the disadvantage that products bound with them don't bend past the point of lying flat. Combs are inserted by hand, which makes them advantageous for just

a few products and rather costly for large quantities. Unit costs do not drop very rapidly as quantities increase.

Double loops of wire. This binding allows the product to lie open doubled over but, unlike spirals, keep the pages lined up across from each other. They are durable, come in several colors and give a more finished look than spirals.

Double-loop bindings have the disadvantages of not allowing for insertion of new pages and having a maximum capacity of about 1 inch. They cannot be printed on the spine but can be casebound, yielding a handsome (and expensive) book. Most trade binderies can insert double wire, but not many printers can.

Other mechanical bindings

Tinning refers to clamping metal strips along the tops or bottoms of calendars. Although tinning machines are simple, binderies that have them are hard to find. Begin by asking your printer.

Screw-and-post binding. Sometimes known as Chicago screw, this works similar to side stitching and has similar design considerations. Users can, however, take the product apart by removing screws from posts, allowing them to insert additional sheets.

Screws and posts are available in many lengths, from ¼" to 3". The binding accommodates a wide range and variety of materials but, because it's a hand operation, is appropriate only for relatively short runs.

Plastic grip bindings. These are applied by quick and in-plant printers to relatively thin reports and presentations. Some styles are removable; others are permanent. Materials are inexpensive and easy to assemble.

....

66 *My printer puts an 'Open last' label on one box of every job. Inside that box is a slip with the job number, date and quantity of last printing. Our stock clerk sends me the slip and I just call the printer to reorder. We never run out and the printer automatically gets repeat business.* **99**

9-10 QUALITY IN FINISHING AND BINDING

Before paying for a printing job, pull at least twenty production samples at random. With small jobs, check when you receive delivery. With larger jobs, complete your inspection within ten days. Tell your printer or bindery about any problems within two weeks of delivery. Check the following features:

- trims with 90° corners square with copy
- drills, punches, scores, perforations and folds per specifications (See Visual 7-8 for tolerances)
- folds square with copy and free from gusset wrinkles
- no printer makeready or unacceptable signatures included
- pages in correct sequence and no missing pages
- bound pages run grain parallel to the spine
- covers bound and trimmed square with insides
- binding that withstands reasonable pull testing
- number of products in shipment conforms to number claimed in manifest and invoice and on boxes
- products don't stick together or show signs of abuse by machinery
- cartons within the shipment the same size, weight and quantity per carton— carton weight per your specifications
- no more than one partial carton per shipment
- every carton identified with title or job name of contents, quantity and other information per your specifications.

Ring binders. These come with solid or padded covers, pockets inside or out, and a variety of ring shapes, sizes and configurations. If you have material drilled for a ring binder, make sure that operators doing the drilling have a sample of the binder. Because binders are printed after manufacture and usually in small lots, they are screen printed and provided to a printer or bindery by an outside vendor. You can cut costs by buying ring binders directly from a supplier listed in a classified directory under "Binders— Loose-Leaf."

Mechanical bindings allow for unlimited use of inserts, foldouts and pockets. Like side stitching, they require generous margins at the binding edge. Make sure your layout allows at least ¼″ for no image along the binding.

CASE BINDING

Nothing beats case binding for durability, good looks or high cost. The method, illustrated in Visuals 9-9 and 9-11 and also known as edition binding, results in the hardbound book.

Case binding begins with sewing signatures along the spine. Thread makes a stronger and more elegant adhesive than glue. Because the machine most commonly used for sewing signatures is made by Smythe, most signatures are Smythe sewn. There are, however, other patterns of sewing, such as saddle, cleat and McCain. If your book is for a market that has technical production specifications, such as school textbooks, check into what kind of sewing is required.

After signatures are sewn, they are gathered and trimmed on three sides. The stack is put inside a case made of binders board covered with paper, cloth, plastic or leather. The case is held to the signatures by glue along the spine and between end sheets.

To cut costs, some publishers skip the sewing by inserting perfect-bound or burst-perfect-bound forms into cases. Case binding can also mix with other techniques, such as comb wire and side stitching.

Printers and trade binderies who specialize in books customarily offer case binding. Most large cities have a small bindery specializing in

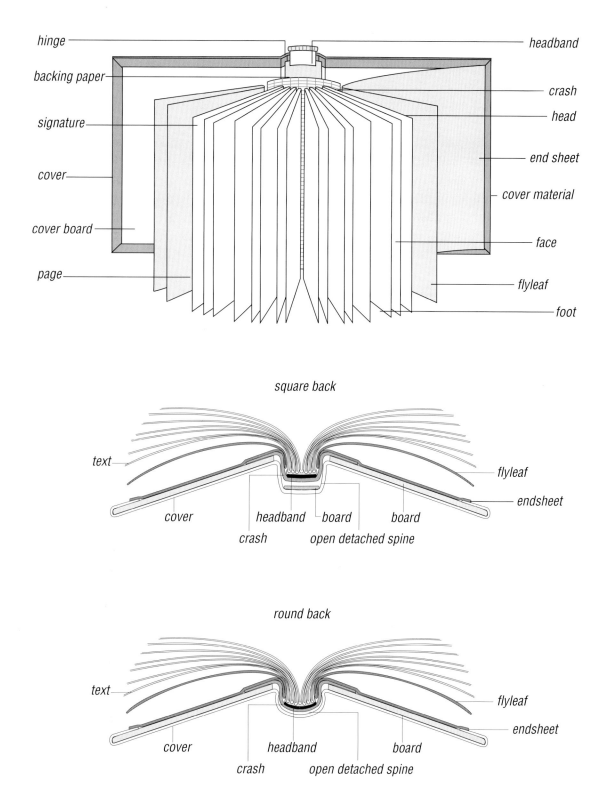

hinge

backing paper

signature

cover

cover board

page

headband

crash

head

end sheet

cover material

face

flyleaf

foot

square back

text

flyleaf

endsheet

cover   headband   board   board

crash   open detached spine

round back

text

flyleaf

endsheet

cover   headband   board

crash   open detached spine

9-11 Case binding Case-bound books can have covers made from many materials such as leather, buckram cloth, woven cloth and synthetic paper. Each material comes in a variety of patterns and grades. Binderies can case bind with round or square backs. Which material and style you prefer depends on your taste and budget.

Because of the large variety of materials and techniques available, case binding requires planning months ahead of production. Consult with both your printer and your bindery to assure that printing and coating harmonize with binding.

short runs, book restoration and presentation volumes involving handcrafted case bindings. Leather coverings and handmade end papers yield lavish books at equally lavish prices.

Because case binding combines so many components, writing specifications is complicated. You must decide about end sheets, square or round backs, amount and quality of binding, headbands, cover material and dust jackets. Sales representatives at trade binderies help you decide. You would also benefit by advice from an experienced book publisher.

SELECTIVE BINDING

Regardless of what binding method you use, you can bind versions of a product custom made for specific audiences. For example, you could produce one version of a clothing catalog for cold climates and another for mild climates. Or one version showing red coats and another showing the same coats in blue. Or ten versions with different covers and order forms but having identical page copy.

Selective binding allows versions of a product tailored to demographic factors, such as age, income, education and job title—any variable you can identify in a database. National magazines use selective binding to present a different mix of display ads to different audiences all reading the same editioral matter. Some even present different editorial matter. Used for this purpose,

....

" When we did our first book, we thought we did a good job of market research, but we still guessed totally wrong about what percentage of the run to perfect bind and what percentage to case bind. In less than a year we ran out of the soft cover, but had 1,300 of the hard cover still sitting in our warehouse. With every book since then, we only bind half the run. We leave the other half as flat sheets at the bindery until we learn what kind of binding the market wants for that particular title. "

selective binding is a form of target marketing.

Machines capable of selective binding link your database to their binding lines. A computer reading your database instructs the machine to skip or add a signature, insert the correct order form or apply the proper version of a cover. If your publication is destined for the mails, the database also governs the ink-jet or laser printer writing labels and personal messages.

Although selective binding permits many combinations of signatures and other elements, it cannot handle variations in trim size. Products may have different page counts but must be the same height and width.

Effective use of selective binding begins with planning and design. You need to know precisely how much flexibility of assembly you have and where the ink-jet or laser printer can write. Inserts must fall precisely at signature breaks and personalized printing occur only on pages intended to receive it. You have zero margin for error, especially with your database.

Selective binding is most popular with saddle stitched magazines and catalogs, where it can cut costs by reducing waste and speeding production. When conforming to USPS regulations for commingling, it can also reduce postage costs and speed delivery.

CONVERTING

A printed sheet changed into a substantially new product—a box, point-of-purchase display, or envelope—has been converted.

Converting companies, like binderies, work primarily with printers. Unlike binderies, however, converters tend to specialize in products such as envelopes. Further specialization occurs in the category of boxes: Some companies focus on boxes and displays made from corrugated paper while others make them from chipboard. The chipboard products are known in the trade simply as paper boxes.

When working with any trade service, experience is the key to success. If you are a graphic arts novice, you'll probably get the best quality and service by letting your printer deal with converters. As you gain experience, you benefit by dealing with converters directly.

PACKING

The method of packing the final product affects shipping and storage and may also influence effectiveness and profit. No one wants damaged goods.

Bindery operators should pack materials tightly to prevent sliding and scratching. Rubber or paper bands or shrink-wrap should go around small bundles before they are put into boxes. Specify how many items you want per bundle. Books that are not shrink-wrapped, either individually or in bundles, should have slip sheets between each book. Workers should band cartons on skids.

Many industries have special standards for shipping and storage that affect specifications to binderies. For example, buyers for many retail outlets order by the gross, so binderies should put products in boxes containing either 72 or 144 units.

If you want each box to contain a specific number of items, make that requirement clear when you specify the job. Your printer may have to order boxes to meet your requirements.

At least part of almost every printing job is stored in a warehouse, back room or bottom drawer. Packing must assure convenience and longevity. Convenience simply means in packages suitable in weight and size for people who must deal with them. Store materials flat, not standing on end. Light and moisture may affect quality during storage because ink fades and paper absorbs moisture. To avoid problems in six months or a year, discuss storage conditions thoroughly before specifying packaging.

Printers and trade binderies offer several forms of packing. Many jobs require a combination.

Bulk packing is the least expensive form of packaging, and many jobs require nothing more. Bindery workers simply load pieces into boxes. Remember that boxes of printed matter are heavy. A box containing five thousand fliers on 8½″ × 11″ coated stock can easily weigh 50

> **I don't care what downtown studio plans the job, I want to see a dummy before it goes to production. Specifications, too. I wouldn't stay in the bindery business very long if my people didn't remeasure trim and fold marks and check measurements against specs. You'd be amazed at how many designs I see for work that won't fit our machines.**

pounds. And the weight adds up. If you plan to stack six or eight boxes on top of each other, make sure the cartons are sturdy and the bottom ones full. The U.S. Postal Service, UPS and other transportation agencies have their own limits on weight and size to keep in mind when planning how you want items packaged.

Workers in bindery should put your materials in cartons that are all the same size and weight and contain the same number of printed pieces. Only one partial carton per shipment may contain less than each of the other cartons.

Shrink-wrapping is the process by which a plastic film surrounds and seals the products. You can see the items inside, but they are wrapped so tightly that they don't rub during transit and they stay dry during storage.

Shrink-wrapping is suitable for anything from fliers to books. You can have each item, such as each book, shrink-wrapped, or you can wrap bundles of items. Unless you specify some particular number, bindery workers wrap as they find convenient—perhaps a handful to each package. Shrink-wrapping also works for entire boxes and even pallets loaded with boxes. The plastic keeps material fresh during storage.

Pallets (also called skids) are standard wooden platforms used in every industry for shipping and storage. A pallet easily holds a ton of printed material packed in boxes. If you expect delivery on pallets and don't have a forklift and loading dock, ask for delivery by truck with a liftgate.

Some trade binderies can handle retail packaging styles, such as skin, bubble and blister wrap, although these techniques are more often done by specialized businesses. If your printing is part of a retail product, confirm that you know packaging requirements. Organizations such as Goodwill Industries offer inexpensive retail packaging services.

Customers often don't think much about labels and may simply get printing delivered with samples of their products taped to the outside of boxes. To make labels clear, tell your printer what information you want on the outside of boxes and packages. Bindery workers can write or stencil the information on each box, or, for larger jobs, they print peel-off labels.

FINAL COUNTS

Whether orders are for 1,000 books, 5,000 posters or 100,000 envelopes, they get counted at the end of bindery.

Controlling quantity is difficult. Printers figure enough extra paper at the beginning of the job to allow for waste along the way. If everything goes smoothly, you'll have a few more pieces than you ordered and perhaps at no extra cost. If it's essential, however, that you have no less than the number you ordered, tell your printer as part of the specifications. Trade customs allow a 10 percent variation on orders up to 10,000 pieces. To ensure you get "no less than," your printer may insist on doubling percentage tolerances for overruns.

Pay careful attention when you pick up materials or receive delivery. Trade customs and business ethics both dictate that you claim shortages promptly. The best time to notice a problem is when the job is still on the printer's counter, loading dock or truck. Take time to spot-check several boxes, then count the cartons to determine that everyone agrees on the totals.

Short counts can happen for several reasons. Perhaps the estimated ratio of waste to finished product just didn't work out. The ratio was, after all, only the printer's guess based on averages and experience. Perhaps some of your material is "lost"—still on a skid at the bindery or printer or in boxes on a truck headed for the other side of town. Perhaps there is

" We worked all weekend to finish printing those posters. The customer needed only 300, but they had to look perfect. We took extra care to spot rejects. Monday morning we shipped them via overnight delivery in plenty of time for the gallery opening. On Wednesday the customer called asking where the posters were. The fancy overnight service had lost them. All their insurance would pay was the cost of paper and ink. Not a penny for our time or, worse, our customer's lost business. We reprinted them, but of course the most likely buyers had been at the opening when there were no posters. "

a systematic error, such as boxes labeled as containing 500 really having 520.

On short counts you can either go back to press to complete the job or get a credit. From the printer's standpoint, going back to press costs far more than cutting the price. From your standpoint, the printed pieces are probably more important than the money. Don't hesitate to insist on going back to press if the additional material is crucial. If you do insist, however, don't feel surprised if that printer loses interest in you as a future customer.

STORAGE AND TRANSIT

Most printers and binderies are not in the warehouse business. When your job is finished, they want you to have it. There are, however, two exceptions. Books and similar materials require a lot of storage space and may stay in inventory a long time. Printers who specialize in these products may offer inexpensive warehouse space. The other exception is material that must be imprinted later. It makes sense to keep that inventory in your printer's warehouse.

Storage at the printer's can be convenient and

cheap, but it also requires some commonsense precautions. Check actual warehouse conditions to verify that the space is reasonably secure and free from moisture, dust and risk of fire. Double-check your insurance situation to learn who would pay for damaged or lost goods. Finally, ask about accessibility. Don't wait until next summer's convention to learn the whole print shop goes on vacation in July.

Printers send your goods wherever you like at standard shipping costs. When shipping by common carrier, the printer's shipping depart-ment probably contracts with reliable services. If in doubt, check with a couple of freight companies yourself.

You need to keep track of jobs received and put into inventory. To assure correct monitoring, you need a working relationship with storage and distributing people in your organization. Tell them when to expect the boxed products and how to handle them when delivered. Ask them to recommend how to pack the job and what procedures they want for packing slips, bills of lading and other paperwork. ■

10. WORKING WITH PRINTERS

To keep up-to-date about working with printers, visit our Web site (www.gettingitprinted.com).

Printing companies vary greatly in size, equipment, market and business goals. Intelligent print buying requires finding the right printer for each job.

To manage a variety of printing jobs, you need to know the benefits that several printers can offer. You may have two or three partnerships with printers for routine work, but you should know how to work with other printers when your regular shops are not appropriate.

Printers have niche markets in which they compete most efficiently. Working with a variety of printers assures maximum control over quality, schedule and price. To control costs, you must use clear, accurate specifications as the basis for printing contracts.

Shopping for the right printer does not mean soliciting bids for every job. On the contrary, your regular printers should represent the lowest procurement costs. Those printers should know your needs and workflow so well that you don't have to worry about nickels and dimes on each individual job. You should feel that you can rely on your key printer partnerships.

In this chapter, you learn how to locate printers suited to your jobs and develop partnerships that benefit both you and them. You discover how to cooperate with printers to achieve quality and service. You learn criteria for evaluating contracts and quotations, and for analyzing invoices.

Even with the guidelines, you often find yourself in a gray area where only experience can shape your judgment. The chapter concludes with information about trade customs and tips about how to negotiate if things go wrong.

YOUR REGULAR PRINTERS

Most printing buyers like working with only one or two printers for routine jobs. Some routine jobs, such as business forms, stationery and newsletters, are generic to every business and organization. Others, such as technical manuals, magazines or posters, are specific to your particular responsibilities.

Your regular printers should know your organization so well that you trust them to take care of your printing needs. They become part of business relationships in the graphic arts that might also include a graphic designer and a prepress service.

With any regular printer, you may save money by negotiating a quantity discount. For example, whenever your monthly invoice exceeds a specific figure, such as five thousand dollars, you might pay 2 percent less than invoice. At ten thousand dollars per month, you might pay 3 percent less.

Having regular printers helps plan jobs to take best advantage of equipment in their shops. Presses at quick printers are quite similar from one shop to the next, but it helps if you know your printer can run 12″ × 18″ paper so that 11″ × 17″ products can have bleeds. Computers are similar from shop to shop, but the operator at your shop may work magic with your favorite application.

Quick printers. A quick printer as one of your regular printers saves time and money with

---

10-1 USEFUL PRINTER WEB SITES

Many printers maintain Web sites to support customer service. Following is the kind of information that a printer's site may provide.

Company information
- contract terms and conditions
- special products and workflows
- font library and equipment lists
- prepress guidelines
- procedures for after-hours help
- staff directory
- location map and parking info
- awards and certifications (ISO, etc.)
- regulatory compliance
- investor relations

Chat rooms and bulletin boards
- service and technical staff
- other customers

Industry information
- trade customs and associations
- classes and seminars
- books, articles and videos

- glossary of terms
- planning tools (carton weights and sheet counts, ppi, etc.)
- international standards (paper sizes and weights, etc.)
- production guidelines (SWOP, GRACOL, etc.)
- links to other sites

Forms
- to submit specifications and alterations
- to receive quotes and invoices

Job status
- search: by purchase order, job or account number
- schedule: proofs, press check, delivery
- quality: densitometer and dot gain read-outs
- quantity: final counts, number per box

For links to Web sites that demonstrate many of these features, visit the site for this book (www.gettingitprinted.com).

....

basic quality, one- and two-color jobs in relatively short runs. With those jobs, the average commercial printer would take longer and have to charge more than the job is worth.

As a consistent customer of a quick printer, you should have several advantages over the walk-in trade. Ask for monthly billings rather than individual invoices. Look for special service, such as overnight printing and after-hours pickup. Expect instant notice when your job is ready or delayed.

Commercial printers. As a consistent customer of a commercial or publication printer, you may get priority press time and delivery scheduling. Staff may know your wishes with regard to packaging and delivery. You may get extended credit terms or get news about special values in paper.

Commercial and publication printers have a more complex mix of equipment than quick printers. Being a regular customer helps you learn how to plan for a press that may be a perfector, a multicolor unit or both.

Managers who buy a lot of printing use five or six printers regularly. A book publisher knows about several book printers. The marketing director for a restaurant chain needs to know about menu printers and perhaps about some screen printers for aprons and T-shirts.

Regular printers are especially convenient for reruns because the job already meets their specifications. They have computer files or flats. You can order by fax or E-mail. With routine jobs, letting the original printer do the reruns usually works out best.

Partnering. Many customers create partnerships with printers that go far beyond producing printed pieces. Partnerships emphasize service and may include anything from graphic design to shipping and storage.

Because so many printers can produce products at satisfactory quality and price, your preferences for partnership printers depends largely on service. Visual 1-6 suggests that range of services found in many partnerships.

Partnerships help streamline workflows, especially regarding prepress for routine jobs. You test and agree what applications work best and how to format and transmit files. You teach your printer what you expect regarding quality and schedule. Your printer teaches you what to expect regarding file corrections and proofs.

Customers and printers base partnerships on long-term contracts that may deal with training and cash flow in addition to printing. To learn more about partner agreements, ask for advice from a printing buyer for a magazine, catalog or book publisher in your area.

OCCASIONAL PRINTERS

You may find that your regular printers cannot do jobs such as catalog sheets or presentation folders as fast or inexpensively as some other printer.

Knowing when to consider alternatives to your regular printers requires judgments about individual jobs. You must decide whether a job is too large or small, has quality standards too high or low, or has some other aspect that makes it unsuited to one of your regular printers. For example, if you want five thousand booklets that are two-color, sixteen pages, saddle stitched and in the good quality category, your regular commercial printer is probably the best bet. If you want fifty thousand booklets that include premium quality four-color process work, it makes sense to get quotations from some other printers.

Moving beyond your regular printers requires understanding the various kinds of printers available and the kinds of work in which they specialize.

Commercial printers fall roughly into categories capable of producing small, medium and large jobs. A shop suited to small jobs has eight to fifteen employees and small presses capable of printing one or two colors at a time. The shop has simple bindery equipment and probably gets film or plates from a prepress service. You may discuss work directly with the owner or manager.

Printing companies suited to medium jobs have fifteen to twenty employees and a blend of presses giving them great flexibility in scheduling and the kinds of items they can print. Shops of this size compete with each other for business in a local area. You meet mainly with sales reps but might also deal with some of the production supervisors.

At a printer seeking volume jobs, equipment and staff handle large amounts of paper and printed goods. The shop may have fifty to one hundred or more employees and both web and sheetfed presses. Press time, especially for the webs, is scheduled weeks or months in advance. People in prepress and bindery know how to deal with complicated jobs. Some larger printing companies specialize because their web presses are configured to make specific products, such as telephone directories.

Size is a poor guide to the quality of work. Shops with small presses as well as those with large presses may do showcase work. Both kinds of shops may also give you disappointing results. Routine work from ABC Litho may look identical to XYZ Graphics' maximum effort. Intelligent buying means knowing what you can reasonably expect from a specific printer. Don't settle for less, but don't ask for more.

SPECIALTY PRINTERS

Many printers target their equipment, supplies, workflow and marketing to a particular category of products. For example, printers specializing in publications have prepress links and web presses configured to work with magazine and catalog publishers. A publications printer might also

10-2 TOURING THE PLANT

Plant tours help you predict how satisfied you may feel working with a printer. To get the most out of a tour, look for the following features.

Clean. Quality printing requires clean paper, film and presses. Pay attention to details that reveal attitudes. Are yesterday's soda cans on the light tables? Is the loading dock littered with broken pallets?

Well organized. Efficient workflow requires orderly plant layout, staff with clear job definitions, and materials and files in a logical storage system. How quickly can the printer assemble data about a specific job?

Customer oriented. Staff in all departments should seem happy to see you, not frustrated that you interrupted their work. Customer service reps need offices in key locations, not hidden from production workers.

Product oriented. Staff should explain how equipment relates to the products that you produce, not just point to powerful computers and big presses.

Proud. True professionals feel proud of their work and workplace. Look for award certificates in the lunchroom as well as the reception room.

When you tour a printing company, you see many printed pieces in various stages of production. Seeing those pieces helps you learn what kinds of jobs the printer does and who some other customers are.

have facilities for selective binding and operate a mailing service.

A specialty printer focuses on doing only one kind of job, so materials and procedures stay consistent from prepress through bindery. For this reason, a specialty printer produces a specific product more efficiently than a commercial

> **People in sales and production have different interests. Sales people work on commission, so want to generate work and satisfy customers. Production people work on wages, so concentrate on efficiency and the needs of the plant. Sometimes the two sets of interests prevent jobs from going smoothly.**

printer that produces brochures today, posters tomorrow and booklets next week.

Large specialty printers benefit from buying vast amounts of only a few kinds of papers. For example, a book printer may buy 100,000 pounds of 55# natural offset every few weeks. A printer specializing in software documentation may keep 50,000 pounds of #3 50# matte handy just to get through the night shift. The typical commercial printer can't compete with that kind of buying power. On the other hand, at a specialty printer you choose from six or eight house sheets, not from the large selection that commercial printers offer.

Specialty printers are known by product, as in "book printer" or "envelope printer." Some common products that printers specialize in include advertising inserts, books, checks, direct mailers, envelopes, financial documents (stocks and bonds), business forms, greeting cards, labels, publications (magazines and catalogs) and scientific journals.

Classified directories list specialty printers under the products in which they specialize. The companies also advertise in periodicals oriented to potential buyers of their products. For example, printers who specialize in large quantities of four-color fliers advertise in trade magazines for gift and jewelry industries.

PRINTING AWAY FROM HOME
Printers compete in national and international markets for products such as catalogs, books, direct mailers and showcase quality annual reports. Customers using printers who specialize in methods such as gravure and holography also deal at a distance. And many customers deal with printers on the Web for everyday newsletters, brochures and stationery.

Experienced printing buyers routinely send specifications and files over long distances and deal with proofs and shipments over the same distances. They may travel personally to the printers only for a press check.

Specialty printers in the national market can frequently produce a job at 30 or 40 percent less than the lowest local bidder. In addition, focused equipment and workflow makes production schedules shorter than schedules for commercial printers doing the same job. With large jobs, you may save much more than the extra costs of doing business at a distance. Moreover, distant printers are often represented locally by brokers or sales representatives in daily contact with the distant shop.

You may feel nervous about sending jobs to out-of-town shops, thinking the printer needs personal contact. Dealing with a distant printer does limit close supervision. Whether it is worth the risk depends on your quality requirements, schedule and the cost savings. If in doubt, ask for references to local customers. Most previous customers feel happy that they learned to work with distant printers.

When considering an out-of-town printer, keep in mind that you might need to visit the plant. If your job is three hundred thousand annual reports or twenty million inserts, travel expenses are incidental. On many small jobs, however, expenses can wipe out cost savings.

International markets. Experienced printing buyers shop in Asia and Europe as well as in North America. Buying printing abroad requires expertise in international financing and customs arrangements, matters best left in the hands of a printing broker during your first few experiences.

Dealing with printers in other countries involves learning their standard paper sizes, which are different from those used in North America, and understanding nuances in process colors, whose hues may look slightly different because of techniques of making inks. Other countries also have different standards for patterns of punching and hardware for ring binders. What works at home may not work overseas.

IN-PLANT PRINTERS

Many businesses, governments and school systems have their own print shops, called in-plant printers. If your organization has an in-plant printer, you should know what kinds of jobs the shop does and how it operates from a business standpoint.

In-plant print shops are an administrative arrangement unrelated to size, skill, equipment or specialization. Both the U.S. Government Printing Office and an ancient laser printer in a church office fit the definition.

The in-plant printer for a state government or large private company might offer the same full range of services as a large commercial printer. The typical in-plant, however, more closely resembles a quick or small commercial printer. Using copiers and small presses, the shop handles the everyday basic and good quality jobs.

In-plant print shops exist for reasons of convenience, cost and security. Taking the job down the hall or to an adjacent building, especially for people in large, noncommercial areas, such as college campuses, is more convenient than going outside. Staff at in-plants build their inventories, equipment and services to fit the needs of the host organization.

Because in-plant printers do not operate for profit and have no costs for sales or marketing, printing jobs cost less than from independent printers. Further savings occur when staff at the in-plant knows postage regulations and paper needs as they relate to your products.

Many businesses believe security offers the main reason for having an in-plant print shop. In-plants do not serve the public, so information such as new prices stays confidential.

Critics of in-plants argue that the advantages sound fine in theory but don't work in practice.

10-3 COMPLETING THE JOB

Don't let the press of tomorrow's job keep you from completing today's project. Take the following four steps to help you, and others who follow you, produce the job next time or work with the same printer again:

1. Compare bills of lading and invoices with specifications and change orders. Note whether the printer delivered on time and the correct quantity and quality.

2. Use Visual 10-12 to analyze the invoice before approving payment.

3. Verify possession of all materials relating to the job and write down their locations:
   • mock-ups, dummies and proofs
   • photos and illustrations
   • computer files
   • press sheets and finished samples
   • specifications and change orders
   • quotes and invoices

4. Write down anything about the job that would make it cost less or improve its workflow next time.

They claim that their in-plants appear less convenient than working with some nearby businesses, especially when the in-plants seem part of a complex bureaucracy. They say that most jobs don't need security. Most important, they assert that in-plants don't have to compete for work, so they don't control cost and quality as well as outside printers.

Sometimes the complaints are justified, but you should view them in their proper context. Although using the same equipment and materials as the world of independent printers, in-plants have a different set of management problems.

Customers often bring in-plants poor files that outside printers would reject or would correct at additional costs. In addition, in-plants get the routine jobs, such as forms, pads and staff

> **❝ People who don't know what they are doing with a large printing job could really help themselves by hiring an experienced graphic designer for a few hours as a consultant. It might cost a couple of hundred dollars to get proofs examined or help with doing a press check, but it could save thousands. ❞**

....

directories. More challenging work goes outside, contributing to the stereotype that in-plants can't do quality printing. Some in-plants do excellent work on material that demands it, even winning awards for products, such as annual reports.

Because in-plant printers don't have to compete in the commercial market, they often have old equipment that wasn't very high quality to begin with. They may get 100 percent out of their machinery, but that still may not be very good.

To get the best possible work from your in-plant, give its staff good originals, adequate time and appropriate respect. Equally important, know what you can reasonably expect. Think about your in-plant as you would any other printer: right for some jobs and wrong for others.

The typical manager of an in-plant print shop knows many printers in your locality. The manager can help you write specifications and prepare files for outside jobs. Taking advantage of this knowledge leads to managing all jobs better.

LOCATING PRINTERS

Finding printers suited to your jobs requires hard work but pays many dividends when it develops dependable relationships.

Classified directories do not distinguish between quick and commercial shops, but their ads and listings help tell who's who. The names of quick printers include words such as "jiffy," "rapid" and "instant." Commercial printers are more likely to include a family or regional name

and to call themselves "full service."

The largest printers tend to have the smallest ads. Professional buyers know who they are.

In addition to listing companies under the classification "Printers," classified directories have a variety of other categories for printing. Most are related to the names of products, such as "Bags—Paper" and "Postcards."

Regional trade associations of printers publish buyer guides that describe the equipment found at member companies. The guides are free to printing buyers. You can locate the association in your region by calling the national headquarters of Printing Industries of America (PIA) in Alexandria, Virginia.

Several national magazines publish annual directories of graphic arts services. Companies pay for listings, which focus on equipment. The directories concentrate on specialty printers for products such as magazines and catalogs.

Qualifying a printer. To learn details about a printer you might use, call the likely candidate and ask to speak with someone in sales. Explain that you want to become better acquainted with shops whose services you might use. Start the conversation by asking about the shop, not by describing the kinds of printing you need done.

Many printers tell prospective customers that the shop can print anything. You, however, need to know what the shop does best. Jobs that the shop does best are also those jobs most likely to arrive on schedule, within budget and according to specifications.

To help find the right printer for the right job, ask the following questions:

• "What jobs do you produce entirely in your own shop?"

When a printer takes part of a job to another vendor, such as a bindery or even another printer, you become involved in another set of workflows and quality expectations. You get best results when you stay under one roof.

• "What is your ideal job—the job most profitable for you and most likely to exceed customer expectations?"

This question tells printers that you respect

their business requirements but that you also expect them to focus on what they produce most efficiently. Make it clear that you want to avoid the "we do it all" mentality.

• "Who are some of your most satisfied customers?"

Any vendor should feel willing—even proud—to tell you about current customers. Ask for phone numbers or E-mail addresses. Let the printer know that you intend to consult the references.

In addition to sending you samples of printed pieces, printers like to provide equipment lists. The typical list starts with specifications for computer hardware and software, then describes sizes and brand names of presses and bindery machines. After a while, the lists from plants of the same size all look the same.

Equipment lists mean little to novice printing buyers and lots to old pros. As you gain experience, you become more able to relate the printer's machinery to your jobs. But keep your focus on your jobs, not the printer's hardware.

If you consider a printer from the standpoint of a long-term partnership, ask what experience the shop has with such arrangements. Ask to see sample contracts and to learn names of other partner customers.

LOCATING PRINTING BUYERS

Experienced buyers can help you find and qualify printers suited to your needs.

Many large organizations have at least one employee who buys printing. Book and magazine publishers call the employee a production manager. Other companies with printing as a primary component of their business, such as catalog retailers and map publishers, use the same title.

Most people who buy printing have job titles that include words such as sales, marketing, public relations, investor relations and communications. Although not called production managers, they perform the same functions of sourcing vendors, then specifying and coordinating jobs. While juggling other aspects of their job duties, these people may contract for $100,000 to $10,000,000 per year on printing.

Skilled printing buyers feel eager to share their experiences with each other and with newcomers. Somewhere your local network of old-timers includes someone willing to mentor you.

Look for local printing buyers in large hospitals, agencies, businesses, associations or other organizations similar to yours. You can find them at local meetings and conferences of the following organizations.

AAF. American Advertising Federation (Washington, DC).

AMA. American Marketing Association (New York City).

ASAE. American Society of Association Executives (Washington, DC).

IABC. International Association of Business Communicators (San Francisco).

PRSA. Public Relations Society of America (New York City).

STC. Society for Technical Communication (Washington, DC).

If you can't find local branches of these organizations, call their national offices or visit their Web sites for the names of local contacts. For links to Web sites for these and other organizations, visit the site for this book (www. gettingitprinted.com).

Some regions have clubs and special events for printing buyers sponsored by associations of printers. Events include trade show seminars about topics that appeal to print buyers. To learn about activities in your area, call your regional affiliate of Printing Industries of America or the PIA headquarters in Alexandria, Virginia.

Interviewing a printing buyer. When you call a printing buyer or a customer who has been referred by a printer, start by describing the kinds of jobs you have. Make it clear that you want to locate or qualify a printer for specific kinds of printed pieces.

After describing your needs, explain what aspects of printing jobs are most important to you. For example, you might say something like the following:

• "I need to keep a tight lid on costs. Does this printer stick with contract terms?"

• "I don't want to worry about quality from

10-4 WHY TO WRITE SPECIFICATIONS

Specify every printing job in writing, even the most simple and routine. Written specifications along with a comprehensive mock-up ensure clear communication between you and everyone else involved in the job.

Good specifications are complete, precise, and use language that graphic arts professionals understand. Specs benefit you in the following ways.

Ensure accurate comparisons. When each vendor quotes on identical specifications, you can compare prices accurately and fairly.

Look professional. Clear, carefully written specifications convey your self-confidence. You expect appropriate quality, attentive service, and reasonable price.

Provide a checklist. Specification forms help you review the entire production se-

quence and save you time in getting quotes. They make it obvious if you forgot an important detail.

Keep costs down. Specifications written on a standard form notify printers that you are soliciting competitive bids.

Reduce guesswork. Good specifications help printers figure costs exactly, identify ways to save money and spot potential problems.

Help monitor changes. Almost every set of specifications changes at least a little as the job goes through production. With the original specifications as a guide, you can keep track of alterations.

Make payment easier. By comparing the final bill to the specifications, you can see exactly what was called for, what was done, and how alterations affected the final price.

---

job to job. After the shop learns what I consider critical, can I depend on consistent quality?"

• "Everything we do needs just-in-time delivery. Has this printer ever failed to meet the contracted deadline?"

• "When I show up on time for a press check, will this printer be ready for me or will I usually have to wait?"

Don't hesitate to ask some open-ended questions, such as the following:

• "If something goes wrong with a job, how does this printer handle the situation?"

• "How good are people in prepress at explaining why I have to prepare files in a certain way?"

If you consider a long-term partnership with a printer, ask about its employee turnover and overall stability as a company. People throughout your organization and the printer's will spend a lot of time coordinating workflows. Make sure the human relationships stay relatively constant.

PRICING PRACTICES

Printers offer either formula pricing or custom pricing. Which method works best for you depends on the job and the relationship you want to have with the printer.

Formula pricing. Printers base formula prices on specifications that fit their equipment, materials and workflow. Quick printers, for example, typically have price charts showing costs per hundred copies using one ink and standard papers. Formula pricing means you know exactly what the job will cost before you send files.

Many specialty printers and printers on the Web use formula pricing. You can order envelopes, self-cover direct mailers, four-color fliers and even books whose unit costs you compute from price lists. These printers keep costs low by using a limited choice of paper weights, sizes, formats and trims and often by grouping jobs from different customers onto the same press sheets.

When you can use one of the formats a shop

offers, formula pricing may save you hundreds or thousands of dollars on jobs for which the message is more important than customized production. Deviating from the standard format, however, means that your job may cost the same as it would at any commercial printer.

Custom pricing. Commercial printers figure a custom price for each job. Estimators compute the costs of paper, preparation and press time, and other factors they consider relevant. They calculate what each job costs to produce and how much the printer needs to earn a profit. Estimators may also take into account how fast you want work finished, the quality level you want and your reputation as an easy or demanding customer.

After computing a price, a printer gives you a quotation, also called an estimate. The quote is an offer to produce a job for a specific price. When you sign the quote or refer to it in a purchase order, you have a contract.

REQUESTING ESTIMATES

Learning how much a printing job will cost begins with clear, written specifications accompanied by a dummy or desktop printout. Even the most simple job can run into problems, so don't make printers guess about anything. Make everything clear by writing it down and providing an example.

Printers feel reluctant to give rough quotes or ballpark figures. They figure prices using complex software, so a reasonable guess takes as much work as a firm quote. Furthermore, customers sometimes forget that a guess is not a quote, a memory lapse that may cause hard feelings when the invoice arrives.

Some printers give firm quotes based only on files, not specifications. They know that customers often overlook factors while writing specifications. Printers who follow this practice should make it clear by writing on the quotation forms that the price is subject to preflighting.

10-5 WHEN TO SOLICIT QUOTATIONS

Some customers get quotes too often. They would be better off simply handing most jobs to their regular printers. Other customers don't get quotes often enough. They spend too much money by not shopping and by not keeping their regular printers competitive.

You can take a balanced approach to shopping for printing by using the following guidelines.

Costs. Get quotes when you think the job will cost an amount that you consider significant. That might be five hundred dollars or fifty thousand dollars.

Familiarity. Get quotes when you're dealing with a printer, process or product that's new to you. When handling your first job using separations or perfect binding, you probably lack sufficient experience to judge whether costs from your regular printer are reasonable.

Quantities. Get quotes when you might find significant savings at different quantities. The printer that bids low on ten thousand brochures might bid high on twenty-five thousand. Price breaks vary greatly from one printer to the next.

Competition. Get quotes on a routine job every couple of years just to remind your regular printer not to take your business for granted.

The number of quotes to solicit depends on how familiar you are with general printing costs, particular printers and the specific job. For most jobs, you don't need more than three quotes—assuming each comes from a printer well suited to the job. With complicated jobs that might run either sheetfed or web, and jobs where you might use an out-of-town printer, you don't need more than four or five quotes.

Every printing job is unique, every print shop has a special blend of machines and skills, and some shops want business more than others. These factors mean that prices on the same job may vary widely from shop to shop. Quotes from printers looking at identical specifications can vary as much as 50 percent even when every shop is well suited to the job.

Business conditions affecting individual printers influence what they quote on a job from one week to the next. A small shop might need business and give you a terrific price. A month later that same shop might have so much business that the quote on the same job is 50 percent more. A large shop might have an opportunity to gang your job with others or run it on paper it bought on a special offer.

Printers actually produce only one job for every seven or eight quoted. If you ask for quotes but never contract a job, you'll soon be ignored. Don't abuse printers' eagerness to figure costs. For example, don't ask a small commercial printer to bid on four thousand copies of a two hundred-page, perfect-bound book. Only ask for quotes from printers suited to the job.

The printer whose quote was too high today may still be right for tomorrow's job. Thank the unsuccessful bidders and tell them you look forward to dealing with them again.

Breaking out costs. You can form a better picture of job costs by asking printers to quote prices in categories. Quotes that show the cost of paper as a separate item help you compare printers and spot ways to cut costs at the last minute. Quotes that show separate prepress costs help you identify tasks that you might do yourself.

Estimating software helps the printer isolate costs but doesn't produce printouts that do the same for customers. Nevertheless, asking your printer to break out costs helps you pinpoint ways to improve your purchasing power.

EVALUATING QUOTATIONS

When evaluating quotes from printers, check first that the price actually relies on your specifications. The quote should refer to your job or purchase order number.

The professionalism of the quote tells a lot about a printer. Look for an answer to every question about cost, condition of copy, type of proofs, packaging and delivery time. Quotes should arrive when promised. A printer that is efficient, thorough and on time with quotations is likely to be that way with jobs, too.

Printing jobs often include services such as foil stamping or case binding that a printer must subcontract. Printers should know what these buyouts will cost before quoting the price of the total job. Don't consider quotes that leave open lines saying something like "plus cost of dies."

The cost of paper may be an exception to the above rule about open price lines. Printers may be unable to anticipate price increases and therefore feel forced to tell you "paper prices subject to current rates."

Most printers hold quoted prices firm for thirty or sixty days. The time limit might mean you must sign the contract within that number of days or might mean that you actually bring in the job. Ask if you are unsure. And don't hesitate to ask for a little more time to think things over.

Remember that dollar amounts on quotation forms are not the only costs of printing. If working with the low bidder means considerable travel time and expense, the price might not look so attractive after all. The peace of mind that comes with close control over a job may be worth a few extra dollars, especially when you are new to a process or product. Think about procurement costs, not just printing costs.

As the last step in evaluating quotes, ask yourself what the job is worth to you and whether dollar amounts seem reasonable. Concentrate on value to yourself. For example, if selling a new product depends on a premium quality brochure, don't risk using a printer whose quality you doubt. If you launch your membership drive with a mailing on the first of the month, don't risk using a printer with a reputation for late delivery.

When you solicit quotations, one of your regular printers may not submit the low bid.

If the difference seems slight, ignore it. Stable business relationships are worth far more than a few dollars saved on a particular job. If, however, your regular printer seems much too high, offer a chance to quote again. Maybe the printer will reduce the price to keep your steady business. Or maybe the estimator simply made a mistake.

Accept a quote in writing to assure the contract is clear and enforceable. Sign the form and return it along with your purchase order.

Pricing overs and unders. Printers rarely deliver the exact quantity you order. With inexpensive pieces, such as newsletters and business cards, you get overs at no additional cost and get no price reduction for receiving a few less. With more costly items, however, your printer may bill you for overs and credit you for unders.

When you sign the contract, verify that you agree on the amount you should pay per unit for overs or be credited for unders. Breaking out costs helps with the arithmetic. Unit costs for overs and unders should reflect only variable costs, such as paper and press time, not fixed costs, such as prepress.

INTERPRETING ALTERATIONS

Almost every printing job has at least one alteration. Some have many. Understanding how alterations affect costs helps keep budgets under control.

An alteration, also known as a change order, is any adjustment you make after giving files or art to a prepress service or printer. Changes could occur in copy, specifications or both.

Some of the most common alterations:

• Page count, when your membership drive proved so successful that your directory needed another half signature.

• Paper, when your printer couldn't get what you wanted or you decided to try something different that cost less or performed better.

• Copy, when you discovered a typo in the president's name or that prices just changed.

• Ink color, when design decided that the red was too red or that brown would look better than green.

• Halftones or separations, when half the originals turned out too grainy to enlarge.

• Quantity, when your boss learned that registration was down for this year's trade show.

10-6 DECIDING QUANTITIES

To decide what quantities to tell printers as bases for their price quotes, follow these steps.

1. Make the best guess that you can using procedures within your own organization. Don't let anticipated printing costs influence this number.

2. Using the quantity that you determined in step one as a starting point, compute two additional quantities, each between 5 percent and 10 percent higher.

3. Include the three numbers on your specifications.

Examples
• If you need 5,000 brochures, ask for quotes on 5,000 and 5,500.

• If you need 1,500 manuals, ask for quotes on 1,500, 1,600 and 1,700.

• If you need 40,000 envelopes, ask for quotes on 40,000, 42,000 and 44,000.

Reasons
• Inventory control begins with you, not your printer.

• Closely grouped quantities let your printers explore possible price breaks while keeping the job suited to the shop.

• Pricing different quantities helps establish the value of overs and unders.

Most alterations take place during prepress, not during presswork or bindery. Mistakes fixed after seeing a proof will cost someone money. If your printer made the mistake, there should be no charge to you. If you made the error, you pay.

You can find something wrong with any printing job at any stage of production. The question is whether you want to change it—whether it really matters. Always ask what alterations will cost before deciding to make them. When computing the costs of changes, remember to figure time for you and your staff. All that running around keeps you from getting the current job done and the next one started.

The cost of alterations varies from almost free to very expensive, depending on the nature of the changes and at what stage they occur. Follow the rule of thumb that a change costing five dollars on the desktop costs fifty dollars in prepress and five hundred dollars on press.

Alterations are invoiced to you, as compared to errors by a prepress service or printer that are not billed. Depending on when you make it, a change in type or ink color may cost nothing. Increasing quantity or upgrading paper, however, may yield a huge difference from the original quote for your job.

Unfortunately for both printers and customers, no one keeps track of alterations very well. Customers give hurried instructions verbally over the phone. A sales or customer service rep jots a hasty note along with other hasty notes relating to other jobs. Notes go into a purse or pocket. By some miracle, most of the alterations get made correctly. But miracles aren't good enough if they don't include your job.

To control costs and ensure accuracy, make

10-7 ANALYZING A JOB FOR PAYMENT

Regardless of how carefully you plan and monitor printing jobs, final bills are often higher than you expect. Before you authorize payment, check each aspect of the job carefully. Examine the invoice and compare it to specifications. Keep in mind the following points.

Completeness. Examine one piece closely to determine that it has the reverses, tints, photos and other features the invoice says you received.

Quality. Study several pieces taken from different boxes to verify that the job meets the correct standard of quality.

Paper. Verify that the printer used the paper specified in the contract.

Quantity. Confirm that you have the right amount. Compare your delivery records with your invoice. Count the contents of a box or two.

Alterations. Make sure that charges for alterations cover only changes you asked for or agreed to.

Extra charges. Evaluate extra charges to make sure you understand why they appear and agree that you should pay them.

Schedule. Note whether delivery was on time and, if not, whether the contract allows a penalty for late delivery.

Shipping. If charges seem out of line, ask for copies of postal receipts, manifests or bills of lading.

Taxes. If your invoice includes a sales or value-added tax, verify that local laws hold you liable.

Arithmetic. Check that accountants correctly figured all totals and discounts.

Examine invoices for reruns especially carefully. Some printers think of reruns as cash cows and charge accordingly. Remember that your rerun required much less prepress than the first run. And keep in mind that paper prices fluctuate. Stock that cost the printer $1,250 last year might cost $1,190 this year.

every change order, no matter how trivial, in writing. Even if you decide on a change while meeting with the printer, confirm it in writing. Fax, E-mail or hand it to your printer.

NEGOTIATING PROBLEMS

Despite everyone's best efforts, a printer occasionally delivers a job that doesn't satisfy you. When that happens, you must express your unhappiness, and listen to the printer's point of view to help you arrive at a solution that works for each of you.

Before you pick up the phone or rush to the print shop, ask yourself how serious the problem really is. If it's a critical error, you can't accept the job. This situation is rare. If it's a major defect, you need to judge its impact. This happens once in a while. If it's a minor flaw, you may choose to ignore it. Every job contains at least one minor flaw.

You have a right to reject a job that doesn't match the specifications on which your contract was based. Only exercise that right when you discover a critical error. Rejecting a job is hard on your printer and probably hard on you, too. Printers work on small profit margins that you destroy when you refuse a job. From your standpoint, refusing a job means missing your deadline and perhaps losing a client.

Notify the printer at once. Don't delay. Even if you need a few days to determine the extent of the problem, let the printer know immediately that you don't feel satisfied. If possible, get the printer involved in inspecting the shipment to verify the situation.

When considering a problem with quality, you need to explain your viewpoints clearly. Use the quality features listed in Visual 7-8 to organize your presentation to your printer. Tell your printer exactly what you don't like. Explain how the problem affects your message.

Successful resolution requires getting the printer to agree that (1) a problem exists and (2) reponsibility lies with the printer, not with you. You can't negotiate a solution until you establish these two facts.

After you and your printer agree on the facts, you can move toward a resolution. Your printer will ask you how you want to handle the situation. The most common technique is to deduct 10 or 20 percent from the invoice for the job.

Some disputes turn on the question of who takes responsibility for settling the matter with the printer. If a graphic designer or broker coordinated the job and brokered the printing, that person is the printer's customer and should settle any problems. If the poor work took place at a bindery or other trade service subcontracted by the printer, you deal with the printer, not the trade shop.

Responsibility and money go hand in hand. The person who presents you with the bill is the person to confront about problems.

Long-term impacts

Resolving a problem requires that you feel clear about the relationship you want with the printer after you have settled today's issue. You might

10-8 through 10-12 Requests for quotation Each printer quoting your job needs identical information. If specifications vary, you can't compare prices. Write your specifications on a form such as the one in Visual 10-8. Even when you write precise specs, printers may interpret requests differently. To ensure clear understanding, send a dummy along with your request for quotation.

While insisting that printers give quotes based on identical specifications, don't hesitate to ask about additional costs on a small number of alternatives. Inquire about the cost of equivalent paper that may be a house sheet, or for prices on one or two alternate quantities. Keep an open mind about cost-cutting alternatives, but insist on seeing prices on your specifications as well as on alternatives suggested by the printer.

Notice three particular features on the Request for Quotation form:

1. The form does not ask for detailed information about fonts, file formats and versions of software. Prepress changes so fast that no standard form can stay current. This form simply says that you will send the job on film or files prepared to the printer's specifications.

2. The form allows you to request breaking out the cost of paper. We suggest that you ask for paper costs separately, especially for long print runs.

3. The form has several places to write comments. Every printing job calls for a unique blend of requirements for prepress, presswork, paper and finishing that no standard form can anticipate. You can see comments from the printing buyers written on the forms in Visuals 10-9 through 10-12 on pages 176 and 177.

10-8 REQUEST FOR QUOTATION

Overview

Organization name _____

Address _____

Contact person _____ Phone _____ Fax _____

E-mail address _____ Mobile phone/pager _____

PO # _____ Date _____ Customer # _____

Job name _____ Job # _____

Date quote needed _____ Job to printer _____ Delivery needed _____

☐ new job ☐ exact reprint ☐ reprint with changes   Previous job # _____

Comments

Prepress

Proofs and plate-ready   ☐ film   ☐ files supplied to printer's specifications   ☐ see mockup

Prepress service _____ Contact _____

Phone _____ Fax _____ Job # _____

Comments

Printing

Quantity   1) _____   2) _____   3) _____

Comments

Quality   ☐ basic   ☐ good   ☐ premium   ☐ showcase   ☐ SWOP   ☐ GRACOL   ☐ SNAP

Comments

Format   Trim size _____ x _____   Page count _____   ☐ bleeds   ☐ plus cover   ☐ self-cover

Comments

Ink colors   side one   side two

cover   _____   _____

text   _____   _____

insert   _____   _____

_____   _____   _____

Comments

Coating ☐ varnish ☐ UV ☐ aqueous ☐ spot ☐ flood ☐ dull ☐ gloss ☐ tint_____

Comments

Other printing ☐ die cut ☐ foil stamp ☐ emboss/deboss ☐ other_____

Comments

Paper

	weight	brand	color	finish	grade
cover	_____	_____	_____	_____	_____
text	_____	_____	_____	_____	_____
insert	_____	_____	_____	_____	_____
	_____	_____	_____	_____	_____
	_____	_____	_____	_____	_____

Show cost of paper separately ☐ no ☐ yes   Suggest alternate stocks ☐ no ☐ yes

Comments

Finishing and binding

Trim to _____ x _____   Fold to _____ x _____   Type of fold_____

☐ see dummy   ☐ score   ☐ perforate   ☐ drill   ☐ punch   ☐ number   ☐ film laminate

☐ plastic comb   ☐ spiral plastic   ☐ spiral wire   ☐ double loop wire   ☐ paste   ☐ saddle stitch

☐ side stitch   ☐ perfect   ☐ burst perfect   ☐ lay flat   ☐ case   ☐ binding side _____

Comments

Packing and delivery

Label cartons_____

☐ bulk pack   ☐ band   ☐ shrink wrap in bundles of_____   maximun carton weight _____

☐ pallet pack   maximum pallet size/weight_____

☐ will call   ☐ deliver   ☐ ship via _____

Comments

10-9 REQUEST FOR QUOTATION: BROCHURE

Overview
Organization name *Elk Ridge Properties*
Address *One Herd Lane, Mitchell, VA 20124*
Contact person *Elizabeth Tousley* Phone *757 131-6676* Fax *757 131-0033*
Email address *ERP@ELK.COM* Mobile phone/pager *1-757-437-0086*
PO # *353* Date *4-5-2000* Customer # *10-266*
Job name *Pine Ridge Brochure* Job # *293*
Date quote needed *4-10* Job to printer *5-1* Delivery needed *5-15*
☐ new job ☐ exact reprint ☑ reprint with changes Previous job # *ERP 224*
Comments *Changes to logo both sides*
OK to lift film from prior flats.

Prepress
Proofs and plate-ready ☐ film ☑ files supplied to printer's specifications ☐ see mock up
Prepress service *Priestly Productions* Contact *Joanna*
Phone *757-523-6032* Fax *523-5929* Job # *67*
Comments

Printing
Quantity 1) *40,000* 2) *45,000* 3) *50,000*
Comments

Quality ☐ basic ☐ good ☑ premium ☐ showcase ☐ SWOP ☑ GRACOL ☐ SNAP
Comments

Format Trim size *9* x *15 7/8* Page count ____ ☑ bleeds ☐ plus cover ☐ self-cover
Comments *rack brochure*

Ink colors	side one	side two
cover		
text	*4-color*	*4-color plus varnish*
insert		

Comments

Coating ☑ varnish ☐ UV ☐ aqueous ☐ spot ☐ flood ☑ dull ☐ gloss ☐ tint ____
Comments

Other printing ☐ die cut ☐ foil stamp ☐ emboss/deboss ☐ other ____
Comments

Paper

	weight	brand	color	finish	grade
cover					
text	*70#*	*Satinglo*	*white*	*semi gloss*	*# 1*
insert					

Show cost of paper seperately ☑ no ☐ yes   Suggest alternate stocks ☑ no ☐ yes
Comments

Finishing and binding
Trim to *9* x *15 3/4"* Fold to *9* x *3 3/8"* Type of fold *Parallel*
☑ see dummy ☐ score ☐ perforate ☐ drill ☐ punch ☐ number ☐ film laminate
☐ plastic comb ☐ spiral plastic ☐ spiral wire ☐ double loop wire ☐ paste ☐ saddle stitch
☐ side stitch ☐ perfect ☐ burst perfect ☐ lay flat ☐ case ☐ binding side
Comments

Packing and delivery
Label cartons *ER - Pine Ridge*
☐ bulk pack ☐ band ☑ shrink wrap in bundles of *100* maximum carton weight *50#*
☐ pallet pack maximum pallet size/weight
☐ will call ☐ deliver ☑ ship via *Tillamook Fast Freight*
Comments *split ship: 1/2 to One Herd Lane*
1/2 to Tyberg's Corner Park
118 Beacon dr. in Leesburg

Copyright © 1998 Mark Beach and Eric Kenly, from Getting It Printed, North Light Books, 1507 Dana Ave., Cincinnati, Ohio, 45207

10-10 REQUEST FOR QUOTATION: NEWSLETTER

Overview
Organization name *Ajax TriState Health - Public Relations*
Address *633 Mosher Rd. Boise, ID 87301*
Contact person *Beverly Blessing* Phone *208-822-0200* Fax *822-0330*
Email address *BBLESS@MNH.COM* Mobile phone/pager *208-445-5843*
PO # *FS 128* Date *3-2-99* Customer #
Job name *Spring Newsletter* Job # *54*
Date quote needed *3-9* Job to printer *3-12* Delivery needed *3-20*
☑ new job ☐ exact reprint ☐ reprint with changes Previous job #
Comments *deadline critical*

Prepress
Proofs and plate-ready ☐ film ☑ files supplied to printer's specifications ☑ see mock up
Prepress service *Carraway Cares* Contact *David Bulls*
Phone *208-747-5582* Fax *747-2898* Job # *00044*
Comments

Printing
Quantity 1) *500,000* 2) *525,000* 3) *550,000*
Comments

Quality ☐ basic ☑ good ☐ premium ☐ showcase ☐ SWOP ☐ GRACOL ☐ SNAP
Comments

Format Trim size *11* x *17"* Page count *8* ☑ bleeds ☐ plus cover ☐ self-cover
Comments

Ink colors	side one	side two
cover		
text	*black + Trumatch grn 20-A5*	
insert	*black only on envelope*	

Comments

Coating ☐ varnish ☐ UV ☐ aqueous ☐ spot ☐ flood ☐ dull ☐ gloss ☐ tint ____
Comments

Other printing ☐ die cut ☐ foil stamp ☐ emboss/deboss ☑ other *return envelope*
Comments *see files and proofs for art and instruction*

Paper

	weight	brand	color	finish	grade
cover					
text	*60#*		*white*	*vellum*	*book*
insert					
Remittance Envelope	*50#*	*Self Seal*	*blue*	*wove*	*bond*

Show cost of paper seperately ☐ no ☑ yes   Suggest alternate stocks ☐ no ☑ yes
Comments

Finishing and binding
Trim to *11* x *17"* Fold to *8 1/2* x *11"* Type of fold *see example*
☑ see dummy ☐ score ☐ perforate ☐ drill ☐ punch ☐ number ☐ film laminate
☐ plastic comb ☐ spiral plastic ☐ spiral wire ☐ double loop wire ☐ paste ☑ saddle stitch
☐ side stitch ☐ perfect ☐ burst perfect ☐ lay flat ☐ case ☐ binding side
Comments *Staple envelope into upper half of centerfold*
— so it will not interfere with horizontal fold.
#10,000 fold once only.

Packing and delivery
Label cartons *Spring newsletter*
☑ bulk pack ☐ band ☐ shrink wrap in bundles of ____ maximum carton weight ____
☑ pallet pack maximum pallet size/weight ____
☐ will call ☑ deliver ☐ ship via ____
Comments *ship to Bradley Mailing Services*
200 Verin Street
Baise, Idaho rear entrance
208-823-9642
deliver 10,000 to Mosher Rd. address

Copyright © 1998 Mark Beach and Eric Kenly, from Getting It Printed, North Light Books, 1507 Dana Ave., Cincinnati, Ohio, 45207

10-11 REQUEST FOR QUOTATION: POSTER

Overview
Organization name _Cooper Mountain Jazz_
Address _9000 Juniper Place_ _Rapido, CA 99229_
Contact person _Jeanne Gilchrist_ Phone _412-326-7030_ Fax _326-1123_
Email address _JGIL@ART.COM_ Mobile phone/pager _1-412-488-9973_
PO # _0177_ Date _5-1-2001_ Customer # _____
Job name _Festival poster_ Job # _20_
Date quote needed _5-10-2001_ Job to printer _5-20-2001_ Delivery needed _5-30-2001_
☑ new job ☐ exact reprint ☐ reprint with changes Previous job # _____
Comments

Prepress
Proofs and plate-ready ☑ film ☐ files supplied to printer's specifications ☐ see mock up
Prepress service _Beta Wave Inc._ Contact _Consuella Chan_
Phone _412-277-9202_ Fax _412-277-4494_ Job # _CO-OP 321_
Comments

Printing
Quantity 1) _1,000_ 2) _1,200_ 3) _____
Comments

Quality ☐ basic ☐ good ☐ premium ☑ showcase ☐ SWOP ☐ GRACOL ☐ SNAP
Comments _We need to know which press you use_

Format Trim size _23_ x _35_ Page count ____ ☑ bleeds ☐ plus cover ☐ self-cover
Comments

Ink colors   side one   side two
cover   _4-color plus trumatch 38-B 1_
        plus varnish
text
insert

Comments _Consistency of spot color is imperative_

Coating ☑ varnish ☐ UV ☐ aqueous ☑ spot ☐ flood ☐ dull ☑ gloss ☐ tint _____
Comments

Other printing ☐ die cut ☐ foil stamp ☐ emboss/deboss ☐ other _____
Comments

Paper

	weight	brand	color	finish	grade
cover					
text	100	Ascentia	bright	matt	#1
insert					

Show cost of paper seperately ☐ no ☑ yes   Suggest alternate stocks ☑ no ☐ yes
Comments

Finishing and binding
Trim to _23_ x _35_ Fold to ____ x ____ Type of fold _____
☐ see dummy ☐ score ☐ perforate ☐ drill ☐ punch ☐ number ☐ film laminate
☐ plastic comb ☐ spiral plastic ☐ spiral wire ☐ double loop wire ☐ paste ☐ saddle stitch
☐ side stitch ☐ perfect ☐ burst perfect ☐ lay flat ☐ case ☐ binding side _____
Comments _Please quote seperately: cost of 1,000_
inserted in mailing tubes.

Packing and delivery
Label cartons _Jazz Fest posters 2001_
☐ bulk pack ☐ band ☑ shrink wrap in bundles of _200_ maximun carton weight _____
☐ pallet pack   maximum pallet weight _____
☐ will call ☑ deliver ☑ ship via _Best way - your carrier_
Comments _Please call ahead to arrange delivery_
326-7030 - before 3:PM

10-12 REQUEST FOR QUOTATION: BOOK

Overview
Organization name _Central State Communications - Marketing_
Address _2700 Prescott Circle #700, Highland Park, Il 60635_
Contact person _Jan A. Dainsburg_ Phone _424-822-0300_ Fax _822-1982_
Email address _JANSAN@NYC.COM_ Mobile phone/pager _1-424-321-6900_
PO # _CR016_ Date _7-5-2010_ Customer # _623_
Job name _Customer Cook Book_ Job # _62_
Date quote needed _7-30_ Job to printer _8-1_ Delivery needed _9-1_
☑ new job ☐ exact reprint ☐ reprint with changes Previous job # _____
Comments

Prepress
Proofs and plate-ready ☐ film ☑ files supplied to printer's specifications ☐ see mock up
Prepress service _Harrison Imaging_ Contact _Brad Kren_
Phone _424-292-0632_ Fax _292-5112_ Job # _CSC 014_
Comments

Printing
Quantity 1) _5,000_ 2) _5,500_ 3) _6,000_
Comments

Quality ☐ basic ☑ good ☐ premium ☐ showcase ☐ SWOP ☐ GRACOL ☐ SNAP
Comments _cover must be premium_

Format Trim size _5_ x _8_ Page count _120_ ☐ bleeds ☑ plus cover ☐ self-cover
Comments

Ink colors   side one   side two
cover   _4-color plus foil_   _black only_
text   _black and Pantone 185_   _black and Pantone 185_
        red   _red_
insert _black_

Comments

Coating ☑ varnish ☐ UV ☑ aqueous ☐ spot ☐ flood ☐ dull ☐ gloss ☐ tint _____
Comments _cover only_

Other printing ☐ die cut ☑ foil stamp ☐ emboss/deboss ☐ other _____
Comments _cover only_

Paper

	weight	brand	color	finish	grade
cover	12pt	Kromecote	white	C 1S	caste coat
text	70#	Damson	cream	smooth	#2
insert	7pt	Springhill	salmon	—	tag

Show cost of paper seperately ☐ no ☑ yes   Suggest alternate stocks ☐ no ☑ yes
Comments

Finishing and binding
Trim to _5_ x _8_ Fold to ____ x ____ Type of fold _____
☑ see dummy ☐ score ☑ perforate ☐ drill ☐ punch ☐ number ☐ film laminate
☑ plastic comb ☐ spiral plastic ☐ spiral wire ☐ double loop wire ☐ paste ☐ saddle stitch
☐ side stitch ☐ perfect ☐ burst perfect ☐ lay flat ☐ case ☑ binding side _8"_
Comments _last page is order form: perforation_
card stock

Packing and delivery
Label cartons _Customer Cook Book - Marketing_
☐ bulk pack ☐ band ☐ shrink wrap in bundles of ____ maximum carton weight _25#_
☑ pallet pack   maximum pallet size/weight _____
☑ will call ☑ deliver ☐ ship via _____
Comments _Please deliver 500 to Hilton Hotel, 200 Marriott St._
attention: James Sears, Food Bank convention.
Hold remainder in your will call.

I wish customers would tell us when they feel unhappy with our work. When we print a job that they find unsatisfactory for whatever reason, it's probably because one of us wasn't clear with the other. A good percentage of any job turning out right is both printer and customer knowing what to expect. **"**

....

want one of the outcomes on the following list:

• Forget that you ever heard of this printer.

• Maintain a long-term relationship with this printer and protect quality and service of future jobs.

• Get the next job from this printer for bare-bones costs.

• Stick with this printer but ask for a different sales rep.

Negotiating requires that you know how strongly you feel. Arguing with your printer may save you some money and enhance your reputation as a sophisticated customer. Haggling also takes time and energy and may detract from an otherwise smooth business relationship. Make sure the rewards justify the effort.

INDUSTRY QUALITY GUIDELINES

The graphic arts industry has several sets of quality guidelines for different kinds of products and processes. Guidelines are specific about such topics as screen ruling, dot gain and ink density. For example, SWOP guidelines apply to film, proofs and web printing for magazines and catalogs on #5 groundwood paper.

Following are some of the guidelines and organizations used by printers in North America.

CGATS. Committee for Graphic Arts Technologies Standards.

GRACOL. General Requirements for Applications in Commercial Offset Lithography.

SNAP. Specifications for Non-Heatset Advertising Printing.

SWOP. Specifications for Web Offset Publications.

Printers in other parts of the world may not use any of these guidelines but may have their own. For example, many printers in Europe follow Euroscale standards.

Quality guidelines are developed by trade associations of printers and printing customers. They are suggestions, not standards, and have no legal standing unless included with your contract. And they change along with new technology and processes.

To learn about guidelines relating to your printing jobs, consult with your prepress service or printer. You can also learn about guidelines from the Graphic Arts Technical Foundation (GATF) in Pittsburgh, Pennsylvania, or the Graphic Communications Association (GCA) in Alexandria, Virginia.

For links to Web sites about production guidelines, visit the site for this book (www.gettingit printed.com).

Some large companies develop guidelines unique to their own products and packaging. For example, print buyers at Microsoft specify quality for manuals, labels and cartons. Rand McNally and the National Geographic Society have guidelines for maps; *Newsweek* and *Time*, for magazines; and *USA Today*, for newspapers. Corporate guidelines, often developed in consultation with vendors, become standards when made part of contracts for printing.

ISO certification. In addition to using guidelines specific to the industry, many printers become certified by the International Standards Organization (ISO). Certification requires a trained auditor to verify that the printer meets the standards it set for itself. A company must pass a yearly audit to keep its certification.

Technically speaking, ISO credentials verify consistency, not quality. ISO verifies that customers can depend on processes and standards that the printer established. Manufacturing companies in many fields, not just printing, use the ISO program.

ISO reviews originated in Europe and are more important there than in North America. Many international companies rely on ISO standards when they source vendors.

10-13 TERMS AND CONDITIONS OF SALE

Contracts for printing jobs deal with many business issues in addition to specifications. Terms are usually printed on the back of the document and become part of the agreement when you sign the contract.

Many printers reproduce standard trade customs on their quotation forms or contracts and then label the trade customs as terms and conditions. Other printers modify the published customs to suit their business needs. Customers and vendors often negotiate fur- ther changes relating to specific jobs.

When you use a purchase order to buy printing, the business terms on your purchase order may be different from those on a printer's contract. It may be unclear whether the buyer's terms or the printer's terms govern the contract.

The printer's terms prevail when they were part of the offer to supply the service and you accepted them by signing the contract.

CLARIFYING TRADE CUSTOMS

The prepress and printing industries have practices concerning issues such as credit, delivery and insurance. The practices, known as trade customs, are codified and published by industry organizations such as Printing Industries of America (PIA), National Association of Printers and Lithographers (NAPL) and the Graphic Arts Technical Foundation (GATF).

Trade customs are guidelines—starting points for discussion and for contract terms. They have only vague legal standing unless a printer includes them as part of your contract. Trade customs in contracts become terms and conditions of sale, as explained in Visual 10-13.

Printing trade customs deal with many key issues in the relationship between customers and vendors. In the following paragraphs, we discuss the most important of these issues.

Quotations. An offer to print a job at a certain price is good for a specific length of time, usually thirty days. Contracts are not, however, clear about whether the thirty-day period begins on the date of the quotation, the date that you sign the contract or the date on which you deliver the job.

Cancellations. If you cancel a job, your printer may ask for payment for materials ordered or work performed. Materials include paper. Work performed includes prepress.

Ownership. Your printer may claim ownership to materials prepared at your request. The issue of ownership relates to physical objects, such as mock-ups and film, and to rights to creative work, such as designs.

If you feel concerned about ownership, you can ensure that you own materials and rights before signing a contract. Strike out the ownership clauses on the printer's contract and insert the phrase "All work performed is work for hire." We wrote more about copyright at the end of chapter one.

Specifications. Printers base price estimates on your specifications. If your files need corrections or don't match your specifications, or if you change your mind about matters such as quantity or schedule, your printer may compute a new price.

Alterations. When you change any aspect of original specifications at any stage in the job, your printer can compute a new price. Consult page 171 for a list of most common alterations.

Contracts usually state that printers explain, in writing, charges for alterations. You have a right to review documentation before paying the final invoice. To communicate clearly, make your change orders in writing.

Proofs. You are responsible if you don't order proofs, don't review them quickly or don't put your approval or changes in writing. Furthermore,

" I used to contract our jobs to eight different printers and expected them all to walk through fire for me. One day my supervisor asked me about our status in the eyes of our vendors. She wondered whether I would provide superior service to every minor customer. I consolidated our work from eight printers to two. Those two don't just walk through fire, they dance in the flames. And I spend lots less time chasing our jobs all over town. "

the printer can charge extra if you arrive late for a press check or make last-minute changes.

Color proofing causes the most headaches. Trade customs say that you must accept "a reasonable variation in color between proofs and the completed job," but the customs don't define "reasonable variation."

Overruns and underruns. Contracts vary in the percent of overruns or underruns that constitute acceptable delivery, but 10 percent is common and the invoice is adjusted accordingly. If you need "no less than" a certain quantity, make sure to include that requirement in your specifications.

Insurance. Your printer insures your property while in the shop, but the insurance has little relationship to the property's actual value or your lost business if it's destroyed. Always keep backups as your only true insurance. If you supply photos or original art of unusual value, deal with a printer or insurance company that provides extra coverage.

Delivery. Your job is delivered when ownership passes from your printer to you. If the printer delivers to your address, you own the job when the truck unloads. If the printer ships via common carrier, you own the job when it leaves the shop.

Schedule. Printers stay on schedule when customers stay on schedule. If you fall behind, your printer might not deliver by the date on the contract.

Storage. If you want your printer to store files, film or other materials, make storage time and accessibility part of your contract. Most printers will not store printed products.

Claims. You report defects, damages or shortages in writing within fifteen days of delivery. Failure to report within fifteen days means you accept the job as meeting specifications.

Liability. Your printer won't pay more than the printed value for defective goods or missed deadlines, and especially won't pay for lost profits. Furthermore, you can't hold your printer liable for printing your job that violates a copyright or trademark or that has libelous or obscene content. ∎

GLOSSARY

This glossary includes the technical and business terms used in this book. Many definitions are abbreviated from those found in the book *Graphically Speaking*, which also includes terms about type, design, printing and products not found in the following pages.

A

A sizes   ISO paper sizes for standard trim sizes on products that don't involve bleeds or trimming outside edges.

A4 paper   ISO paper size 210mm × 297mm used for letterhead.

acid-free paper   Paper made from pulp containing little or no acid so it resists deterioration from age. Also called archival paper.

additive color   Color produced by light falling onto a surface. The additive primary colors are red, green and blue.

advertising printer   Printer that specializes in products such as free-standing inserts and direct mailers.

advertising specialties   Items such as a calendars, coffee cups, hats, matchbooks and pencils printed with advertising.

against the grain   At right angles to the grain direction of the paper being used. Also called across the grain and cross grain.

allocation   Quantity of a product, such as a brand of paper, that is rationed to distributors and customers until a specified date.

alteration   Any change made by the customer after sending files to the printer.

anti-offset powder   Fine powder lightly sprayed over the printed surface of coated paper as sheets leave a press.

antique finish   Roughest finish offered on offset paper.

application   Computer program used for specific tasks such as word processing, editing photographs or laying out pages.

aqueous coating   Coating in a water base and applied like ink by a printing press to protect and enhance the printing underneath.

archival paper   Alternate term for acid-free paper.

archive   Cache of documents and files saved for possible use in later jobs.

B

B sizes   ISO paper sizes about 18 percent bigger than A sizes for printing large items such as charts, maps and posters.

backup   Printing on one side of a page that must align correctly with printing on the other side.

basic size   The standard size of sheets of paper used to calculate basis weight in the U.S. and Canada.

basis weight   In the U.S. and Canada, the weight, in pounds, of a ream (500 sheets) of paper cut to the basic size. Also called ream weight and substance weight (sub weight). In countries using ISO paper sizes, the weight, in grams, of one square meter of paper. Also called grammage and ream weight.

bible paper   Very thin, opaque paper used for products such as bibles and dictionaries. Also called India paper.

bit   Smallest unit of information used by a computer.

bitmap   Computer image consisting of pixels or halftone dots.

black point   Reference point defining the darkest area in an image.

blade coating   Method of coating paper that ensures a relatively thick covering and level surface, as compared to film coating. Also called knife coating. Gloss, dull and matte papers are blade coated.

blanket   Rubber-coated pad, mounted on a cylinder of an offset press, that receives the inked image from the plate and transfers it to the surface to be printed.

bleed   Printing that extends to the edge of a sheet or page after trimming.

blueline   Prepress proof where all colors show as blue images on white paper. *Blueline* is a generic term for proofs made from a variety of materials having similar appearances that may also be called blueprint, position proof, silverprint, Dylux and VanDyke.

board paper General term for paper over 110# index, 80# cover, or 200 gsm that is commonly used for products such as file folders, displays and postcards. Also called paperboard.

body stock Paper on which the text or main part of a publication is printed, as compared to cover stock.

bond paper Category of paper used for writing, printing and photocopying. Also called business paper, communication paper and writing paper.

book paper Category of paper suitable for books, magazines, catalogs, advertising and general printing needs. Book paper is divided into uncoated paper (also called offset paper) and coated paper (also called art paper, enamel paper, gloss paper and slick paper).

brightness Measure of light reflected from paper.

bristol paper General term referring to paper six points or thicker with basis weight between 90# and 200# (200-500 gsm). Used for products such as index cards, file folders and displays.

broke Trimmings, defective sheets, and other unprinted paper collected at the mill and from converters and printers. Broke is preconsumer waste that mills recycle back into pulp.

broken carton Carton of paper from which some of the sheets have been sold. Also called less carton.

build a color To overlap two or more screen tints to create a new color. Such an overlap is called a build, color build or tint build.

bulk Thickness of paper relative to its basis weight.

bulking dummy Dummy assembled from the actual paper specified for a printing job.

burn To expose a printing plate to light.

burst perfect bind To bind by forcing glue into notches along the spines of gathered signatures before affixing a paper cover. Also called burst bind, notch bind and slotted bind.

buy out To subcontract for a service that is closely related to the business of the organization.

Also called farm out. Work that is bought out is called outsourced or referred to as being out of house.

byte Unit of computer memory consisting of eight bits.

C

C sizes ISO paper sizes with correct dimensions to make folders and envelopes for products trimmed to A sizes.

C1S and C2S Abbreviations for coated one side and coated two sides.

calender To make the surface of paper smooth by pressing it between rollers during manufacture.

caliper Thickness of paper or other substrate expressed in thousandths of an inch (mils or points), pages per inch (ppi), thousandths of a millimeter (microns) or pages per centimeter (ppc).

camera-ready copy Mechanicals, photographs and art that are fully prepared for reproduction according to the technical requirements of the printing process being used.

carload Selling unit of paper that may weigh anywhere from 20,000 to 100,000 pounds (9,090 to 45,454 kilos), depending on which mill or merchant uses the term. Abbreviated CL.

carton Selling unit of paper weighing approximately 150 pounds (60 kilos). A carton can contain anywhere from 500 to 5,000 sheets, depending on the size of sheets and their basis weight.

case Covers and spine that, as a unit, enclose the pages of a casebound book.

case bind To bind using glue to hold signatures to a case made of binder board covered with fabric, plastic or leather. Also called cloth bind, edition bind and hard bind.

cast-coated paper High-gloss, coated paper made by pressing the paper against a polished, hot, metal drum while the coating is still wet.

catalog paper Coated paper rated #4 or #5 with basis weight from 35# to 50# (50 to 75 gsm) commonly used for catalogs and magazines.

CCD Abbreviation for charged coupled device such as a camera or scanner that uses arrays of photocells to capture images.

change order   Alternate term for alteration.

chipboard   Solid (not corrugated) cardboard.

choke   Technique of slightly reducing the size of an image to create a hairline trap or to outline. Also called shrink and skinny.

chroma   Strength of a color as compared to how close it seems to neutral gray. Also called depth, intensity, purity and saturation.

CIE   Abbreviation for Commission International de l'Eclairage, the organization that developed color standards used in PostScript and other software.

clean color   Subjective term meaning vivid or pure.

CMYK   Abbreviation for cyan, magenta, yellow and key (black), the process colors.

coated paper   Paper with a coating of clay and other substances that improves reflectivity and ink holdout.

cockle finish   Slightly puckered surface on bond paper.

collateral   Printed pieces, such as newsletters and brochures, that support or supplement display or broadcast advertising.

color balance   Refers to amounts of process colors that simulate the colors of the original scene or photograph.

color break   In multicolor printing, the point, line or space at which one ink color stops and another begins.

color cast   Unwanted color affecting an entire image.

color control bar   Strip of small blocks of color on a proof or press sheet to help evaluate features such as density and dot gain.

color correct   To adjust the relationship among the process colors to achieve desirable colors.

color curves   Instructions in software that allow users to change or correct colors. Also called HLS and HVS tables.

color gamut   The entire range of hues possible to reproduce using a specific device or process.

color matching system   System of numbered ink swatches that facilitates communication about color.

color model   Way of categorizing and describing the infinite array of colors found in nature.

color separation   1. Technique of using a camera, scanner or computer to divide continuous-tone color images into four halftone negatives. 2. The film, proof or printed product resulting from color separating.

color sequence   Order in which inks are printed. With process colors, the sheetfed sequence is often black first, then magenta, cyan, and yellow last. The web sequence is often cyan, magenta, yellow, with black either first or last. Also called laydown sequence and rotation.

color shift   Change in image color resulting from changes in register, ink densities or dot gain.

comb bind   To bind by inserting the teeth of a flexible plastic comb through holes punched along the edge of a stack of paper. Also called GBC bind.

commercial match   Acceptable difference between the color on a sample of ink or paper, or the color on a proof, and the color achieved on press.

commercial printer   Printer producing a wide range of products such brochures, posters, booklets, stationery and business forms. Also called job printer because each job is different.

commercial register   Informal trade recognition that acceptable quality allows slight variation of register throughout the press run.

commodity   Refers to paper or printing produced quickly and in high volumes, thus relatively inexpensive.

composite proof   Proof of halftones and separations in position with graphics and type.

composition   The arrangement of type, graphics and other elements on the page.

comprehensive dummy   Simulation of a printed piece complete with type, graphics and colors. Abbreviated comp.

compressed files   Files with nonessential data deleted to make them easier to store and transmit.

condition   To keep paper in the pressroom for a few hours or days before printing so that its moisture level and temperature equal that in the pressroom. Also called cure, mature and season.

continuous-tone copy   All photographs and those illustrations having a range of shades not made up of dots. Abbreviated contone.

contract proof Any proof that the customer considers final.

converter Business that makes products such as boxes, bags, envelopes and displays.

cool colors Blues, greens and browns.

corrugated board Board made by sandwiching fluted kraft paper between sheets of paper or cardboard. Used for making boxes.

cover paper Category of thick paper used for products such as posters, menus, folders and covers of paperback books.

creep Phenomenon of middle pages of a folded signature extending slightly beyond outside pages. Also called feathering, outpush, push out and thrust.

crop marks Lines near the edges of an image indicating portions to be reproduced. Also called cut marks and tic marks.

crossover Type of art that continues from one page of a book or magazine across the gutter to the opposite page. Also called bridge and gutter jump.

customer service representative Employee of a printer who coordinates projects and keeps customers informed. Abbreviated CSR.

cutoff Circumference of the impression cylinder of a web press, therefore also the length of the printed sheet that the press cuts from the roll of paper.

cut sizes Paper sizes used with office machines and small presses.

CWT Abbreviation for hundredweight using the Roman numeral C=100.

cyan One of the four process colors.

D

DCS Abbreviation for desktop color separation, a format for four PostScript files for a color image.

dandy roll Wire-mesh drum on a papermaking machine that presses watermarks and surface patterns into paper while it is still 90 percent water.

deboss To press an image into paper so it lies below the surface.

deckle edge Edge of paper left ragged as it comes from the papermaking machine instead of being cleanly cut. Also called feather edge.

densitometer Device used to measure light reflected or transmitted from paper or film.

density 1. Regarding ink, the relative thickness of a layer of printed ink. 2. Regarding color, the relative ability of a color to absorb light reflected from it or block light passing through it.

device independent colors Hues identified by wavelength or by their place in systems such as those developed by CIE. 'Device independent' means a color can be described and specified regardless of how it is reproduced.

die cut To cut irregular shapes in paper or paperboard using a die.

digital camera Camera that captures images using CCDs, not film.

digital plate Plate burned from a computer file, not film.

display type Type larger than 14 points.

Dmax/Dmin The points of maximum/minimum density in an image or that a device can capture.

doctor blade Flexible metal strip on a gravure press that controls the thickness of ink.

dot area Refers to the percentage of ink coverage that a screen tint allows to print. Also called screen percentage.

dot gain Phenomenon of halftone dots printing larger on paper than they are on films or plates.

dots-per-inch Measure of resolution of input devices such as scanners and output devices such as laser printers and imagesetters. Abbreviated dpi.

double black duotone Duotone printed from two halftones, one exposed for highlights and the other exposed for midtones and shadows.

double burn To burn a plate twice to different negatives or files and thus create a composite image.

doubling Printing flaw created by slight bounce of blanket against paper.

drawdown Sample of inks specified for a job applied to the substrate specified for a job. Also called pulldown.

drop out Halftone dots or fine lines eliminated from highlights by overexposure during camera work. The lost copy is said to have dropped out.

dry trap To print over dry ink, as compared to wet trap.

dual-purpose bond paper Bond paper suitable for printing by either lithography (offset) or xerography (photocopy). Abbreviated DP bond paper.

dull finish Flat (not glossy) finish on coated paper; slightly smoother than matte. Also called suede and velvet.

dummy Simulation of the final product. Also called mock-up.

duotone Black and white photograph reproduced using two halftone negatives, each shot to emphasize different tonal values in the original.

duplex paper Thick paper made by pasting together two thinner sheets, usually of different colors. Also called double-faced paper and two-tone paper.

duplicator Offset press made for quick printing.

Dylux Brand name for photographic paper used to make blueline proofs. Often used as alternate term for blueline.

dynamic range Practical limit of a scanner or press to capture or reproduce an image.

E

emboss To press an image into paper so it lies above the surface. Also called cameo and tool.

emulsion Coating of light-sensitive chemicals on papers, films, printing plates and stencils.

emulsion down/emulsion up Film whose emulsion side faces down (away from the viewer) or up (toward the viewer) when ready to make a plate or stencil. Abbreviated ED/EU. Also called E up/down and face down/face up.

encapsulated PostScript file Computer file containing both images and PostScript commands. Abbreviated EPS.

end sheet Sheet that attaches the inside pages of a case bound book to its cover.

English finish Smooth finish on uncoated book paper; smoother than eggshell, rougher than smooth.

engraving Printing method using a plate, also called a die, with an image cut into its surface.

ep Abbreviation for envelope.

EPS Abbreviation for encapsulated PostScript.

equivalent paper Paper that is not the brand specified, but looks, prints, and may cost the same.

estimate Price that states what a job will probably cost. Also called bid, quotation and tender.

eye markers In flexography, color control images consisting of small squares of process color printed outside of image areas.

F

fair use Concept in copyright law allowing, without permission from copyright holder, short quotations from a copyrighted product for purposes of reviewing or teaching.

feeding unit Component of a printing press that moves paper into the register unit.

felt finish Soft woven pattern in text paper.

felt side Side of the paper that does not make contact with the Fourdrinier wire during papermaking.

fifth color Spot color run in addition to process colors.

film coating Method of coating paper that leaves a relatively thin covering and rough surface, as compared to blade coating.

fine papers Papers made specifically for writing and printing.

finish 1. Surface characteristics of paper. 2. General term for trimming, folding, binding and all other postpress operations.

fixed costs Costs that remain the same regardless of how many pieces are printed.

flat color Alternate term for spot color.

flat Stripped film ready for platemaking.

flexography Method of printing on a web press using rubber or soft plastic plates with raised images. Also called aniline printing. Abbreviated flexo.

flood To print a sheet completely with an ink or varnish.

foil stamp Method of printing that releases foil from its backing when stamped with the heated die. Also called block print.

font Complete assortment of uppercase and

lowercase characters, numerals, punctuation and other symbols of one typeface.

form   Each side of a signature. Also spelled forme.

form web   Press using rolls 8½″ to 10″ wide to print business forms, direct mailers, catalog sheets, stationery and other products whose flat size is typically 8½″×11″.

format   Size, style, shape, layout or organization of a layout or printed product.

form bond   Lightweight bond made for business forms. Also called register bond.

formula pricing   Prices shown on a grid or spreadsheet.

for position only   Refers to inexpensive or low resolution images used to indicate placement and scaling, but not intended for reproduction. Abbreviated FPO.

fountain solution   Mixture of water and chemicals that dampens a printing plate to prevent ink from adhering to the non-image area. Also called dampener solution.

four-color process printing   Technique of printing that uses black, magenta, cyan and yellow to simulate full-color images. Also called color process printing.

Fourdrinier machine   Machine used to make paper by catching furnish on a wire called a Fourdrinier wire.

FPO   Abbreviation for the term for position only.

free sheet   Paper made from cooked wood fibers mixed with chemicals and washed free of impurities. Also called woodfree paper.

full web   Press using use rolls 35″ to 40″ wide to print sixteen-page signatures whose flat size is typically 23″×35″. Also called sixteen-page web.

furnish   Mixture of fibers, water, dyes, and chemicals poured from the headbox onto the Fourdrinier wire of a papermaking machine. Also called slurry and stock.

G

gang   1. To halftone or separate more than one image in only one exposure. 2. To reproduce two or more different printed products simultaneously on one sheet of paper during one press run. Also called combination run.

gathered   Signatures assembled next to each other in the proper sequence for binding. Also called stacked.

GCR   Abbreviation for gray compenent replacement.

ghosting   1. Phenomenon of a faint image appearing on a printed sheet where it was not intended to appear. 2. Phenomenon of printed image appearing too light because of ink starvation.

gloss finish   Shiny finish on photographic paper or coated printing paper.

GRACOL   Abbreviation for General Requirements and Applications for Commercial Offset Lithography.

grade   General term used to distinguish among printing papers, but whose specific meaning depends on context. Grade can refer to the category, class, rating, finish or brand of paper.

graduated screen tint   Screen tint that changes densities gradually and smoothly, not in distinct steps. Also called degrade, gradient, ramped screen and vignette.

grain direction   Predominant direction in which fibers in paper become aligned during manufacturing. Also called machine direction.

grain long/short paper   Paper whose fibers run parallel to the long/short dimension of the sheet.

grammage   Basis weight of paper expressed in grams per square meter (gsm).

graphic arts   The crafts, industries and professions related to designing and printing on paper and other substrates.

graphic design   Arrangement of type and visual elements along with specifications for paper, ink colors and printing processes that, when combined, convey a visual message.

gravure   Method of printing using metal cylinders etched with millions of tiny wells that hold ink.

gray balance   Printed cyan, magenta and yellow halftone dots that accurately reproduce a neutral gray image.

gray component replacement   Technique of

replacing gray tones in the yellow, cyan and magenta files with black. Abbreviated GCR.

gray levels Number of distinct gray tones that can be captured by a scanner or reproduced by an output device.

gray scale Strip of gray values, ranging from white to black, used to calibrate exposure times for film and plates. Also called step wedge.

gripper edge Edge of a sheet held by grippers on a sheetfed press, thus going first through the press. Also called feeding edge and leading edge.

groundwood paper Newsprint and other inexpensive paper made from pulp created when wood chips are ground mechanically rather than refined chemically.

guillotine cutter Large cutting machine whose blade trims paper evenly across a stack of sheets. The blade is brought down from above, hence the term "guillotine."

H

hairline Subjective term referring to very small space, thin line or close register.

half web Press using rolls 17″ to 20″ wide to print eight-page signatures whose flat size is typically 17″ × 22″.

halftone A photograph or continuous-tone illustration that has been converted to dots for reproduction.

hard copy/proof Type and images on paper or proofing material.

heat-set web Web press equipped with an oven to dry ink, thus able to print coated paper.

hickey Spot or imperfection in printing, most visible in areas of heavy ink coverage, caused by dirt on the plate or blanket.

high-fidelity color Color reproduced using six, eight or twelve separations.

high-key photo Photo whose most important details appear in the highlights.

highlights Lightest portions of an image.

histogram Vertical bar chart showing tonal range in an image.

HLS Abbreviation for hue, lightness, saturation. Also called HVS.

holography Printing method using a laser to emboss images precisely overlaying each other on a thin piece of film to produce a three-dimensional image.

house sheet Paper kept in stock by a printer and suitable for a wide variety of printing jobs. Also called floor sheet.

hue A specific color such as yellow or green.

hundredweight 100 pounds in North America, 112 pounds in the United Kingdom. Abbreviated CWT.

I

imagesetter Laser device for outputting film or plates.

image trap Slight overlapping of images to ensure they appear registered.

imposition Arrangement of pages so they will appear in proper sequence after press sheets are folded and bound.

impression 1. Referring to an ink color, one impression equals one press sheet passing once through a printing unit. 2. Referring to the speed of a press, one impression equals one press sheet passing once through the press.

impression cylinder Cylinder, on a press, that pushes paper against the plate or blanket, thus forming the image

impressions per hour Measure of speed of a printing press. Abbreviated iph.

imprint To print new copy on a previously printed sheet, such as imprinting an employee's name on business cards. Also called surprint.

ink balance Relationship of the densities and dot gains of process inks to each other and to a standard density of neutral gray.

ink fountain Reservoir, on a printing press, that holds ink.

ink holdout Characteristic of paper that prevents it from absorbing ink, thus allowing ink to dry on the surface of the paper. Also called holdout.

ink-jet printing Method of printing by spraying droplets of ink through computer-controlled nozzles.

ink trap Ink printed over a previously printed image.

in-plant printer Department of an agency, business or association that does printing for a parent organization. Also called captive printer and in-house printer.

integral proof   Color proof of separations shown on one piece of proofing paper. Also called laminate proof.

interpolation   Increasing input resolution by using software to create new pixels based on the nature of neighboring pixels.

ISO sizes   Metric paper sizes.

J

job lot paper   Paper that didn't meet specifications when produced, has been discontinued, or for other reasons is no longer considered first quality.

job ticket   Form used to specify the production schedule of a job and the materials and processes it needs. Also called docket, production order and work order.

JPEG   Abbreviation for Joint Photographic Experts Group.

K

Kelvin   System for expressing the temperature of light.

kerning   Adjusting space between pairs of letters to make them appear better fitted.

keylines   Lines on a mechanical or negative showing the exact size, shape and location of photographs or other graphic elements. Also called holding lines.

kiss die cut   Die cut through face materials but not backing.

knockout   Alternate term for reverse.

kraft paper   Strong paper used for wrapping and to make grocery bags and large envelopes.

L

laid finish   Finish on bond or text paper on which grids of parallel lines simulate the surface of handmade paper.

lap   Edge of a signature that a machine grips during binding operations.

laser   Acronym for light amplification by stimulated emission of radiation; very intense light that can be precisely focused.

laser bond   Bond paper made especially smooth and dry to run well through laser printers.

laser-imprintable ink   Ink that will not fade or blister as the paper on which it is printed is used in a laser printer.

lay-flat bind   Method of perfect binding that allows a publication to lie fully open.

leading   Amount of space between lines of type.

ledger paper   Strong, smooth bond paper used for keeping business records. Ledger paper is usually sub 28 or 32. Also called record paper.

legacy materials   Art, film or files from previous print jobs for incorporating into a new job.

legal paper   North American term for bond paper trimmed to 8½″×14″ sheets.

legible   Referring to type having sufficient contrast with its background that readers can easily perceive the characters.

letter paper   In North America, 8½″×11″ sheets. In Europe, A4 sheets.

letterpress   Method of printing from metal type and other raised surfaces. Also called block printing.

lettershop   Alternate term for mailing service.

letterspacing   Distance between individual letters. See also kerning and tracking.

lightweight paper   Book paper with basis weight less than 40# (60 gsm).

line copy   Any high-contrast image, including type.

linen finish   Embossed finish on text paper that simulates the pattern of linen cloth.

lithography   Method of printing using plates whose image areas attract ink and whose non-image areas repel ink. Non-image areas may be coated with water to repel the oily ink or may have a surface, such as silicon, that repels ink.

long run   Relatively large quantity to print in relation to the size and speed of press used.

loose proof   Proof of a halftone or color separation that is not assembled with other elements from a page. Also called first proof, random proof, scatter proof and show-color proof.

low-key photo   Photo whose most important details appear in the shadows.

lpi/lpcm   Lines per inch/centimeter, unit of measurement for the size of halftone dots.

M

M weight Weight of 1,000 sheets of paper in any specific size.

magenta One of the four process colors.

mailing service Business that addresses, sorts and bundles mailings according to USPS standards.

makeready 1. All activities required to prepare a press or other machine for a specific printing or bindery job. Also called setup. 2. Paper used in the makeready process at any stage in production.

making order Order for paper that a mill makes to the customer's specifications.

mark up To add a percentage to the cost of goods or services obtained for a customer.

matte finish Flat (not glossy) finish on photographic paper or coated printing paper.

measured photography Technique of exposing original photos to place critical details within the tonal range of the printing process.

mechanical Camera-ready assembly of type, graphics and other copy complete with instructions to the printer. Also called an artboard and pasteup.

metamerism Phenomenon of color appearing different under difference light sources.

midtones Tones created by halftone dots between 30 percent and 70 percent of coverage.

mill order Order for paper that will be filled from inventory at a mill, not inventory at a paper merchant.

mini web Press using rolls 11″×14″ wide to print brochures, newsletters and other products whose flat size is typically 11″×17″.

mock-up Alternate term for dummy.

modem Device for transmitting digital data over analog telephone lines.

moiré Undesirable pattern resulting when halftones and screen tints are made with improperly aligned screens, or when a pattern in a photo, such as a plaid, interferes with a halftone dot pattern.

mottle Spotty, uneven ink absorption. Also called sinkage. A mottled image may be called mealy.

multicolor printing Printing in more than one ink color (but not four-color process). Also called polychrome printing.

N

native file File still in the application in which it was originally created.

natural color Very light brown color of paper. May also be called antique, cream, ivory, off-white or mellow white.

NCR paper Abbreviation for No Carbon Required paper, a brand name for carbonless paper.

nested Signatures assembed inside one another in the proper sequence for binding. Also called inset.

neutral gray Gray with no hue or cast.

non-heatset web Web press without a drying oven, thus not able to print on coated paper. Also called cold-set web and open web.

O

object-oriented image Alternate term for vector image.

off-shore sheet Term used in the United States and Canada for paper made overseas.

offset printing Printing technique that transfers ink from a plate to a blanket to paper instead of directly from a plate to paper.

opacity 1. Characteristic of paper that prevents printing on one side from showing through to the other. 2. Characteristic of ink that prevents the substrate from showing through.

outsource To buy a service from an outside vendor rather than performing the service in house.

overlay proof Color proof consisting of clear plastic sheets laid on top of each other with their images in register. Also called layered proof.

overrun Quantity printing delivered that is more than the quantity ordered.

overprint To print one image over a previously printed image, such as printing type over a screen tint. Also called surprint.

P

page One side of a leaf in a publication.

page count Total number of pages that a publication has. Also called extent.

page proof Proof of type and graphics as they will look on the finished page complete with elements such as headings, rules and folios.

panel One page of a brochure, such as one panel of a rack brochure. One panel is on one side of the paper. A letter-folded sheet has six panels.

parent sheet Any sheet larger than 11″×17″ or A3.

pass One complete sequence of activities, such as a pass through a manuscript to check spelling or a pass through a press to lay down varnish.

pasteup To paste copy to mounting boards and, if necessary, to overlays so it is assembled into a camera-ready mechanical. The mechanical produced is often called a pasteup.

PDF Abbreviation for Portable Document Format.

perfect bind To bind sheets that have been ground at the spine and are held to the cover by glue. Also called adhesive bind, cut-back bind, glue bind, paper bind, patent bind, perfecting bind, soft bind and soft cover.

perfecting press Press capable of printing both sides of the paper during a single pass. Also called duplex press and perfector.

pica Anglo-American unit of typographic measure equal to .166 inch (4.218mm). One pica has 12 points.

PICT A Macintosh format for defining images.

pixel Short for picture element consisting of spots made by a scanner or digital camera.

plate Piece of paper, metal, plastic, or rubber carrying an image to be reproduced using a printing press.

plate-ready film Stripped negatives or positives fully prepared for platemaking.

pleasing color Color that the customer considers satisfactory even though it may not match originals.

PMS Obsolete reference to Pantone Matching System. The correct trade name of the colors in the Pantone Matching System is PANTONE Colors, not PMS Colors.

point 1. Regarding paper, a unit of thickness equaling .001 inch. 2. Regarding type, a unit of measure equaling $1/12$ pica and .013875 inch (.351mm).

Portable Document Format Adobe file format allowing convenient sharing of files between the Internet, prepress devices and other media.

post-consumer waste Paper that has been printed and returned to a paper mill instead of going into a landfill.

PostScript Software that controls desktop printers and imagesetters.

ppi/ppcm Pixels per inch/centimeter, unit of measurement for input resolution and display on monitors.

preliminary proof Any proof examined prior to making a contract proof.

prepress Color correcting and separating, stripping, platemaking and other functions performed by the printer or prepress service prior to printing.

preconsumer waste Paper that has not been printed, including trimmings leftover from converting paper into products such as envelopes, roll ends and damaged paper that printers couldn't use, and waste at the mill itself.

preprint To print portions of sheets that will be used for later imprinting.

press check Event at which makeready sheets from the press are examined before authorizing production to begin.

press proof Proof made on press using the plates, ink and paper specified for the job. Also called strike off.

price break Quantity at which unit cost of paper or printing drops. In the United States and Canada, price breaks for paper are typically at four cartons, sixteen cartons, 5,000 pounds, and 20,000 pounds.

printer font Font produced by software in an output device.

printer spreads Files prepared so they are imposed for printing.

printing Any process that transfers to paper or another substrate an image from an original such as a film negative or positive, electronic memory, stencil, die or plate.

printing plate Surface carrying an image to be printed.

printing unit Assembly of fountain, rollers and cylinders that will print one ink color. Also called color station, deck, ink station, printer, station and tower.

process colors The colors used for four-color process printing: yellow, magenta, cyan and black.

procurement cost Total cost of a printing job, including staff time, storage and overhead.

proof Test sheet made to reveal errors or flaws, predict results on press and record how a printing job is intended to appear when finished.

publication printer Printing company specializing in magazines, catalogs and other products that are typically web printed and saddle stitched.

publishing paper Paper made in weights, colors and surfaces suited to books, magazines and catalogs.

Q

quality Subjective term relating to expectations by the customer, printer and other professionals associated with a printing job and whether the job meets those expectations.

quarter tones Tones between shadows and midtones (¾ tones) and between highlight and midtones (¼ tones).

quick printing Printing using small sheetfed presses and cut sizes of bond and offset paper.

quotation Price offered by a printer to produce a specific job.

R

raster image processor Computer that converts files to bitmapped images ready to output on a imagesetter.

readable Characteristic of printed messages that are easy to read and understand.

reader spread Files prepared in two-page spreads as readers would see the pages.

ream 500 sheets of paper.

ream marked Sheets of paper in a carton or on a skid with markers placed every 500th sheet.

recycled paper New paper made entirely or in part from old paper.

reflective copy Products, such as fabrics, illustrations and photographic prints, viewed by light reflected from them.

register To place printing properly with regard to the edges of paper and other printing on the same sheet. Such printing is said to be "in register."

register marks Cross-hair lines on mechanicals and film that help keep flats, plates and printing in register. Also called crossmarks and position marks.

repeatability Ability of a device, such as an imagesetter, to produce film or plates which yield images in register.

reprographics General term for xerography, diazo, and other methods of copying used by designers, engineers, architects, or for general office use.

resolution Ability of a device to record or reproduce a sharp image.

reverse Type and images reproduced by printing ink around their outline, thus allowing the underlying color of paper to show through and form the image. Also called knockout.

RGB Abbreviation for red, green and blue, the additive primary colors.

RIP Abbreviation for raster image processor.

roman type Style considered normal for a given typeface.

rule Line used as a graphic element to separate or organize copy.

ruleup Map or drawing showing how a printing job must be imposed using a specific press and sheet size.

S

saddle stitch To bind by stapling sheets together where they fold at the spine. Also called pamphlet stitch, saddle wire and stitch bind.

satin finish Alternate term for dull finish on coated paper.

scanner Device that converts an analog image, such as a photo, to a digital image.

score To compress paper along a straight line so it folds more easily and accurately. Also called crease.

screen angles Angles at which screens intersect with the horizontal line of the press sheet. The common screen angles for separations are black 45°, magenta 75°, yellow 90° and cyan 105°.

screen percentage Alternate term for dot area.

screen font Font produced to appear on a computer monitor.

screen printing Method of printing by using a squeegee to force ink through an assembly of mesh fabric and a stencil.

screen ruling Number of rows or lines of dots per inch or centimeter in a screen for making a screen tint or halftone. Also called line count, screen frequency, screen size and screen value.

screen tint Color created by dots instead of solid ink coverage. Also called fill pattern, shading, tint and tone.

screw and post bind To bind using a bolt that screws into a post. Bolts and matching posts are available in lengths ranging from ¼ inch to 3 inches.

scum Undesirable thin film of ink in non-image areas. Scumming may appear on portions of a sheet or across the entire sheet and results from poor ink/water balance. Also called blush, catch up, haze, and toning.

selective binding Placing signatures or inserts in magazines or catalogs according to demographic or geographic guidelines.

setoff Undesirable transfer of wet ink from the top of one sheet to the underside of another as they lie in the delivery stack of a press. Also called offset.

shadows Darkest areas of a photograph.

sheetfed press Press that prints sheets of paper.

sheetwise Technique of printing one side of a sheet with one set of plates, then the other side of the sheet with a set of different plates. Also called work and back. One-up jobs require sheetwise printing.

shingling Allowance made to compensate for creep. Creep is the problem; shingling is the solution. Also called stair stepping and progressive margins.

short run Relatively small quantity to print in relation to the size and speed of press used.

shrink wrap Method of wrapping packages or products in clear plastic film then using heat to tighten the film around the item.

side stitch To bind by stapling through sheets along one edge. Also called cleat stitch and side wire.

signature Printed sheet folded at least once, possibly many times, to become part of a publication.

soft copy/proof Type and images viewed on a monitor.

specialty printer Printer whose equipment, supplies, workflow and marketing is targeted to a specific category of products.

specifications Complete and precise written description of features of a printing job. Abbreviated specs.

specular highlight Highlight area with no printable dots, thus no detail. Also called catchlight and dropout highlight.

spiral bind To bind using a spiral of continuous wire or plastic looped through holes. Also called coil bind.

spoilage Paper which must be recycled due to mistakes or accidents.

spot color Any color created by printing only one ink. Also called flat color.

spread 1. Technique of slightly enlarging the size of an image to accomplish a trap with another image. 2. Two-page arrangement of copy. See also reader spread and printer spread.

standard viewing conditions Background of 60 percent neutral gray and light that measures 5000 Kelvin—the color of daylight on a bright day.

step and repeat Prepress technique of exposing an image in a precise, multiple pattern to create a flat or plate.

stochastic screen Halftone with dots that vary in placement, not size. Also called FM screen.

strip To assemble images on film for platemaking.

substance weight Alternate term for basis weight, usually referring to bond papers. Also called sub weight.

subtractive color Color produced by light reflected from a surface. Subtractive color includes hues in color photos and colors created by inks on paper.

subtractive primary colors Yellow, magenta and cyan. In the graphic arts, these are known as process colors because, along with black, they are the ink colors used in color-process printing.

supercalendered paper Groundwood paper

calendered using alternating chrome and fiber rollers to produce a smooth, thin sheet for magazines, catalogs and directories. Abbreviated SC paper.

SWOP Abbreviation for Specifications for Web Offset Publications.

T

tagged image file format Computer file format used to store images from scanners and video devices. Abbreviated TIFF.

target ink densities Densities of the four process inks as recommended for various printing processes and grades of paper.

text paper Designation for printing papers with textured surfaces such as laid or linen. Some mills also use text to refer to any paper they consider top-of-the-line, whether or not its surface has a texture.

thermography Method of printing using colorless resin powder that takes on the color of underlying ink. Also called raised printing.

three-quarter web Press using rolls 22″ to 27″ wide to print eight-page signatures whose flat trim size is typically 17″ × 22″. Also called eight-page webs.

TIFF Abbreviation for tagged image file format.

tonal range Difference between the darkest and lightest areas of copy.

tone compression Reduction in the tonal range from original scene to printed reproduction.

total area coverage Total of the dot percentages of the process colors in the final film. Also called maximum density, total dot density and total ink coverage.

tracking Adjusting space between all letters to make them fit.

trade customs Business terms and policies codified by trade associations to provide guidelines for contracts.

trap See ink trap and image trap.

typeface Design identified by a name such as Helvetica or Times.

type style Characteristic such as bold, italic or roman.

U

uncoated paper Paper that has not been coated with clay. Also called offset paper.

undercolor removal Technique of making color separations such that the amount of cyan, magenta and yellow ink is reduced in midtone and shadow areas while the amount of black is increased. Abbreviated UCR.

underrun Quantity printing delivered that is less than the quantity ordered.

unit cost The cost of one item in a print run computed by dividing the total cost of the printing job by the quantity of products delivered.

unsharp masking Technique of adjusting dot size to make a halftone or separation appear in better focus. Also called edge enhancement and peaking.

up Term to indicate multiple copies of one image printed in one impression on a single sheet. Two up means printing the identical piece twice on each sheet.

UV coating Liquid applied to a printed sheet, then bonded and cured with ultraviolet light.

V

value The shade (darkness) or tint (lightness) of a color. Also called brightness, lightness, shade and tone.

variable costs Costs that change depending on how many pieces are produced.

varnish Liquid applied as a coating for protection and appearance.

vector image Besier curves. Also called object oriented.

vellum finish Somewhat rough, toothy finish on paper.

VOC Abbreviation for volatile organic compounds, petroleum substances used as the vehicles for many printing inks.

W

warm colors Yellows, oranges and reds.

wash up To clean ink and fountain solutions from rollers, fountains, screens and other press components.

waste Paper which is recycled as a result of

normal makeready, printing or bindery operations.

watermark   Translucent logo in bond paper created during manufacture.

web press   Press that prints from rolls of paper, cutting it into sheets after printing. Also called reel-fed press.

white point   Reference point defining the lightest area in an image.

wire side   Side of the paper that rests against the Fourdrinier wire during papermaking, as compared to felt side.

with the grain   Parallel to the grain direction of the paper being used.

work and tumble   To print a sheet so that the same combination of images is printed on both front and back using the same set of plates. Work and tumble uses opposite gripper edges.

work and turn   To print a sheet so that the same combination of images is printed on both front and back using the same set of plates. Work and turn uses the same gripper edges.

work for hire   Creative work for which the creator agrees that the client owns the copyright to the finished product.

working film   Intermediate film that will be copied to make final film after all corrections are made. Also called buildups.

wove finish   Somewhat smooth, slightly patterned finish on bond paper.

wrong reading   An image that is backwards when compared to the original. Also called flopped and reverse reading. ■

INDEX

....

....

illustrated, 136
EPS files, 23, 61-62
equipment lists, 166
equivalent weights, 91-93
estimates. *See* quotations
eye markers, 131

fade-resistant ink, 108
felt text paper, 99
fifth ink color, 34, 49
files,
    application, 59
    archiving, 75-76
    compressed, 62
    formats, 61-62
    information to accompany, 63
    managing, 5
    plates from, 75
    preflighting, 64
    saving, 75-76
film,
    ownership of, 76
    photos from, 40
    plates from, 75
    proofs from, 71
    pros and cons, 68
    storing, 76
film coated paper, 99
final counts, trade custom, 158
fine papers, 79, 82
finishing, quality guidelines chart, 124-125
fixed costs, 8
flats. *See* film
flaws, quality guidelines chart, 124-125
flexography, 106, 132
    illustrated, 133
    plates for, 75
    unit costs, 8
Flightcheck, 65
Flightpro, 65
fluorescent ink, 108
fluorescent lights, effects of, 26
foil stamping, 142-143
    costs and schedule, 144
    effect on ink color, 108
    illustrated, 143
folding, 90, 116, 146
    illustrated, 147
fonts. *See* type fonts
format, of cameras, 42
form bond paper, 98
formula pricing, 167

four-color process,
    illustrated, 30
    and ink-jet printing, 131
    register of, 119
Fourdrinier wire, 81
    illustrated, 80
Framemaker, 61
FreeHand (Altsys), 59
free sheet, 82
French fold, illustrated, 147
furnish, 81

gamut, 28, 31
ganging, 96
    halftones and separations, 48
    quality guidelines chart, 124-125
gate fold, illustrated, 147
GATF, 34, 48, 178, 179
    color control images, 34
gathering, 148
    illustrated, 149
GBC binding, 153
GCA, 178
ghosting, 121
    illustrated, 122
gloss coated paper, 99
gluing, 150
good quality printing, 117
    defined, 7
    dot gain, 66
    evaluating photos for, 39
    quality guidelines, 121
    quality guidelines chart, 124-125
Goodwill Industries, 158
GRACOL, 53, 178
grain,
    of paper, 90, 115, 146
    of photos, 39
grammage, 92
graphic designers, 9-11
Graphic Interchange File (GIF), 62
gravure, 106, 136, 164
    illustrated, 137
    plates, 74
gray balance, proofing, 73
gray component replacement, 52
gray levels, illustrated, 47
gripper edge, 113
groundwood paper, 79, 82, 99
gusset wrinkle, 146
Gutenberg, 132

hairline,

register, 119
rule, 20
halftones, 43
    effects of dot gain, 65
    embedding, 62
    illustrated, 43
    quality guidelines chart, 124-125
    screen printing, 134
    screen ruling for, 21, 46
heat-set web press, 116
hue, 29
    illustrated, 28
hickies, 121
    illustrated, 123
high-fidelity color, 52
high finish, 99
highlights, 48, 55, 56
    illustrated, 41
histogram, 43
holography, 143, 164
house sheets, 86, 173
hundredweight, 97

IABC, 167
IBM, 130
ICC, 28
illustrations, 23, 59
Illustrator (Adobe), 59
imagesetters, 14, 17, 59, 68, 118
image trap, 66, 118
    illustrated, 68
imaging services. *See* prepress
imposition, 66
    illustrated, 67, 149
impression, 116
imprinting, 129
incandescent lights, effects of, 26
index paper, 105
Indigo, 100, 130
infographics, 61
ink, 106-108
    analine, 133
    costs of, 106
    density of, 119-120
    and foil stamping, 108
    fountain, 113
    holdout, illustrated, 100
    and laser printing, 107
    for on-demand printing, 131
    soy, 107
    trapping, 121
ink-jet printing, 130-131
in-plant printers, 165-166
inserts, illustrated, 148

More Great Books for Knock-Out Graphic Design!

2001 Artist's & Graphic Designer's Market—Completely updated, with 500 new listings! Find out who's looking to buy. This book lists 2,500 markets for design and art work—from stock illustration and clip art firms, to computer game companies, to magazine and book publishers. You'll find names, addresses, phone numbers, Web sites and E-mail addresses—along with submission guidelines and pay rates. You'll also find hot advice from industry "insiders." *#10663/$24.99/720 pages/paperback*

Streetwise Guide to Freelance Design & Illustration—Get the business smarts you need to start and maintain a thriving career—by yourself, for yourself! The book guides you through every step—from equipping your studio, promoting yourself and pricing your services to taxes, contracts and copyrights. Includes interviews with designers and illustrators who are already "out there." *#31111/$24.99/144 pages/66 color illus./paperback*

Fresh Ideas in Photoshop—Today's designers are pushing Photoshop to its limits. Here's a current gallery of the most innovative and adventurous work done in Photoshop. You'll get 100+ case studies—posters, self-promotions, packaging, brochures, fine art and other projects—complete with EXTENSIVE details from the creators on concept, design and production. *#31114/$29.99/144 pages/209 color illus.*

Make Your Scanner a Great Design and Production Tool, Revised Edition—Designer/scan-master Michael Sullivan shares expert tips, step-by-step techniques and neat ideas for using your scanner creatively and producing high quality output. You'll find out what the technical stuff (scaling, screen frequency, dpi) means to you. You'll also learn the capabilities of your specific scanning hardware and software, and how to find the right scanner and storage media for your needs. *#31113/$28.99/160 pages/222 color, 120 b&w illus./paperback*

Graphic Design Tricks & Techniques—This book contains 300+ use-'em-today tips from designers, photographers, typographers and printers across the country. On every page, you'll find great ideas for saving time and money, and doing cool design. You'll get tips on how to check dot gain; streamline the production of projects; create low-cost animations for multimedia projects; manage your type library; get the most out of a photo shoot; work with engraving and varnishes; get creative with clip art and stock photos; and lots, lots more. *#30919/$27.99/144 pages/99 color, 19 b&w illus./paperback*

Digital Focus: The New Media of Photography—Digital manipulation has forever changed the art of photography. This book's 300+ full-color images chronicle the digital excellence and technical artistry of the industry's leading photographers. Sections include business, fashion, food, medical, people, sports and Web sites. *#30978/$39.95/176 pages/300 color illus.*

Cool Type—Contains the trend-setting typework of 46 international artists and studios—the likes of Edward Fella, Chip Kidd, Lucille Tenazas and Why Not Associates. With a complete spread or two per designer, this book shows cutting-edge type used in actual designs—everything from annual reports and on-line design to CD packaging and magazine covers—with information from the designers on how each typeface was inspired, created or manipulated. *#30887/$34.99/144 pages/292 color illus.*

Graphic Design: Inspirations and Innovations 2—This book tells behind-the-scenes stories of how designers have taken every "challenge"—from computer snafus to ridiculous deadlines to overlooked typos—and turned out great finished pieces. (Talk about quick, creative thinking!) Includes work from Modern Dog, Stefan Sagmeister, Galie Jean-Louis, John Sayles and Mirko Ilic and more than 30 other designers. *#30930/$29.99/144 pages/177 color illus.*

Great Design Using Non-Traditional Materials—Take a close look at how 55 resourceful designers have used unusual materials—anything from pizza boxes to Super Sculpey—to turn typical projects into memorable and uniquely appropriate pieces. Step-by-step, you'll find out how 12 of these intriguing pieces were conceived, designed and produced using corrugated cardboard, chipboard and handmade paper; found objects and unique bindings; acrylics, glass and mixed media; and textiles, wood and metal. From experts in each medium, you'll get production tips, cost-cutting advice and fresh ideas. *#30805/$29.99/144 pages/178 color illus.*

Graphic Artists Guild Handbook: Pricing & Ethical Guidelines, 10th Edition—Based on a survey of more than 20,000 designers and illustrators, the Guild Handbook gives you the most complete, specific and up-to-date look at the going rates for all types of design and illustration services—including Web and CD-ROM design. You'll also find current information on copyrights, trademarks and tax issues. Updated sample contracts. Tips on negotiating the best deals. And lots more. *#31509/$32.95/350 pages/paperback*

Even More Great Design Using 1, 2 & 3 Colors—An international collection of 170 excellent limited color designs. You'll find lots of great ideas for working effectively with one, two and three colors—like innovative uses of reverse area printing, halftone printing and colored paper. The work includes posters, stationery, packaging, annual reports and more. Work is shown big, with color chips. *#30955/$39.95/192 pages/300+ color illus.*

Designer's Guide to Marketing—Forty case studies show how designers develop and apply marketing strategy in direct mail, annual reports, retail design, packaging and other projects. You'll find clear, easy-to-understand explanations of marketing basics—like how to focus in on your target market; track your client's competition; try out your ideas on a test market; and gather information from the Internet, focus groups and other sources. *#30932/$29.99/144 pages/112 color, 24 b&w illus.*